The Evolution of Human Pair-Bonding, Friendship, and Sexual Attraction

The Evolution of Human Pair-Bonding, Friendship, and Sexual Attraction presents an evolutionary history of romantic love, male-female pair-bonding, same-sex friendship, and sexual attraction, drawing on sexuality research, gay and lesbian studies, history, literature, anthropology, and evolutionary science.

Employing evolutionary theory as a framework, close same-sex friendship is examined as an adaptive trait that has harnessed love, affection, and sexual pleasure to navigate same-sex environments for both men and women, ultimately benefiting their reproductive success and promoting the inheritance of traits for friendship. Chapters consider the desire to form close same-sex friendships and ask if this is embedded in our biology, concluding that most humans have the capacity to form loving, meaningful, and sexual relationships with men and women.

This book takes on a unique interdisciplinary approach and is essential reading for those studying and working in sexuality research, anthropology, sociology, evolutionary psychology, and gay and lesbian studies. It will also be of interest to marriage and family therapists as well as sex therapists.

Dr. Michael Kauth is Director of LGBT Health in the Department of Veterans Affairs and Professor of Psychiatry at Baylor College of Medicine. He has authored several papers and books on LGBT veteran health, implementation science, and the evolution of sexual attraction.

The Evolution of Human Pair-Bonding, Friendship, and Sexual Attraction

Love Bonds

Michael R. Kauth

Routledge
Taylor & Francis Group

NEW YORK AND LONDON

First published 2021
by Routledge
52 Vanderbilt Avenue, New York, NY 10017

and by Routledge
2 Park Square, Milton Park, Abingdon, Oxon, OX14 4RN

Routledge is an imprint of the Taylor & Francis Group, an informa business

Library of Congress Cataloging-in-Publication Data
Names: Kauth, Michael R., author.
Title: The evolution of human pair-bonding, friendship, and sexual
attraction: love bonds/Michael R. Kauth.
Description: New York, NY: Routledge, 2021. | Includes bibliographical
references and index.
Identifiers: LCCN 2020026680 | ISBN 9780367427245 (hardback) |
ISBN 9780367427269 (paperback) | ISBN 9780367854614 (ebook)
Subjects: LCSH: Sexual attraction. | Mate selection. | Friendship.
Classification: LCC HQ23 .K3168 2021 | DDC 306.82–dc23
LC record available at https://lccn.loc.gov/2020026680

ISBN: 978-0-367-42724-5 (hbk)
ISBN: 978-0-367-42726-9 (pbk)
ISBN: 978-0-367-85461-4 (ebk)

Typeset in Sabon
by Deanta Global Publishing Services, Chennai, India

Contents

Illustrations

Chapter 1

Initial Introductions

Human relationships fascinate me, particularly erotic and loving relationships both in the present and the past. I am curious how people have related to each other to survive and find comfort, safety, or meaning in their lives, along with pleasure. Specifically, I am curious why humans so readily form romantic pair-bonds and close friendships. Both are passionate, intimate, long-term attachments. Are they related? What are the functions of romantic pair-bonds and close friendships? Academic disciplines either have very different explanations for these phenomena or none at all. There are few common threads across disciplines. Some disciplines, like the evolutionary sciences, focus explanations on the far distant past and on reproduction, while others, like sexual science, concentrate on the present and on sexual attraction and pleasure, mostly ignoring human evolution and history. Other disciplines, like history, simply tell the story in context, often with a sociopolitical narrative, and still others, like gender studies, critical theory (*à la* Foucault), and some gay and lesbian studies, see human reproductive or mating pair-bonds and close friendships as unique to each culture but in relationship to social conventions, with no underlying or universal basis. I find these explanations incongruent, incomplete, and unsatisfying. In this book, I attempt to present an integrated, interdisciplinary account of the origin, function, and history of human reproductive, mating pair-bonds and devoted same-sex friendships across cultures. I offer a narrative analysis that integrates several disciplines. I view erotic/sexual attraction and love as the mechanisms that created these critical, intimate, long-term attachments that have been so prevalent and successful through human history. Social customs then emerged to further support these vital relationships. I also hope to demonstrate that Western cultural centrism and current conceptions of marriage, friendship, and sexuality—how we view ourselves—have blinded us and misled scientists into ignoring or reimagining the past to conform to our narrow modern views about sexual kinds of people. In the end, I propose a paradigm shift away from siloed academic disciplines and contemporary Western centrism and toward an integrated, interdisciplinary approach to human sexuality, relationships, and evolution. This is easier said than done, but much more interesting than explaining human phenomena from a singular perspective.

With regards to human relationships, humans are remarkably social creatures who, for the most part, like to be together, unlike some other animals. Humans often maintain close relationships with kin all their lives and even stay connected to extended kin. Humans also show an amazing affinity for close associations with non-relatives. Generally, people *like* other people and prefer to live in groups, close to each other. There are individual exceptions, of course, and people often distrust out-groups. However, cooperative, personal human associations are more the rule than the exception. Other species live in groups. Many species of fish live in schools. Many kinds of birds flock together. Dolphins, penguins, flamingoes, elephants, horses, wolves, deer, baboons, and chimpanzees also prefer to live in groups. Living in groups is an effective strategy to protect against predators. Group living also facilitates food acquisition and care for vulnerable young. Anthropologists generally agree that humans live in groups for many of the same reasons that benefit other species that live in groups (Gurven, 2012; Marlowe, 2012).

Beyond just group-living, humans pursue close companionship in at least two specific forms. Throughout history, humans have formed passionate, intimate, long-term relationships with non-relatives in mating pair-bonds and devoted friendships. Other species sometimes form long-term mating pair-bonds. Many birds, for example, mate for life. Mammals do this less often, preferring other mating strategies. Less than 10% of mammals form long-term mating pair-bonds (Lukas & Clutton-Brock, 2013). Individuals in many species also form long-term preferential alliances in what looks like friendships. For instance, dolphins, elephants, and chimpanzees frequently form long-term peer alliances (Seyfarth & Cheney, 2012). Humans, however, form long-term different-sex (male-female) mating pair-bonds and devoted same-sex friendships on an extraordinary scale.

Both different-sex mating pair-bonds (or marriage) and same-sex friendships are pervasive across human cultures and take various forms (Beer, 2001; Brown, 1991). I am most interested in socially monogamous mating pair-bonds as erotic and loving relationships. Social monogamy refers to committed togetherness, not sexual exclusivity, but more on that in later chapters. Anthropologists note that, in many cultures, humans spend a considerable amount of time and energy longing for, locating, choosing, and keeping a reproductive mate. Volumes have been written about this process. Whole families and the community are sometimes involved in these efforts, and elaborate public ceremonies formalize and celebrate the pair-bond. Marriage is the cultural construction for formal mating pair-bonds, but marriage is quite varied. Every culture has a tradition of marriage. The United States has one of the highest annual marriage rates (6.9/1,000) in the world, with nearly 2.5 million marriages each year (Centers for Disease

Control, 2017a). Among European countries, Lithuania boasts the highest annual marriage rate at 7.5 marriages per 1,000 citizens (Eurostat, 2019). Globally, formal marriage ceremonies, or weddings, are a $300 billion-dollar industry that employs approximately 750,000 people (Bourque, 2017). Although marriage rates have been on the decline in the United States and worldwide in recent years, marriage is far from disappearing. Increasingly, couples opt to live together and even start a family without the formal ritual of marriage. Living together in a committed family relationship is a mating pair-bond just the same.

Anthropologists also show that close personal relationships also take a variety of forms, just like marriage. I am most interested in affectionate long-term attachments between unrelated same-sex individuals that are both erotic and loving. I will argue that friendship may be just as valuable and necessary as marriage, although friendship as a topic has received far less social and scholarly attention than finding a reproductive mate. In many past cultures, devoted male friendships—passionate, intimate, long-term attachments—have been formalized in public ceremonies and recognized by the community (Williams, 1992a). Across historical cultures, devoted male friends have been called "sworn brothers", "adoptive brothers", "blood brothers", or other terms (Miller & Donovan, 2009/2013). Historians have recorded devoted male friendships in many past cultures, and uniformly these friendships have been revered. While people today value good friends, contemporary cultures no longer recognize "sworn brothers" or romantic same-sex friendships as in previous cultures. Modern friendships have been de-eroticized, while people themselves have become sexualized based on their sexual attractions. Today, Western people often identify themselves by their sexual attractions, consistent with the modern idea that people *are* their sexuality (Halperin, 2012). This idea is perpetuated, accidentally or on purpose, by sexual scientists who focus on individual differences between sexual kinds of people. Conventional sexual identities include *heterosexual* (different-sex attracted), *gay* or *lesbian* (same-sex attracted), and *bisexual* (both different- and same-sex attracted). Less conventional, idiosyncratic identity terms narrow or broaden the scope of one's attractions, such as *asexual* (no attraction), *queer* (not exclusively heterosexual), *pansexual* (attraction to people regardless of gender), and even *sapiosexual* (attraction to highly intelligent people). Because people have been sexualized and friendships have been de-eroticized in contemporary cultures, friends may find themselves worrying that affection or intimacy will be interpreted by their friend or by observers as "gay", thus, jeopardizing the friendship.

Gender and gay and lesbian scholars remind us that, for the past several hundred years in Western culture, same-sex sexual attraction and behavior, especially among males, have been severely stigmatized and punished. While Western cultures have experienced tremendous social changes in recognizing the rights and dignity of lesbian, gay, bisexual, transgender, and queer (LGBTQ) people in recent years, these are relatively recent changes, and not everyone has benefited. Gay and queer kids still get kicked out of their homes, and sexual orientation-motivated violence is the third most common hate crime in the United States (Federal Bureau of Investigation, 2019). In many states, LGBTQ Americans can be fired from their jobs because their employer dislikes their sexuality or gender expression. Few states have LGBTQ discrimination protections (Freedom for All Americans, 2018). At the same time, conservative religious groups demand the right to discriminate against LGBTQ people as "religious freedom" (People for the American Way, 2019).

Anthropologists and gay and lesbian historians have noted that contemporary Western culture conceptualizes friendship and marriage quite differently than it did even a few hundred years ago and differently from most historical cultures. For instance, contemporary culture allows mixed sex socializing and friendships, as well as gay marriages. Today, Western people often think of their spouse as their best friend and view their best friend more like a cousin who is fun to have around, but not too familiar. Given that marriage and friendships have long histories, are these recent social changes in Western culture simply superficial? Of course, cultures define marriage and friendships somewhat differently. However, knowing human cultural histories can aide in spotting persistent social characteristics from variable ones. Knowing human cultural histories also helps in identifying beliefs, customs, and discourse that create a social reality for any particular culture and point in time. What, if anything, is persistent about human mating pair-bonds and devoted same-sex friendships through history?

The evolutionary sciences attempt to explain how we got to this point by looking at the distant past: that is, the reason why humans evolved to look, think, and act like we do is a function of solving ancient problems of survival and reproduction. Characteristics that have persisted through history and across cultures, like reproductive mating pair-bonds and devoted same-sex friendships, may be adaptive. Backward engineering these traits may reveal clues to specific challenges faced by our early ancestors in their environments. Thus, an evolutionary analysis of human mating pair-bonds and devoted friendships can help us understand our development and how we came to think and behave in certain ways. An evolutionary analysis provides a broader, deeper context of human development. However, an evolutionary analysis cannot tell us if evolved traits are adaptive today because the environment that most people live in today is quite different from the environment of our early ancestors. In fact, some adaptive traits, evolved in ancient, long-gone environments, may conflict with life in contemporary environments. If evolved human traits may not be adaptive today because our modern manufactured environment is so different from the savannahs of Africa where the traits developed, then why undertake an evolutionary analysis? Is an evolutionary analysis really worthwhile? I think it is. We are better informed when we understand that human bodies and brains are works in progress but adapted to environments that are wildly different from today. Our bodies and brains are constantly playing catch-up with the demands of the ecology, and now our social culture and technology are evolving at an ever accelerating pace. Knowing human evolutionary history can help us be more understanding when evolved human traits conflict with changing social environments and social values.

Academic disciplines like evolutionary biology, anthropology, developmental biology, paleontology, archaeology, genetics, evolutionary psychology, ancient history, classical studies, literature, art history, sexual science, gender studies and critical theory, and gay and lesbian studies, all referenced in this text, use different methodologies to examine different phenomena at different points in time based on different assumptions. In many ways, these disciplines present partial truths. No discipline has the Truth, although the rigor and precision of some disciplines allow them to be more confident of what they know. Each discipline is a little like the blind men and the elephant; it can only describe the part of the phenomenon it examines. No one experiences the entire animal. In a sense, I am collecting and integrating perspectives from different disciplines to piece together a more comprehensive picture of the origin, function, and history of human mating pair-bonds and same-sex friendships. I am looking for common threads through disciplines and historical cultures. I approach this task cautiously, because interpreting findings from different fields is fraught with risk. What is more, the pieces of data come from different puzzles. While there are links between puzzles, the final puzzle picture, like the one presented here, can only be strongly suggestive because the fit is imperfect, and there are many missing pieces.

In this book, I examine human different-sex mating pair-bonds and devoted same-sex friendships as adaptations. From an evolutionary framework, the adaptive value of male-female mating pair-bonds seems obvious since these relationships directly benefit reproductive success, although there are alternative mating strategies. The adaptive value of devoted same-sex friendships may be less obvious but makes sense in the context of sex-segregated environments. Drawing on findings from several evolutionary sciences, I will show that at least since the early division of labor, and perhaps long before that, humans have largely lived in sex-segregated environments. In these environments, devoted same-sex friendships directly benefited survival by facilitating navigation of the same-sex social environment to defend against threat and acquire resources. Further, devoted same-sex friendships likely indirectly benefited reproductive success by facilitating the acquisition of a quality mate as well as resources to protect and support one's family. Over time, these adaptive traits spread through the population, and social customs developed to reinforce marriage and close friendships. As a result, the desires to have a reproductive mate and form a family and make a close, long-term friend is written in our biology, while culture determines the forms these attachments take.

As part of this story, I also explore how evolution exploited erotic/sexual attraction, love, and sexual pleasure to support both human mating pair-bonds and same-sex friendships. Drawing on anthropological studies and field observations, I will show the extensive prevalence of devoted male friendships among contemporary hunter-gatherers and among native people upon first contact. Drawing on ancient history, classical studies, and litera-ture, I will show a long history of devoted male friendships across diverse cultures up to the near present. I will introduce limited evidence of close female friendships because this information is quite scarce. A major implica-tion of these findings and the idea that devoted same-sex friendships are an adaptation is that most men (and probably most women) have the capacity for attraction to male and female partners. Yet this conclusion runs coun-ter to how Western culture views sexuality and counter to sexual science research that shows most people identify as exclusively heterosexual. How can that be? Drawing on data from sexual science, I will show that sexual arousal patterns for men and women show much more variability than is predicted from self-reports of exclusive attractions. Drawing on gender and gay and lesbian studies, I observe that culture has a lot to do with how people experience sexual attraction (and which kinds) and how they define themselves. Scientists exist within the same culture and even perpetuate social conventions! In the end, I hope to present a fuller, richer account of reproductive mating pair-bonds, same-sex friendships, and human sexuality.

Building on the Past Work of Scholars

This book builds on the scholarship of many brilliant, insightful experts. While this work is presented in later chapters, I want to highlight a few texts that significantly influenced my thinking about sexual attraction, mat-ing, and friendship. Among these is an engaging history of the evolution of human sexuality by archaeologist Timothy Taylor in *The Prehistory of Sex: Four Million Years of Human Sexual Culture*. Rather than focus exclusively on reproductive sex, Taylor examined how a range of sexual attractions and behaviors shaped early human culture, especially gender, clothing, religious practices, prostitution, burials, art, and love. Helen Fisher's *Anatomy of Love* is another powerfully influential text that made the case that romantic love is an adaptive trait. Fisher presents an impressive amount of cross-cul-tural data to support her position. She argues that romantic love facilitated and maintained (at least in the short-term) monogamous male-female human pair-bonds, because pair-bonding benefited raising children to reproductive age. In her view, long-term pair-bonds enhanced reproductive success among early humans, and love was the glue that held couples together. While Fisher focused on heterosexual (different-sex) love and relationships, obviously gay and lesbian people experience love and form intimate relationships too. This observation suggested to me that romantic love is the glue that bonds all long-term couples. For love to bond effectively, the desire to love and be loved should occur independently of one's ability to reproduce. Fisher barely noted same-sex love and only briefly mentioned friendship in the 2016 second edition of *Anatomy of Love*.

An important and easily accessible text on evolutionary psychology is David Buss's *The Evolution of Desire*. Using Charles Darwin's sexual selection theory as a framework, Buss explains how mate choice and mate competition have shaped human bodies, behavior, and psychology. He engagingly describes the impact that ancient evolved traits have on men and women's intimate relationships today. However, Buss gave only five pages to same-sex attraction and drew no summary conclusions. This suggested to me that Buss was unconvinced that same-sex attraction had any adaptive value but chose not to portray same-sex attraction as maladaptive. For readers new to evolutionary theory, a helpful preface to Buss' text is psychologist David Geary's book, *Male, Female: The Evolution of Human Sex Differences*, now in its second edition. Geary effectively demonstrates how sexual selection has produced numerous sex differences among humans. Yet to my disappointment, homosexuality is mentioned only twice in the text.

Another influential text, David Greenberg's *The Construction of Homosexuality* is a sprawling early volume on the cultural history of human homosexuality. Sociologist Greenberg argued that wide variability in meaning and form of same-sex attraction and behavior demonstrates that culture defines our experiences with sexuality. That is, gay/lesbian and straight sexual identities are simply a variation in cultural expressions of sexuality. Greenberg's broad history of homosexuality provides overwhelming evidence that same-sex relationships have existed across many cultures. By contrast, anthropologist Gilbert Herdt narrowly focused on how homosexuality played constructive roles in making boys into men in early human cultures. In describing contemporary hunter-gatherer societies in Melanesia (*Guardians of the Flutes*), Herdt produces convincing evidence that homosexuality was part of an ancient ritualized men-making tradition. What is more, this tradition in Melanesia is similar to men-making rituals found among contemporary African hunter-gatherer cultures, although not all contemporary hunter-gatherers share this pattern. Herdt's work suggested to me that early humans had the capacity for attraction to males and females and that natural selection exploited sexuality for functions other than reproduction.

In a classic text, *Men in Groups*, anthropologist Lionel Tiger proposed that male-male cooperation is an adaptive trait. Tiger effectively argued that early male hunter-gatherers had to cooperate with each other to maximize their acquisition of game, defend against predators, and protect themselves and the community from hostile outsiders. As a result, boys and men evolved to prefer the company of males. Tiger notes that men generally prefer all-male activities, such as team sports, militias, male living quarters, and male clubs. He strongly implies that cooperative male relationships are enjoyable but stops short of calling them affectionate. Tiger also failed to distinguish between close friendship and associations, and he did not speculate about female cooperation and associations. In a more recent text, *A Talent for Friendship: Rediscovery of a Remarkable Trait*, John Terrell asserts that ancient male friendships were more than transactional, and they were affectionate and intimate. Terrell presents fascinating ethnographic data on extensive social networks among contemporary hunter-gatherer societies in Melanesia, demonstrating that New Guinea cultures maintained distant friendships across several communities despite inhospitable terrains and geographic isolation. These friendships were largely social and personal, according to Terrell. Yet Terrell does not extend his conclusions to other hunter-gatherer societies and offers no evolutionary theory of friendship. In another recent book that explores the history of personal friendships across cultures, social psychologist Robin Goodwin and others in *Personal Relationships Across Cultures* also neglected to present a theory of adaptive friendship.

Finally, a hugely influential text on my thinking about sexuality is French philosopher Michel Foucault's *The History of Sexuality: An Introduction.* Unarguably, Foucault's writings about the social construction of sexual orientation changed how academics conceptualize sexuality. Foucault asserts that social discourse in the late nineteenth century invented a new kind of person who was defined by their sexual attraction: The homosexual/gay/ lesbian. Later, in *The Invention of Heterosexuality*, historian Jonathan Ned Katz completed Foucault's thought about the invention of sexual kinds of people by describing the origin of the normative heterosexual in contrast to the deviant homosexual. For most of the past 150 years, heterosexuality and homosexuality have functioned as two sides of the same coin. However, I will make the case that sexual attraction is not a coin, and there are no sides. I conceptualize sexual attraction more like a gelatinous substance that mostly (but not entirely) is molded by the social environment. But more on this later. While there are problems with Foucault's rigid conceptualization of the social construction of sexuality, theorists writing about sexuality must account for the role of social discourse and culture in their evolutionary and biological theories. Simply presenting different sexual beliefs and practices across a few cultures is not enough. Social and evolutionary biological theorists need to explain how their theories account for similarities and differences in human sexuality through history and across cultures.

Similar Ideas about Same-Sex Alliances

In 2000, my own book, *True Nature: A Theory of Sexual Attraction*, was published. In this text, I proposed that erotic attraction fueled intimate same-sex alliances, benefiting both men and women in early hunter-gatherer cultures. I argued that our early ancestors spent much of their time in same-sex activities. Within largely sex-segregated environments, individuals who formed alliances with older, higher status individuals and even peers gained social advantages. I argued that erotic alliances directly aided survival within same-sex environments and indirectly facilitated the acquisition of resources necessary for reproductive success, including a mate, food for the family, and childcare. Thus, natural selection favored men and women who formed close same-sex erotic alliances to manage their sex-segregated social environments. At the time, I did not think of erotic alliances as friendships, and I was unaware of the long history of devoted male friendships across cultures. While I proposed that most people have a capacity for sexual attraction to males and females, this idea may have been lost in the lengthy discussion about the persistence of same-sex sexual attraction.

The same year, two scholars in separate journal articles proposed remarkably similar ideas as mine to explain male-male sexual attraction. I was surprised and pleased to discover others thinking along the same lines. In the first paper, "The Evolution of Human Homosexual Behavior", ecologist Rob Craig Kirkpatrick remarked that male homosexuality is too common to be a fluke or mutation. He hypothesized that male homosexuality may have some adaptive function to be so prevalent among humans. Kirkpatrick reviewed three well-known adaptationist theories of male-male sexual attraction—kin selection, parental manipulation, and balanced polymorphism—and examined evidence for each. Briefly, in *kin selection* theory, non-reproducing same-sex attracted individuals at their own expense benefit the reproductive success of brothers and sisters by contributing to the survival of their siblings' children. In *parental manipulation* theory, parents somehow produce children who will not reproduce to advantage their children with greater reproductive value. Lastly, in *balanced polymorphism* theory, same-sex attraction and different-sex attraction are viewed as two versions of a trait that maintain a stable equilibrium because the heterozygous version is more advantageous than either homozygous versions of the trait. The idea is that the same-sex attraction allele contributes something useful to the phenotype that is missing in the homozygous different-sex alleles alone. Therefore, the trait of same-sex attraction is maintained. After finding little supportive evidence for these three theories, Kirkpatrick proposed that same-sex attraction might be under direct selection by facilitating male-male alliances that increase survival, resource acquisition, and defense. He viewed male alliances as survival strategies and suggested that sexual pleasure might function to enhance the bond. While mainly focused on male-male alliances, Kirkpatrick speculated that similar alliances might also directly benefit women. In the concluding lines of his paper, Kirkpatrick (2000) stated: "The evolution of human homosexuality is tied to the benefits of same-sex affiliation. Natural selection favors same-sex affection; it must be fundamental for both sexes to desire bonds with partners of both sexes" (p. 398).

In the second paper, "The Evolution of Homoerotic Behavior in Humans", evolutionary psychologist Frank Muscarella directed his arguments at evolutionary psychologists who have rejected any adaptive value of same-sex behavior because it does not directly benefit reproduction. Muscarella proposed that same-sex alliances, reinforced by erotic behavior, helped early humans of both sexes to survive. He speculated that adolescents would have been highly vulnerable within ancestral communities and young people likely benefited from same-sex alliances. Muscarella argued that adolescents who bonded with older, higher status same-sex individuals, as well as with same-sex peers, would have been more likely to survive. Thus, same-sex alliances would be directly favored by natural selection. He claimed that even same-sex peer alliances would have offered some protection and support and better assured access to food and shelter. What is more, same-sex alliances would have facilitated acquisition of resources such as a mate, thereby indirectly benefiting reproduction. Muscarella cited evidence of same-sex alliances among non-human primates and across human cultures in support of his hypothesis. He went on to speculate that exclusive sexual interest in one sex may be due to normal variation in the trait of sexual attraction (Muscarella, 2006). Muscarella also proposed that, like different-sex mating pairs, same-sex alliances most likely would have followed a dominant-submissive structure. Dominant-submissive relationships are based on differences in individuals' status and role. Such relationships are common in human and non-human animal worlds and not necessarily abusive or exploitive. In many traditional cultures, adult human males have higher status and decision-making authority than either young adult or adolescent males. Adult females and children generally have low status and little social power in traditional cultures, which does not mean that adult females have no voice in the community or never hold positions of power.

Since its publication, Muscarella's work has received a fair amount of attention and is most closely associated with the *Alliance Formation Theory* of same-sex sexual behavior. While Muscarella and Kirkpatrick both emphasized sexual behavior and pleasure as the erotic bond within alliances, in my book I placed more emphasis on sexual attraction and love as the adhesive bond among same-sex alliances.

Also, in 2000, Michael Ross and Alan Wells published an insightful paper titled, "The Modernist Fallacy in Homosexual Selection Theories: Homosexual and Homosexual Exaptation in South Asian Society". Like

Muscarella, Ross and Wells chided evolutionary psychologists for too quickly concluding that same-sex sexuality has no adaptive value because there is no evidence of adaptation observed in modern culture. The pair argued that more traditional settings, such as small villages in South Asia, rather than university campuses in the United States, are more appropriate places to look for the adaptive value of same-sex sexuality. And that is what they did. Ross and Wells then proposed that same-sex behavior evolved from male-male social affiliation as an *exaptation* to directly aide survival within traditional collective cultures. An exaptation is an adaptive trait that has been co-opted for another function. Ross and Wells' paper further reinforced my own thinking that modern society is too different from traditional cultures to find clear evidence of the adaptive benefits of same-sex alliances. More likely, supportive evidence for devoted same-sex friendships as an adaptation can be found in traditional cultures and in the past.

The texts cited above, and others, greatly influenced my thinking about the evolution of different-sex mating pair-bonds, devoted same-sex friendship, and sexual attraction. Since the publication of *True Nature* two decades ago, research on these topics has blossomed. We know more about the role of oxytocin on social affiliation and romantic love than we did 20 years ago. We know much more about the role of friendship across cultures, as well as the history of homosexuality. We have a better understanding of the prevalence of people with same-sex attractions. We also have a better understanding of practices, relationships, social networks, and culture among contemporary hunter-gatherer societies, which sadly are quickly disappearing. In the past two decades, there has also been a large cultural shift toward greater acceptance of same-sex sexualities and scholarship on sexuality. Twenty years ago, as a non-traditional academic and a federal government employee, I was concerned that writing about sexual attraction, especially same-sex attraction, could mean that I would not be taken seriously by my health research peers. However, I experienced no pushback or rejection, and the cultural climate has steadily improved. Today I have a national leadership role in a federal government health care organization directing policy and the implementation of best practices for the care of military veterans with lesbian, gay, bisexual, transgender (LGBT), and related identities. These days, everyone seems interested in LGBT health. Clinicians want to know what they were not taught in their professional training programs. Researchers now often include questions on sexual orientation and gender identity in their surveys, even if they have no specific interest in these areas. New academic journals like *LGBT Health* and *Transgender Health* have emerged to promote further research. In just a few years, there has been incredible social change, although hostilities against sexual and gender minorities have not disappeared, and scholarship in this area still carries some risk in the current political climate.

Anchor Points

In my view, two main divisions exist within the broad field of human sexual culture/sexual science. On one side, anthropologists, gender and critical theorists, and gay and lesbian studies scholars largely promote *social constructionist* perspectives. My choice of words here recognizes that this old academic debate continues in new forms. On the other side, evolutionary biologists and psychologists, neuroscientists, and laboratory researchers largely take empirical scientific positions. The two sides share little common language, and each side tends to view the other as misinformed at best and the enemy at worst. The stakes are high, and defenses are up. Gender and critical theorists often portray scientific researchers as biased, oppressive of minorities, and self-serving, while biologically inclined researchers frequently present feminist, gender, and gay studies scholars as unscientific social change advocates. Clearly, political and social change are not scientific programs. While social learning is a scientific theory that is often promoted by constructionists, social constructionism as employed by gender and critical theorists is not a scientific approach and is even anti-science (Kauth, 2002). As employed by gender and critical theorists, constructionism has functioned as a strategy for disrupting conventional power dynamics in discourse to reveal alternative narratives outside the dominant narrative. At the same time, science is not free from bias. As an evolutionist, historian, and gay man who worries about the slow pace of social change, I appreciate these different perspectives. While the division between science and constructionism presented here is overly simplified and not new, this contrast is useful for discussing dominant and alternative narratives in human sexuality. More sophisticated versions of constructionist analyses can be found in efforts to show the existence of self-identified same-sex attracted people at a time when none were thought to exist (e.g., Norton, 1997; Robb, 2003) and in explorations of intimate female friendships and sexuality in previous eras (e.g., Marcus, 2007; Vicinus, 2004), some of which are mentioned later.

Evolutionary theory is the overarching framework with which I will examine human different-sex mating pair-bonds and devoted same-sex friendships. Human bodies and psychology evolved over countless generations to survive the African savannah. Ancient humans also lived in social environments as part of families, small groups, communities, and larger bands. Over a long period of time, ancient human bodies, brains, and personalities evolved to survive the complex social environment that humans created for themselves. Ancient humans who were reproductively successful in these environments passed on their genes and heritable dispositions to their offspring until the offspring became us. While I think I make a convincing argument for the evolution of different-sex mating pair-bonds and devoted same-sex friendships in the forthcoming pages, some may be unpersuaded. Some readers may feel unsettled or annoyed that I have not defined mating and friendship in the way they do. For skeptical readers, I hope to at least convey some insights that will lead them to question conventional knowledge about marriage, friendship, and sexuality.

This text is not a primer on evolutionary theory, but there are basic tenets of evolutionary theory that I want to make clear from the start. Here they are in a nutshell. By evolutionary theory, I am referring to neo-Darwinian theory that integrates modern genetics. Darwin originally referred to heritable traits that enhanced an organism's survival and reproduction as *adaptations* (Darwin, 1859/1958). He posited two explanations for the origin and diversity of species: natural selection and sexual selection. *Natural selection* is the process whereby particular heritable traits confer a survival and reproductive advantage to their host within an ecology. Those heritable traits are passed on to offspring. *Reproductive success* refers to the production of offspring who themselves produce offspring, thereby passing on one's genes and heritable traits. Organisms with adaptive traits will out-reproduce their peers who lack those traits, and the adaptive traits will eventually predominate in the population. A large social brain and the ability to walk upright are adaptive human traits that likely evolved by natural selection. The ecology or physical environment broadly refers to climate, water and food sources, natural shelter and resources, and predators and parasites.

Darwin (1871/1981) proposed *sexual selection* to explain costly traits and subgroup differences or varieties within a population. Sexually selected traits include brightly colored feathers, large appendages, and ritual courtship displays. Sex differences within a species are sexually selected traits. Darwin advanced two forms of sexual selection: *intrasexual* (mate competition) and *intersexual selection* (mate choice). While he reasoned that sexually selected traits persist because they confer a reproductive advantage, some traits may be preferred because they are attention-getting or perceived as beautiful, rather than for any fitness benefit (Prum, 2017). Pendulous human breasts and dangling penises are sexually selected traits that may have no adaptive advantage but were selected because early humans found them pleasing. Besides natural and sexual selection, evolution of a species may also occur through non-adaptive mechanisms, such as neutral (non-detrimental) mutations, genetic drift (changes in allele frequencies due to reduced population), and gene flow (migration). These mechanisms are not the focus of this book.

Robert Trivers's (1972) perceptive concept of *parental investment* helped to explain both mate competition and mate choice. Parental investment refers to the costs (time, energy, resources, and lost reproductive opportunities) associated with conceiving, gestating, and raising offspring to reproductive age. In many species, females bear a greater parental investment cost due to having a limited number of eggs, or limited periods of fertility, and a larger investment of personal resources in reproduction (gestation, feeding young, etc.) than males who mainly contribute sperm and have little to do with raising offspring. Because females have more at risk with each pregnancy, females are choosy in who they mate with. Access to females for mating becomes a limited resource. Female mate choice fuels mate competition among males. While mate competition is generally thought of as male-male competition for a reproductive mate, females may also compete to a lesser extent with other females for a mate, especially when males become choosy because they have an increased parental investment.

Generally, male-male competition for reproductive mates promotes the development of sexual weaponry or ornamentation. *Sexual weapons* may include large physical size, large sharp teeth, horns, and aggressive behavior to fight rivals. *Sexual ornaments* can include bright colors, elaborate tails, full manes, and ritualistic behavioral displays to attract a mate's attention. Male-male competition also contributes to the formation of social hierarchies, dominant-submissive roles, and efforts to gain status (Geary, 2010; Tiger, 1969/1984). To reduce intrasexual aggression and maintain or increase social status, males may form temporary coalitions or long-term alliances with unrelated males to defend against threats and acquire quality resources like food and reproductive mates (Symons, 1979; Tiger, 1969/1984). Female-female competition for a reproductive mate is more evident in species that share parenting, like humans (Trivers, 1972). Shared parenting makes an invested male mate a limited resource. To a lesser degree, female-female competition spawns loose social hierarchies and alliances. More often, female alliances are kinship-based, such as mother-daughter or sister-sister alliances (Geary, 2010). Females may also establish temporary coalitions or long-term alliances, often in response to resource disputes and to defend against male aggression. Generally, female alliances tend to be smaller and less stable than male alliances (Buss, 2003).

An important point about evolutionary theory that people sometimes find confusing is that evolutionary theory is concerned with the *why* of a phenomenon, that is, the ultimate or "real" cause of a trait in the sense of origin in the distant past. If a trait has an adaptive function, this likely occurred tens of thousands or even millions of years ago. On the other hand, theories about male sexual attraction regarding prenatal androgen exposure, genetics, or social learning are concerned with explaining *how* the phenomenon develops; that is, the proximate or immediate cause of a trait within the organism's lifetime. As we will see in the next chapter, the ultimate cause of long-term different-sex mating pair-bonds may be that ancient humans who formed mating relationships in this way out-reproduced mating couples that employed alternative strategies. However, the proximate cause of long-term mating pair-bonds might be explained in part as exposure to oxytocin during sexual activity which enhances feelings of affection and love. Proximate explanations are important. However, knowing the *mechanism* for a trait's expression is not the same as knowing the *reason* for its existence. From an evolutionist perspective, human mating pair-bonds are more than an emotional attachment or response to a social convention. The desire to form an intimate, committed, long-term reproductive relationship with a different-sex mate is the result of an evolved trait that resulted in greater reproductive success for our early ancestors.

Because this text employs evolutionary theory as its framework and reproduction is the mechanism for conveying beneficial heritable traits, I will use "male" and "female" to refer to biological sex and its reproductive functions. Biological sex is usually evident by the presence of a penis or a vagina. The presence of these reproductive organs suggests the likelihood of producing sperm and eggs, respectively. There are other indicators of biological sex and reproductive ability that are important, such as sex chromosomes and internal genitalia. However, in the ancient environment of evolutionary adaptedness, an infant's external genitals were visible evidence of its sex that everyone could witness. While some people are born with indeterminate or ambiguous genitalia, these are rare cases and peripheral to the story. I will use "man" and "woman" to refer mainly to gender and gender roles. Every culture recognizes men and women and masculine and feminine gender roles, although their meanings vary. Some cultures recognize more than two genders. The *fa'afafine* of Samoa, for example, represent an alternative gender for individuals with male anatomy and feminine characteristics (and sexual attraction to men) but who do not identify as men or women (Vasey & VanderLaan, 2014). The *tombois* of Sumatra are individuals with female anatomy and masculine characteristics (and attraction to women) but who do not identify as women (Blackwood, 1999). While not exactly a third gender, Western culture has begun to recognize people whose gender identity or expression is not congruent with their sexual anatomy and sex assigned at birth. Such individuals are often referred to as *transgender* people (Centers for Disease Control, 2017b). Transgender individuals may identify as transgender men or women, or simply as men or women, or they may use another gender term. My focus in this book is not on gender identity, nor on so-called *transgender homosexuality*, meaning third- or fourth-gender individuals with male anatomy, feminine or ambiguous gender expression, and sexual attraction to and sexual behavior with masculine men.

This is not a text about homosexuality specifically, although I will describe many loving same-sex relationships. Given the evolutionary and historical framework of this text, I will use "same-sex" to refer to male-male and female-female relationships and sexuality. "Different-sex" will refer to male-female relationships and sexuality. I will occasionally use the term "heterosexual" to refer to contemporary male-female mating pair-bonds and use the term "bisexual" when referring to sexual attraction and sexuality with both males and females. Recently, to improve precision, some sexual scientists have begun to use the terms *androphilia* and *gynephilia* to refer to sexual attraction to men and to women, respectively. These terms avoid ahistorical identity labels and implying binary gender attractions. However, these terms are unfamiliar to most people, awkward, and unnecessarily technical. The combined term *androgynephilia* to refer to attraction to men and women is even more awkward and esoteric. For simplicity and clarity, I use "same-sex" and "different-sex" to refer to sex of partners. I will use these terms or note attraction to both males to females to indicate particular sexual attractions.

Generally, I avoid using the term *homosexual* to refer to same-sex phenomena or to people. The "homosexual" is a socially constructed sexual type of person. "Homosexual" is also not an objective term. From its beginning, the term "homosexual" has been associated with social stigma, mental illness, disease, and immorality. Although the terms *gay* and *lesbian* carry some social stigma, they are more clearly self-identities and not imposed labels or former clinical disorders. I use the terms *gay men* and *lesbian women* to refer to modern sexual identities and the combined term *homosexual/gay/lesbian* when referring to the historical construction of this sexual kind of person. *Heterosexual*, as a normative social role and identity, is not stigmatized. In general, I only use the term "heterosexual" when referring to a modern identity. People in the distant past did not have heterosexual identities. Other terms are defined as they arise in the text. Whole chapters are devoted to mating pair-bonds, devoted friendships, and sexual attraction, so these terms will be addressed later.

Some readers may wonder about my own personal biases and to what extent I am objective. That is a fair concern. I can say truthfully that I have been as objective as I can be. I also acknowledge consciously narrowing the scope of this book to a manageable level and that means making editorial decisions to cover some material and not others. The critical reader can decide if I have left too much out or too much in. Like everyone, I have a particular perspective and biases. Taking a perspective is necessary for storytelling. My aim is to tell an engaging and persuasive story that illustrates the facts as I see them. Some readers may wonder how my personal background has influenced this story. I am a white gay man who spent his childhood in a small, rural, ethnically homogenous Kansas town at a time when being gay was not something people ever said out loud. Everybody worked hard. My father was a laborer, and my mother was a housewife. I am the oldest of their four children. We were lower, middle class at best. We never went hungry, but I do not know how my parents managed to raise a family of six with one small income. My parents were fundamentalist Christians who distrusted education because it led to questioning their authority and questioning God. We attended church at least twice a week. I read constantly as a child because reading was fun and an escape. I am an overeducated, non-traditional academic. My undergraduate degree is in Art History, and my doctorate is in Clinical Psychology. I am an educator, researcher, scholar, health care policy leader, social activist, and husband. I still read voraciously. I love to cook, visit with friends, and travel outside of the United States, where I can experience different languages, cultures, foods, and wine. Readers can decide for themselves whether any of these influences matter to this story.

Map of the Terrain

Now that I have outlined the main themes of this book and set some boundaries, we can look at what lies ahead. In Chapter Two, "Love, Sex, Marriage, and Family", I explore the evolution of human mating pair-bonds and the role of different-sex sexual attraction and romantic love in establishing and maintaining these relationships. Most people readily acknowledge male-female sexual attraction, romantic love, and marriage, as well as their relationship to reproduction, even if they know nothing about evolution. These associations are generally not disputed, making it a good place to begin. Different-sex mating pair-bonds are an ancient sexual strategy employed by our earliest human ancestors because this approach led to their reproductive success. For parents, staying together to raise their large brained, slow-to-develop, social children became the key to their children's survival and to out-reproducing other hominin groups. Thus, long-term different-sex mating pair-bonds are adaptive traits. It is unlikely that occasional sex and pleasure were enough to keep ancient couples together. Romantic love was the likely key to long-term bonding. Later, social conventions around coupling and marriage further promoted and maintained mating pair-bonds. This chapter concludes with the claim that a consequence of different-sex mating pair-bonds as an adaptation is that many men and women yearn to fall in love with another person and establish a family, whether children are desired or not. The modern obsession with romantic love is a byproduct of human mating pair-bonds as an adaptation.

Among our early ancestors, male competition for a mate led to the formation of male social hierarchies, male alliances, and, in part, sex segregation. As tasks became specialized and gendered, social life became more complex and further sex-segregated. After childhood, early humans lived and interacted mainly with same-sex members of the community. In Chapter Three, "Friends with Benefits", I explore the evolution of same-sex alliances and friendships and their functions within early human cultures. Friendships take many forms. I focus on passionate, intimate, long-term, devoted male friendships, rather than alliances or brief coalitions that are more transactional. Devoted male friendships are also qualitatively different than alliances. Within male social communities, devoted male friendships likely functioned to facilitate navigation of the social environment, defend against threat, increase social status, and acquire resources for survival. Thus, devoted male friendships may have been directly selected as an adaptation. For men, acquiring status, protection, and resources increased the likelihood of obtaining a quality mate, thereby indirectly benefiting reproductive success. Emotional bonding through love and sexual affection likely held together devoted friendships, much like mating pair-bonds. We find numerous examples of devoted male friendships among contemporary hunter-gatherer societies in the form of blood brotherhoods and mentoring. A consequence of devoted male friendships as an adaptation is that men should desire to have close, intimate male friends. Although direct evidence is sparse, early human females would have faced similar challenges in navigating a largely female social environment. For women, forming devoted friendships to share workload, gather food, care for children, and defend against hostile women and men in the community would have provided many advantages as well.

In Chapter Four, "Life Partners", I trace the history of devoted male friendships, and a few female friendships, up to the Christianization of the late Roman Empire. One of the earliest examples of written literature is a story about devoted male friends. In the ancient poem *Gilgamesh*, the Sumerian king and his sworn brother Enkidu bond and have several epic adventures together. After Enkidu dies, Gilgamesh struggles with finding meaning in his life. Other famous male friends are described in this chapter, including David and Jonathan among the early Israelites and mythic heroes Achilles and Patroclus from *The Iliad*. The poet Sappho provides the earliest evidence of devoted female friendships in the ancient world. With the Christianization of the Roman Empire, same-sex friendships and marriage changed dramatically and began to take shapes that are more familiar to people today. By the late Roman Empire, radical Christian zealots and Christian emperors began criminalizing and demonizing men who submitted to anal sex, eventually condemning anyone who engaged in same-sex sexual acts. Christian leaders introduced into Western culture a general attitude that condemned sexual pleasure as sinful and blamed male-male sexuality and idolatry for natural disasters, famine, plague, barbarian invasions, and the fall of society. Early Christians viewed devoted male friendships as pagan. The relatively recent disappearance of devoted male friendships in China and Japan can be traced to the domineering, judgmental influence of Western culture as Western contact increased in these countries. The long history of devoted male friendships and probable female friendships provides strong evidence that most men, and likely most women, have the capacity for attraction to males and females and will express such affections when the culture supports it.

By the late nineteenth century, Western culture had invented two mutually exclusive sexual kinds of people: the "heterosexual" and the "homosexual/ gay/lesbian". The invention of exclusive sexual kinds of people was a dramatic break with the history of bisexuality that pervaded previous cultures.

In Chapter Five, "Labeling Love and People", I examine the social construction of the heterosexual and the homosexual/gay/lesbian and how humans have come to experience themselves in these terms. Contemporary sexual science research data also appear to conclusively demonstrate that most people describe themselves as exclusively heterosexual while a small proportion identify as gay or lesbian. However, sexuality research also demonstrates that women are surprisingly flexible in their sexual arousal pattern and not exclusive—despite what they self-report. Similar research shows that men are more fluid in their arousal pattern than they report and contrary to what researchers conclude. New analyses of previously published data actually show that bisexual men experience a continuum of arousal to males and females. How do we reconcile current research data with the long history of concurrent different-sex mating pair-bonds and devoted male friendships? An alternative interpretation of current sex research views scientists and study participants as embedded within culture. By taking a broad historical and cultural perspective, researchers can see how cultures have influenced how humans experience their lives and their sexual attractions. By recognizing how social discourse and culture have constructed social reality, scientists can better understand how people experience their erotic and sexual lives. I call for a shift in research away from identifying individual differences to a focus on the *function* of sexual attractions. Small differences between groups of heterosexuals and groups of gay men and lesbian women tell us little that is substantial. Worse, this approach reinforces the idea that differences between these artificially constructed groups are important. Cross-cultural research that explores the function of sexual attraction in mating and friendship has the potential to tell us much more about the rich role of sexual attraction and sexuality. The interdisciplinary evolutionary model of mating and friendship presented here is an example of that functional approach. This interdisciplinary approach is broader, richer, and more parsimonious than evolutionary theories focused on mating alone.

Acknowledgments

Writing this book has been an intense and stimulating experience. I have learned much along the way that has reinforced my ideas and challenged what I thought I knew. I hope that readers find this book as interesting and enjoyable to read as it was for me to write. I am also very grateful to many people for supporting me in this effort. I appreciate the patient assistance that I received from Routledge in readying this manuscript for publication. While working on this book, I have had numerous conversations with people that have generated ideas or identified problems that I needed to address in this manuscript. In particular, I am grateful to Frank Muscarella for reading and commenting on early rough drafts of chapters and appreciate him overlooking the numerous errors and incomplete thoughts in those drafts.

His comments were insightful and extremely helpful as I put words to the ideas in my head. I have a big thank you for my work colleagues who covered for me on many occasions when I took days off to write. Finally, I am grateful to my husband, Matthew Horsfield, for forgiving my long periods of inattention over two years while I worked on this project every weekend, many evenings, and holidays. I could not have completed this book without everyone's support.

References

Beer, B. (2001). Anthropology of friendship. In N. J. Smelser & P. B. Baltes (Eds.), *International encyclopedia of social and behavioral sciences* (pp. 5805–5808). Kidlington, England: Pergamon.

Blackwood, E. (1999). *Tombois* in West Sumatra: Constructing masculinity and erotic desire. In E. Blackwood & S. E. Wieringa (Eds.), *Female desires: Same-sex relations and transgender practices across cultures* (pp. 181–205). New York: Columbia University Press.

Bourque, A. (2017). Technology profits and pivots in the $300 billion wedding space. *HuffPost*. https://www.huffpost.com/entry/technology-profit-and-piv_b_7 193112

Brown, D. E. (1991). *Human universals*. Boston, MA: McGraw-Hill.

Buss, D. M. (2003). *The evolution of desire: Strategies of human mating – Revised and expanded*. New York: Basic Books.

Centers for Disease Control and Prevention (2017a). Marriage and divorce. National Center for Health Statistics. https://www.cdc.gov/nchs/fastats/marriage-divorce.htm

Centers for Disease Control and Prevention. (2017b). Transgender persons. https://www.cdc.gov/lgbthealth/transgender.htm

Darwin, C. (1859/1958). *On the origin of species by means of natural selection*. New York: New American Library.

Darwin, C. (1871/1981). *The descent of man and selection in relation to sex*. Princeton, NJ: Princeton University Press.

Eurostat. (2019, February 14). Which EU countries have the highest marriage rates? https://ec.europa.eu/eurostat/documents/4187653/9541683/Marriage+rates +2017

Federal Bureau of Investigation. (2019). 2018 hate crime statistics. https://ucr.fbi .gov/hate-crime/2018/resource-pages/hate-crime-summary

Freedom for All Americans. (2018). LGBTQ Americans aren't fully protected from discrimination in 30 states. https://www.freedomforallamericans.org/states/

Geary, D. C. (2010). *Male, female: The evolution of human sex differences* (2nd ed.). Washington, DC: American Psychological Association.

Gurven, M. (2012). Human survival and life history in evolutionary perspective. In J. C. Mitani, J. Call, P. M. Kappeler, R. A. Palombit & J. B. Silk (Eds.), *The evolution of primate societies* (pp. 293–314). Chicago, IL: University of Chicago Press.

Halperin, D. M. (2012). *How to be gay*. Cambridge, MA: The Belknap Press.

Kauth, M. R. (2002). Much ado about homosexuality: Assumptions underlying current research on sexual orientation. *Journal of Psychology and Human Sexuality*, *14*(1), 1–22.

Kirkpatrick, R. C. (2000). The evolution of human homosexual behavior. *Current Anthropology*, *41*(3), 385–414.

Lukas, D., & Clutton-Brock, T. H. (2013). The evolution of social monogamy in mammals. *Science*, *341*(6145), 526–530.

Marcus, S. (2007). *Between women: Friendship, desire, and marriage in Victorian England*. Princeton, NJ: Princeton University Press.

Marlowe, F. W. (2012). The socioecology of human reproduction. In J. C. Mitani, J. Call, P. M. Kappeler, R. A. Palombit & J. B. Silk (Eds.), *The evolution of primate societies* (pp. 469–486). Chicago, IL: University of Chicago Press.

Miller, N. F., & Donovan, J. (2009/2013). *Blood brotherhood and other rites of male alliance* (2nd rev. edn.). Milwaukie, OR: Dissonant Hum.

Muscarella, F. (2006). The evolution of male-male sexual behavior in humans: The alliance theory. In M. R. Kauth (Ed.), *Handbook of the evolution of human sexuality* (pp. 275–311). Binghamton, NY: Haworth Press.

Norton, R. (1997). *The myth of the modern homosexual: Queer history and the search for cultural unity*. London: Cassell.

People for the American Way Foundation. (2019). Who is weaponizing religious liberty? Retrieved from http://www.pfaw.org/report/who-is-weaponizing-religious-liberty/

Prum, R. O. (2017). *The evolution of beauty: How Darwin's forgotten theory of mate choice shapes the animal world—And us*. New York: Doubleday.

Robb, G. (2003). *Strangers: Homosexual love in the nineteenth century*. New York: W. W. Norton & Company.

Seyfarth, R. M., & Cheney, D. L. (2012). The evolutionary origins of friendship. *Annual Review of Psychology*, *64*, 153–177.

Symons, D. (1979). *The evolution of human sexuality*. Oxford: Oxford University Press.

Tiger, L. (1969/1984). *Men in groups*. New York: Marion Boyers.

Trivers, R. L. (1972). Parental investment and sexual selection. In B. Campbell (Ed.), *Sexual selection and the descent of man* (pp. 136–179). Chicago, IL: Aldine.

Vasey, P. L., & VanderLaan, D. P. (2014). Evolving research on the evolution of male androphilia. *Canadian Journal of Human Sexuality*, *23*(3), 137–147.

Vicinus, M. (2004). *Intimate friends: Women who loved women, 1778–1928*. Chicago, IL: University of Chicago Press.

Williams, W. L. (1992a). The relationship between male-male friendship and male-female marriage: American Indian and Asian comparisons. In P. M. Nardi (Ed.), *Research on men and masculinities, vol. 2: Men's friendships* (pp. 186–200). Newbury Park, CA: SAGE.

Chapter 2

Love, Sex, Marriage, and Family
Different-Sex Mating Pair-Bonds as an Adaptation

Romantic love permeates contemporary Western cultures. Most of us want to find someone to love, fall in love, and be loved passionately in return (Baer, 2017; Goodwin, 1999). People rejoice in finding their true love and mourn the loss of love. The bliss of falling in love and the pain of losing love are commemorated in thousands of songs and countless poems, numerous novels and plays, and many television dramas and movies. Self-help books on how to fall in love and keep love's spark alive fill bookstore shelves. When friends get together, almost invariably, the subject turns to who is involved with whom, who is in love, who is struggling to make the relationship work, who is having an affair, and who is thinking about leaving their partner and finding someone who will treat them better. Humans love the subject of love and its struggles.

Western culture is obsessed with different-sex (male-female) romantic love and loving relationships, but Western culture is not alone. In a well-known study of love in other cultures, sociologist Susan Sprecher and colleagues (1994) asked adult men and women in Russia, Japan, and the United States if they would marry someone who had all the qualities in a spouse they wanted if they were not in love with that person. Unsurprisingly, a large majority of Russian, Japanese, and American participants said they would *only* marry for love. A bit surprising, most participants reported they were currently *in* love, with Japanese men being the lone exception. A study of love among college students in 11 cultures (India, Pakistan, Thailand, United States, England, Japan, Philippines, Mexico, Brazil, Hong Kong, and Australia) found similar results (Levine, Sato, Hashimoto, & Verma, 1995). Across most cultures, students said they were unlikely to marry someone they did not love. Men and women in India and Pakistan were the exception, although not all students in India and Pakistan felt that way. The study authors noted that romantic love in marriage was more valued among individualistic, mostly Western cultures like the United States and England than collective cultures like India and Pakistan. In an enormous study of 10,047 young adult men and women across 37 cultures and 33 countries (six continents and five islands), participants rated 18 characteristics associated with choosing a mate (Buss, Abbott, Angleitner, et al., 1990). Across all samples, men and women ranked "mutual attraction—love" as the number one characteristic they valued most when choosing a mate. What is more, men and women agreed on the next three important characteristics: "dependable character", "emotional stability and maturity", and "pleasing disposition". Despite considerable agreement among men and women across cultures, the study authors focused mainly on their disagreements: overall women valued "good financial prospects/good earning capacity" more than men, and men valued "good looks/physical attractiveness" more than women (Buss, Abbott, Angleitner, et al., 1990).

Historians trace the modern concept of different-sex romantic love as a prerequisite to marriage to eighteenth-century Western culture (e.g., Goodwin, 1999; Hatfield & Rapson, 1993). However, there are clear references to romantic love throughout history and across diverse cultures, although marriage was usually not based on love (Jankowiak & Fischer, 1992; Karandashev, 2015; Mitchell, 2004). Cultures expected married couples to like each other and ideally grow to love each other over time. But, romantic love was not restricted to marriage. A lovely Egyptian poem from the New Kingdom (1570 BCE–1544 BCE) illustrates the wonder and disorientation of love. In the fourth stanza of the *Papyrus Chester Beatty I*, a young woman confesses, "My heart flutters hastily, when I think of my love of you; It lets me not act sensibly, it leaps from its place" (Damrosch, 2003, p. 154). We do not know if the woman is single or married or if the young man is intended to be her husband. It does not matter. She could not control who she fell in love with, and we cannot control who we fall in love with.

In an ethnographic study that examined folk tales, love songs, and literature across a variety of cultures, the authors reported clear evidence of romantic love in 147 of 166 cultures (Jankowiak & Fischer, 1992). Only one culture lacked positive evidence of romantic love, which does not necessarily mean that romantic love is non-existent in that culture. Frequent references to romantic love can be found in ancient literature, love spells, and artwork in China, Greece, Rome, Iraq, and Egypt, dating back 5,000 years (Fletcher, Simpson, Campbell, & Overall, 2015; Mitchell, 2004). One of the earliest references to romantic love is a Sumerian love charm (Gregersen, 1996). The magic spell involves cow's milk and fat combined in a ritual bowl that, when applied to a young girl, will motivate her to chase after her male suitor. In the ancient Babylonian poem *Gilgamesh*, written about 1700 BCE, the priestess Shamhat casts a love spell on the wild man Enkidu that gives him an erection for seven days, leading to nonstop sex with the sorceress (Mitchell, 2004). As a result of their magical sexual frenzy, Enkidu is civilized! References to love magic are quite common across ancient and modern cultures, which suggests that many people have not only longed for love but experienced unrequited love and were willing to go to some lengths to manipulate others into falling in love with them. Love magic to induce passion was particularly popular among women during the Roman Empire, for some reason (Knapp, 2013). Among the Trobrianders of Papua New Guinea, all success in love is thought to be due to magic (Gregersen, 1996). Love magic to direct another's romantic feelings can be found among cultures as distinct as the Cree and Navajo Indians of North America and European Roma/Romani (Gregersen, 1996).

While cultures may not view romantic love in the same way, the concept of being in love with someone appears to be universal. So, what is romantic love? Where did it come from? Sigmund Freud (1905/1953) hypothesized that adult romantic love is an extension of maternal love or mother-infant bonding, and he may have been right. Nature is conservative and tends to use available resources in new ways. Modern researchers have viewed romantic love as a combination of attachment (intimacy), caregiving (commitment), and sex (Shaver & Hazan, 1988). Social psychologist Elaine Hatfield and historian Richard Rapson (1993) distinguished between two forms of romantic love, *passionate love* and *companionate love*, although the two are closely linked. They described passionate love as an intense desire to be with the object of affection. Passionate love involves infatuation, desire, longing, and elation when fulfilled and emptiness, distress, and despair when unrequited or rebuffed. Passionate love is what most people would call romantic love. By contrast, companionate love is less intense. Hatfield and Rapson (1993) viewed companionate love as a warm feeling of affection toward the love object that includes sexual interest and activity. Companionate love involves a sense of respect and devotion as well as a feeling of deep connection that follows the intense frenzy of passionate love. While passionate love fades over time, companionate love is relatively long-lasting.

In this volume, I use the term *romantic love* to refer to an intense desire to be emotionally, physically, and sexually intimate with one's object of affection, much like how Hatfield and Rapson described passionate love. Sexual attraction is central to romantic love, even if the pair chooses not to have sex. There is debate about whether attraction precedes or follows love, although to me the order of conscious experience is less important than their close association. The order of experience may depend on unique characteristics of the individuals involved as well as the circumstances of their togetherness. In this chapter, I will focus mainly on different-sex (male-female) sexual attraction, romantic love, and mating pair-bonds. Like Hatfield and Rapson (1993), I use the term *companionate love* to refer to a deep mutual affection that develops over time within a pair-bond and involves at least occasional sexual activity. *Sexual attraction* refers to the desire to be physically intimate and sexual with an individual based on their particular characteristics, which include the individual's biological sex and gender traits. Sexual attraction and desire lead to physiological arousal such as feeling flush (warm), skin sensitivity, nipple hardness, and penile erection or vaginal lubrication, which often precede sexual activity. The term *erotic attraction* refers to a sensual, suggestive, aesthetic quality that causes sexual feelings. *Eroticism* is a broad experience that encompasses sexual attraction. While same-sex attracted people also experience sexual attraction, romantic love, and pair-bonding, loving same-sex friendships are examined in detail in Chapters Three and Four. I address sexual attraction in Chapter Five.

For contemporary different-sex attracted men and women in Western cultures, finding an agreeable sexual partner is relatively easy. Finding love and commitment with a partner is more difficult. A major difficulty in making a loving, committed connection is that men and women have inherently different levels of investment in reproduction that drive their sexual interests and their approach to pairing with a partner. Because of inherent differences between men and women, a couple that stays together must continually work to overcome self-interest and distrust, concerns about fairness, and fear of exploitation in order to maintain the relationship, no matter how sexually attracted and in love they are. In this chapter, I describe how different-sex sexual attraction and love evolved among our early ancestors to bond reproductive mating pairs together at least long enough to ensure the survival of their offspring. I will argue that intense emotional pair-bonding (love) contributed to emotional and sexual exclusivity and an increased desire by the male partner to protect and provide for his mate. In short, romantic love likely developed as a commitment device (Buss, 2006). A committed, long-term couple probably encouraged engagement of kin networks and non-relative community members in childcare because raising children is resource-intensive. Human children need years of physical, social, and cognitive development to successfully manage community life. The reproductive and social interests of the couple and kin, and even community members, led to the cultural development of marriage and kinship rules. The long-term survival of the couple may have provided indirect reproductive advantages to their children when they coupled and produced their own children. As the progeny of these ancient couples, we carry their traits with us.

The Evolution of Different-Sex Mating Pair-Bonds and Romantic Love

Evolutionary theory offers a useful framework for understanding the function of sexual attraction and romantic love. Evolutionary theory helps to explain why humans, unlike most primates, form intimate different-sex mating pair-bonds for relatively long periods of time. The universality of romantic love and mating pair-bonds (often in the form of marriage) suggests that these are naturally selected traits (Buss, 2006; Lieberman & Hatfield, 2006; Miller, 2000). While marriage is practiced differently across cultures, most men and women seek to establish a long-term different-sex mating pair-bond and raise a family.

Among most primates, like the great apes (i.e., chimpanzees, gorillas, orangutans, humans), different-sex attracted males compete with other males for sexual access to females, while females exercise some choice over their reproductive mate (Miller, 2000). Darwin's sexual selection theory (1871/1981) predicts that when fertile females are a limited resource (i.e., more males than females) or when they are choosy, then males will compete amongst themselves and/or engage in courtship displays to win attention from and access to a female. Sexually selected traits like physical size and aggressiveness in males may confer fitness advantages because they contribute to access to fertile females through competition and mate choice. That individual's male offspring may possess similar physical traits and gain similar reproductive advantages. Over generations, male sexual competition and female mate choice produce dramatic changes in physical features and behavior between males and females of a species. In general, strong mate competition and mate choice lead to sexually dimorphic species, such as physically large males with distinct sexual features (weapons or ornaments) and small, drab females. Modest male competition and female choice, or both mate competition and mate choice by males and females, result in sexually monomorphic species, where males and females are similar in size and appearance and difficult to distinguish. It is important to remember that sexually selected traits may not improve reproductive fitness and, therefore, are not always adaptive. Some traits appear to be selected for their aesthetic value alone, such as male birds with unusually long tail feathers that impair flight and long-term survival. Sexually selected traits, especially for aesthetic value, create subgroups within a species.

In multi-male, multi-female groups, which are common among chimpanzees (*Pan troglodytes*), our closest living primate relatives, females compete at times with other females to form *consortships*, or friendships, with favored males (Miller, 2000). Mating with a dominant male in the group may prevent infanticide by other males. Consistent with sexual selection theory, a high ratio of female chimpanzees to males increases female mate competition and contributes to male choosiness in a mate, even though male chimpanzees rarely contribute to parenting of their offspring. Despite the considerable intrigue and buildup around mate choice, non-human primate mating is brief and easy to miss. Among chimpanzees, for example, sex lasts only for a few seconds, and consortships are short-lived.

Generally, in many species, males and females have different mating strategies because they have different reproductive and parental investments within particular ecologies. Males exert energy and risk injury competing with other males for access to fertile females but expend few personal resources to manufacture sperm, which are ejaculated by the thousands a few seconds after penile intromission. Quick sex minimizes the risk of physical attack by another male. The lack of male parental commitment in raising offspring allows for impregnation of other females and additional offspring. Consequently, in many species, males are bigger, physically aggressive, easily aroused sexually, and quick to ejaculate. In contrast, females generally do not compete with other females for a reproductive mate and expend significant personal resources manufacturing ovum. No matter how many males she mates with, females have only one or a few offspring at a time. Once impregnated, the female must nourish both herself and her growing fetus(s) for several months, requiring additional effort and risk to her health. In many species, giving birth is risky for both the mother and newborn(s) due to complications and predators. For several additional weeks or months or years, the mother must continue to nourish the newborn(s) with her own body and protect the infant(s) from physical threat at great personal risk. The mother must pay close attention to her young until they can feed and care for themselves. Gestating, birthing, and raising young are substantial commitments of the mother's personal resources and time. Consequently, in many species, females are more social and nurturing because attentiveness and nurturance increased the chances of offspring survival. In many species, females are only periodically fertile and interested in sex only during those times. In addition, the ecology places pressures on courting, mating, and raising offspring. Like our primate ancestors, early humans experienced ecological and reproductive pressures that shaped their mating strategies, as well as their bodies and minds.

Hominin Evolution

About eight million years ago, in heavily forested eastern Africa, our hominin line shared a common ancestor with chimpanzees (Taylor, 1996). By about four million years ago, our Australopithecine ancestors (e.g., *Australopithecus afarensis* and *africanus*; *Paranthropus robustus*) had begun walking exclusively on their hind legs, perhaps to take advantage of resources in emerging open areas. These creatures looked a lot like tall bonobos (*Pan paniscus*) or pygmy chimpanzees. Australopithecine males had small penises, and females had large clitorises and only modest breasts during periods of breastfeeding (Taylor, 1996). Males were larger than females, suggesting strong male sexual competition and female choice. Both males and females were covered in thick body hair. Dentition suggests that Australopithecines were herbivores. Between three and two million years ago, the climate on the eastern side of Africa became cooler and drier, and the forests receded further. Large mixed woodland and grassland savannahs spread across the continent. New species of animals emerged to take advantage of the open grassland environment, including hominins who became more varied, as did their diets. By about 2.5 million years ago, our direct hominin ancestors lived full-time on the African savannah. By about two million years ago, approximately six different species of hominins, including *Homo erectus* and *Homo ergaster*, had begun to spread across Africa and into Europe and, thus, into widely diverse ecologies (Taylor, 1996). They continued to spread into the Caucasus, China, and finally Java. *Homo erectus* and *Homo ergaster* were likely the first hominins to live in hunter-gatherer societies and control fire. These archaic human ancestors increasingly lost body hair and wore clothing. Some evidence suggests that they recognized gender and had a division of labor. There is also evidence of emerging culture among these groups. Figure 2.1 presents a general timeline of hominin evolution and major events in ancient human history.

By about one million years ago, only a few hominin species remained. By about 300,000 years ago, *Homo neanderthalensis* emerged in Europe and Western Asia, and *Homo sapiens* emerged in Africa and soon began migrating across the planet in waves, perhaps because of climate change and/or famine. Neanderthals and early humans met and interbred even with other archaic humans, such as Denisovans. Neanderthals disappeared by about 25,000 years ago (Taylor, 1996). Anatomically modern humans (*Homo sapiens sapiens*) who looked like us emerged only about 50,000 years ago. A final ice age began about 40,000 years ago and lasted roughly to 12,000 years ago. As a point of reference, the Venus of Willendorf statuette was produced during this ice age around 25,000 years ago. The expanding glaciers pushed south through about 20,000 years ago and lowered sea levels, expanding the coastline. Later, as heavy glaciers receded in the north, land masses rose creating the Bering strait land bridge. The first humans arrived in North American around 13,000 years ago, and at least three waves of migrants followed (Saey, 2018). Migrants reached South America by about 11,000 years ago and reached the Andes just around 4,200 years ago.

In postglacial, Mesolithic communities, humans tended to live in semi-permanent settlements. By about 12,000 years ago, in the Near East, humans began to settle, farm, and domesticate animals (initially sheep and goats) for food (Taylor, 1996). With farming came rules about property, production, gender, and marriage systems designed to keep clan property together. The switch from hunting and foraging to farming took place at different times in at least five or six different parts of the world, including China, India, and the Americas. About 11,000 years ago, farming people began moving out of modern Turkey into Europe and into the Balkans, perhaps because of climate change, natural disasters, or disease (Curry, 2013). As farming people moved into new lands, they cleared large areas of forests. They spread through the Mediterranean and reached Britain by 6,000 years ago. Farmers displaced and eventually replaced hunter-gatherers by clearing forests, creating permanent settlements, and defending their "property". Because farming is labor intensive, farmers needed children for labor and had large families. With farming and permanent settlements came population increases,

General Timeline of Hominin Evolution

| | Early Australopithecines | Later Australopithecines | Early Humans | Early Archaic Homo Sapiens | Late Archaic Homo Sapiens | Modern Humans | | | | | | |

Ardipithecus ramidus

Australopithecus anamensis

Australopithecus afarensis ("Lucy")

Australopithecus sediba

Homo rudolfensis

Homo habilis

Homo ergaster

Homo erectus

Homo heidelbergensis

Homo neanderthalensis

Homo denisova

Homo naledi

Homo sapiens

Homo sapiens sapiens

| Use of simple tools | Larger penises, breasts, some upright walking | Use of made tools, camps | Nakedness, clothing, linguistic communication, controlled fire | Built shelters, hunting with spears | | Speech develops | Cave paintings, figurines | First humans arrive in North America | Anatolian farming people begin migrating | | Roman Republic established | |

Early farming Near East

Pre-conquest Americans arrive

Time of mythic Greeks, writing develops, lactose tolerance, early cities, kingdoms

Western Roman Empire collapses

DRIER CLIMATE   ICE AGES

| 5 million years ago | 3.5 million years ago | 1.8 million years ago | 300,000 years ago | 25,000 years ago | 12,000 years ago | 5,000 years ago | Last 2,000 years |

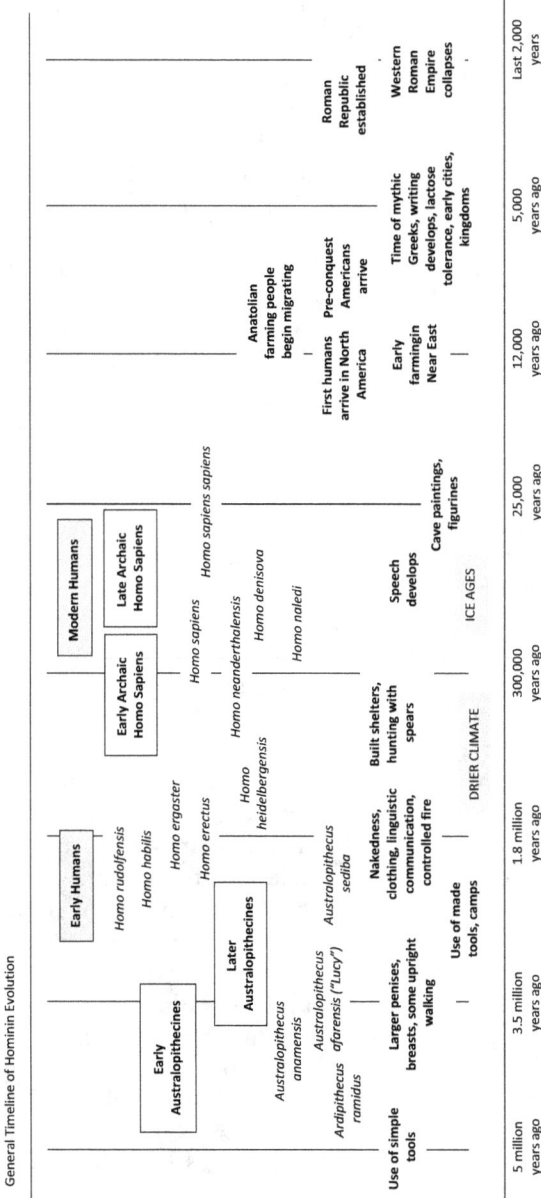

Figure 2.1 General Timeline of Hominin Evolution

establishment of cities, political hierarchy, social classes, trade, craft specialization, development of accounting systems, mathematics, and writing (Taylor, 1996).

Along with labor specialization, clothing and customs likely became even more gender defined around this time. By about 8,500 years ago, there is evidence of pottery designed to manipulate milk fats to produce cheese and yogurt (Curry, 2013). By roughly 7,500 years ago, a mutation allowed some Late Neolithic communities to develop a tolerance to lactose in milk, and farmers began producing milk to drink. By the early Bronze Age, around 5,000 years ago, lactose tolerance had spread across northern and central Europe with waves of farmers, along with cattle herding, demonstrating the recent rapid spread of a beneficial heritable trait in the population. Farmers without this trait had already settled in southern Europe, where lactose tolerance remains less common even today.

The point of this exposition is that about 300,000 years ago relatively naked, big-brained early humans (*Homo sapiens*) who looked much like us appeared. Between about two million and 300,000 years ago, the selective pressures that shaped our physical appearance and differential mating strategies had taken effect. By this time, early human males were modestly larger than females, suggesting a mating pattern of modest-to-moderate polygyny (and polyandry) but mostly monogamy (pair-bonding). Early humans were moderately sexually dimorphic, but far less so than their ancestors. Early human males had broad shoulders, narrow hips, facial hair, a large penis, and dangling scrotum. Early human females had narrow shoulders, narrow waist, broad hips, large buttocks, and visible and permanent breasts. Both males and females had underarm and pubic hair. They had scalp hair that grew. Like their ancestors, early humans were likely hunter-gatherers who established a division of labor; men hunted and collected difficult-to-reach foods (e.g., fruit, nuts, bird eggs, some seafood), while women mostly gathered food (e.g., plants, tubers, fruit). If early humans were like contemporary hunter-gatherers, they lived in small bands of a few dozen people encompassing several families to a few hundred individuals (Lehmann, Lee & Dunbar, 2014). The size of the community may have varied by the richness and stability of the ecology, with larger groups remaining in one place longer and returning to resource rich locales, while smaller groups moved frequently around harsher, more impoverished environments (Haas, Klink, Maggard, & Aldenderfer, 2015). If there is a lifestyle that humans are physically and mentally adapted to, it is a hunter-gatherer way of life. For most of human history, humans have lived as hunters and gatherers. From about two million years ago when the earliest archaic humans first appeared until just 12,000 years ago when farming began, hunter-gatherers lived in a variety of ecologies throughout Africa, Australia, China, and northern Europe. Remarkably, a few isolated hunter-gatherer societies have survived to the present.

Raising Babies

Life on the African savannah was hard. Life outside of the African savannah, along coastal areas or in harsher northern climes of mixed wood and grasslands, was also quite difficult. Living in open areas left individuals vulnerable to harsh weather, predation, and attack by other hominin bands. Injury or illness could be fatal. Food could be scarce at times or difficult to eat when available. The water was dirty and ridden with parasites. These environments would not seem like good places to raise a family, but that is what our early ancestors did. This was home. While very difficult, they did not manage alone. Evidence suggests that early human hunter-gatherers helped each other. They formed cooperative alliances, established loosely organized bands, and maintained extended social networks across large geographic spaces.

Having a large brain helped. Having a large social brain was probably key to early human success in surviving harsh environments and out-reproducing other hominins (Fletcher, Simpson, Campbell, & Overall, 2015). A large brain permitted greater creativity and development of tools—early technology. A large brain facilitated early linguistic and gestural communication and later, spoken language, to better convey intention and manage cooperative alliances, especially as relationships became more complex. A large brain allowed for the development of a theory of mind (i.e., taking another's perspective and deducing their mental states, beliefs, and motivations) to predict other's intentions and promote cooperation. A large brain enabled not just the development of social beliefs, religion, and culture, but also their transmission. A large human brain had numerous advantages but was also costly. It required more energy to operate. A large human brain also needed a big skull, which complicated childbirth and increased risk to the mother (Fletcher, Simpson, Campbell, & Overall, 2015). A creative, social, linguistic brain also necessitated a longer, slower developmental period, extending the length of juvenile development and requiring more nurturing and social interaction, protection, and resources from mother and others. Birthing and raising children with big growing social brains was resource intensive, and hunter-gatherer moms did not do it alone.

Early archaic human mothers needed help gathering food for themselves and their mates, especially during late-term pregnancy and when nursing. Mothers also needed help caring for their children. If a mother and baby survived childbirth, the new mother needed to stay close to her newborn to breastfeed, which could continue for a few years. [Human mothers wean infants at an earlier age than other great apes, which reduces time between pregnancies and increases reproductive output (Hrdy, 2009)]. A new hunter-gatherer mom could not abandon a newborn or small child to get water or search for and prepare food for herself and her family. One solution was *cooperative breeding*, where non-parent individuals, most often kin but also non-relatives, participated in caring and providing for young children in the group. Humans are major cooperative breeders, unlike our primate relatives (Kramer, 2010). Cooperative breeding is relatively rare, occurring in only about 3% of bird and mammal species.

If ancient hunter-gatherers were anything like contemporary hunter-gatherers, early archaic human mothers enlisted childcare assistance from female relatives, particularly sisters and grandmothers, but also from their mate's female relatives, as well as from non-kin females in the group (Benenson, 2013; Hrdy, 2009; Sear & Mace, 2008). Anthropologist Sarah Hrdy (2009) has argued that early human mothers nurtured their children with help from female relatives and non-kin females in the group and received minimal childcare assistance from the fathers. Cooperative breeding increased the chances of survival of human infants. Among contemporary hunter-gatherer societies, children who receive care from relatives and group members are twice as likely to survive to reproductive age as offspring of our great ape relatives (Kaplan, Hill, Lancaster, & Hurtado, 2000). While family members benefited most (genetically) by assisting with childcare for relatives, non-relatives who provided parenting support (*alloparenting*) to group members likely increased their chances of receiving support or provisioning when needed. It is quite possible that non-relative females in small bands cooperated in many shared tasks, including childcare. Non-relative females may even have formed emotional attachments to other women's children while caring for them, although perhaps not quite a mother-child attachment. Among humans, mother-child attachment is a relatively strong and durable hormonal, cognitive, and emotional bond (Broad, Curley & Keverne, 2007). Mothers and children co-evolved predispositions to form a tight emotional bond because strong mother-child attachments enhanced survival. It seems possible that cooperative childcare triggered a form of mother-child attachment. Grandmothers, for example, may have recalled or re-experienced feelings of maternal bonding with their child (now a mother) when holding their grandchild or experienced a new mother-(grand)child attachment. Given a large social brain and a theory of mind, sisters may have felt their mother-bonding disposition triggered when thinking about their sister as a new mother or when holding their sister's child. Similarly, non-relative females in the group may have felt a form of mother attachment when caring for a group member's child, especially if the mother was a close friend.

Fathers also bond with their newborn children, largely in the same way that mothers do, through physical contact and feeding (Figueiredo, Costa, Pacheco, & Pais, 2007). As we will see later, while some fathers in contemporary hunter-gatherer societies participate in childcare, they do so in a more limited way than mothers. Feeding and childcare are almost exclusively the mother's responsibility and a female activity. However, mother and newborn benefit from the father providing high-calorie food, shelter, and protection from hostile males in the community. Thus, father engagement in the family is critical. If the new father loses interest or becomes hostile, both the mother and child are vulnerable. While soliciting provisions from a male lover might work temporarily, the presence of another male may invite harsh aggression from the father and increase the risk of infanticide, unless the culture believes that multiple fathers are needed to produce a child (*partible paternity*) (Hrdy, 2000). Slow development of human children actually extended the period of risk for infanticide (Opie, Atkinson, Dunbar, & Shultz, 2013). Infanticide has very high reproductive costs for mothers and modest costs for fathers.

Infanticide is driven by paternity uncertainty and an unwillingness to invest in a non-relative male's reproductive success. While mothers can be sure that a child is her own, males cannot be certain (Buss, 2003). Males who expend time and resources to raise another male's child experience a significant reproductive loss—their own genes do not get carried forward. One general male strategy to ensure paternity, and thereby minimize infanticide, is mate-guarding. Silverback gorilla males (*Gorilla gorilla*) guard their harem from interlopers (Opie, Atkinson, Dunbar, & Shultz, 2013). However, guarding a harem requires constant vigilance and is not always successful. Interestingly enough, gorillas have the highest rate of infanticide among the great apes. A female strategy to minimize infanticide is to thoroughly confuse paternity by polyandrous mating—mating with several males. Because the mother has mated with several males, no male in the community knows who the real father is. Common chimpanzees live in multi-male, multi-female communities and follow this mating strategy. Consequently, adult male chimpanzees defend and protect young chimps because they have mated with fertile females in the group and could well be the father of any individual. A few human cultures, especially contemporary hunter-gatherers, recognize formal polyandrous relationships often, but not always, because of beliefs in partible paternity (Starkweather & Hames, 2012). There are other factors that support polyandry that I will come back to later. Data from one contemporary hunter-gatherer culture, the Barí of Venezuela, demonstrate that children who have two "fathers" are significantly more likely to survive to age 15 than children with one father (Beckerman et al., 1998). A third general strategy to ensure paternity and reduce the risk of infanticide is *social monogamy* or pair-bonding, which is more common among primates, especially humans (Opie, Atkinson, Dunbar, & Shultz, 2013). Social monogamy refers to a lengthy living arrangement and presumed bonding between an adult female and adult male that includes some mutual effort in raising their young. By keeping a female mate physically close and emotionally committed, the male can feel more confident that he is the father of their offspring. The mother receives some form of support from the father to protect and raise their young. It is worth noting that social monogamy refers to a primary pair-bond and does not necessarily mean sexual exclusivity, especially for males. In many species, but especially among humans, mating strategies are not absolute. More on this later.

There is evidence of different-sex socially monogamous pair-bonds among early archaic humans, which suggests that this is a very old mating strategy (Taylor, 1996). Leading up to modern humans, hominins have shown decreasing physical dimorphism, consistent with species that form socially monogamous pair-bonds (Grueter, Chapais, & Zinner, 2012). Highly polygynous species tend to show sexually dimorphic features, such as large males and small females. As noted earlier, sexual dimorphism is a product of male mate competition and female mate choice. Thus, moderate sexual dimorphism among early archaic humans strongly suggests a trend toward different-sex socially monogamous pair-bonds. This trend also suggests moderate male competition and moderate female choice for a partner who will commit to the relationship/family, although early humans also employed other mating strategies. Quite possibly, early human females' need for committed male mates promoted modest female sexual competition. I will also circle back to this topic later.

Thus, diminishing sexual dimorphism leading up to and including early modern humans strongly suggests that different-sex socially monogamous pair-bonds were an effective mating strategy across ecologies. That is, over many generations and in various environments, early humans who formed monogamous mating pair-bonds out-reproduced those who followed other mating strategies, such as polygyny and polyandry. However, even modern humans exhibit low-to-moderate sexual dimorphism, which indicates that humans sometimes employed other mating strategies and were reproductively successful in these efforts. Thus, for most of human evolutionary history, different-sex mating pair-bonds generally solved the problem of paternity uncertainty, reduced the risk of infanticide, and contributed to family protection and provisioning (Fletcher, Simpson, Campbell, & Overall, 2015). The long history of different-sex mating pair-bonds suggests that humans are predisposed to form mating pair-bonds. While sexual attraction likely ensured that different-sex individuals came together and engaged in procreative sex, romantic love functioned to keep the couple together at least long enough to raise children to reproductive age (Fletcher, Simpson, Campbell, & Overall, 2015). It is important at this point to note that predispositions are tendencies, not automatic actions. In addition, all traits have some variability, even those that are typical in a species. Thus, for a variety of reasons, including trait variability, some people will not feel the urge to pair-bond or produce children.

Sex is Not Enough

For sexually reproducing species, the problem is how to bring male and female bodies together long enough (or often enough) to mate and conceive (Ridley, 1993). Mating is an intimate and vulnerable activity, and conception is not a sure thing. Successful conception may require repeated mating, necessitating repeated close physical contact with another individual and increased risk. Fertile females even in relatively social species, like primates, must risk having a generally larger, aggressive male close enough to penetrate her body in order to mate. The male might harm her physically, even accidentally. While mating, males risk vulnerability to attack by male competitors due to inattention to their surroundings. There is a small possibility of injury by his mate. Physical risks during mating may be the primary reason why sexual activity among many social species, especially primates, lasts only a few seconds. While humans face similar physical risks during sex, human sexual activity is quite long and leisurely compared to other species (Prum, 2017).

For the most part, across species, sexual interest among males and females is largely organized around their relative reproductive investment and competition for a mate. In many species, males produce numerous small gametes that are less costly to generate. Typically, males invest little in raising their offspring. Consequently, across species, a common male characteristic is ready sexual interest (especially in novel partners) and quick ejaculation. Human men generally follow this pattern, although men can engage in sexual intercourse for several minutes before ejaculation, and they are often involved in supporting their children. As noted earlier, in many species, females have a substantial investment in reproduction. As a result, a common female characteristic is sexual interest only when ovulating. Human women are an exception. For women, sexual desire is not closely connected to fertility and appears to be situational, as we will see later.

There is clear evidence across numerous studies that men have stronger sexual drives and prefer more frequent sexual activity with more partners compared to women (Baumeister, Catanese, & Vohs, 2001). Across all stages of long-term different-sex relationships, men report wanting sex more often than women (Ard, 1977; McCabe, 1987). Not surprisingly, this male desire for frequent sex is also evident among gay male couples compared to lesbian female couples (Blumstein & Schwartz, 1983). Further, men think about sex more often than women. In a national study of American adults, more than half the men thought about sex daily, but only one-fifth of women thought about sex as frequently (Laumann, Gagnon, Michael, & Michaels, 1994). It is possible that women are less aware of their sexual thoughts than men. In a series of studies that I explore more in Chapter Five, psychologist Meredith Chivers found that women were often not aware of their own physiological sexual arousal (as measured by blood flow to the vagina) (Chivers, 2005; Chivers, Seto, & Blanchard, 2007). In these studies, women watched short videos of men and women engaged in sexual activity together and alone, as well as scenes of nude men and women exercising alone, while monitoring their physiological sexual arousal. Women's subjective ratings of sexual arousal did not match their physiological arousal pattern. While women reported subjective arousal when viewing explicit sexual scenes, they did not report subjective arousal but evidenced physiological sexual arousal when viewing non-preferred sexual activity, such as women masturbating or exercising. Chivers and colleagues concluded that women are aroused more by the *context* of sexual activity than by the sex of partner (Chivers, 2005; Chivers, Seto, & Blanchard, 2007), which is very different from men. In these studies, men reliably reported sexual arousal. Of course, men also have obvious clues of their arousal because they can see and feel their erection when aroused.

Another difference between men and women is that men regularly act on their sexual desire and arousal by masturbating. Men masturbate much more frequently than women (Laumann, Gagnon, Michael, & Michaels, 1994), even in old age (Bergström-Walan & Nielsen, 1990). In a meta-analysis of 26 studies, men were nearly a whole standard deviation higher than women on masturbation frequency (Oliver & Hyde, 1993). Overall, women are far more likely to report *never* masturbating compared to men (Laumann, Gagnon, Michael, & Michaels, 1994). It is worth noting that globally men are by far the largest consumers of pornography (Porn tube sites are free, 2018) and paid sex (Prostitution revenue by country, 2018). While many women consume and enjoy pornography and some pay for sex, their numbers are quite small compared to men. In short, men and women seem to experience sexual desire and arousal differently. Men find a variety of stimuli sexually arousing and, for men, sexual activity, including masturbation, is nearly always pleasurable (leading to orgasm) and an end in itself. For women, however, sexual context seems to matter more than individual sexual stimuli or partner characteristics. These differences in arousal patterns are consistent with evolutionary theories of differential reproductive investment.

Sexual arousal is not quite enough for reproductive success. Having sex with another individual requires being physically intimate and vulnerable. For males and females in sexually reproducing species, hormones related to sexual desire function to reduce the fear of contact with another individual (who can harm you) and motivate physical contact and sexual activity (which increases the risk of injury). Among mammals, for example, males are sexually primed by testosterone and triggered by visibly receptive behavior by fertile females or her pheromones (or both) to approach and initiate sexual activity (Drea, 2015; Keverne, 1983). Female mammals typically experience sexual receptivity (estrus) and fertility at specific times (e.g., seasonally), which is triggered by a combination of hormones that prompt behavioral signaling of sexual receptivity and lessens the fear of contact with a large male. Among humans, female fertility occurs at specific times, but ovulation is concealed. Unlike most mammals, human females do not display obvious signs that they are ovulating. What is more, sexual interest and receptivity among human females are not limited to specific periods of fertility.

One sexual encounter is usually not enough for conception to occur. Researchers have estimated that female gorillas mate about ten times for every conception as indicated by live birth (Ridley, 1993). Female common chimpanzees mate about 500–1,000 times for every conception, while female bonobos mate about 3,000 times for every conception. Either nature is very inefficient, or pleasurable sexual activity has other functions besides reproduction. For chimpanzees and bonobos, sexual pleasure may function to facilitate emotional bonding, provide reassurance, signal forgiveness, demonstrate concession or submission, or express happiness and fun. The sexual act itself may also signal to others in the community that the pair have a special relationship. Like gorillas, chimpanzees, and bonobos, different-sex attracted humans also engage in sex for social reasons. Common human sexual activities are often non-reproductive, such as kissing, frottage, manual masturbation or use of toys, oral sex, and anal sex, because conception is not the goal. Even when pregnancy is desired, human men and women often engage in sexual intercourse many times before conceiving. A website and video blog in the United Kingdom called *Channel Mum* asked 1,194 couples who wanted to get pregnant about the number of times they had vaginal intercourse before conceiving (Arsenault, 2017). Non-reproductive sexual activities were not counted in this study. On average, couples had vaginal intercourse 78 times before becoming pregnant, or 13 times per month for six months. About half the couples reported that they had vaginal intercourse more frequently once they decided to get pregnant. Ten percent of couples had vaginal intercourse 15–20 times per month, and 5% had intercourse daily. Again, either nature is inefficient, or sexual activity has evolved other functions besides reproduction for humans. It is reasonable to believe that if the couples in the *Channel Mum* survey were trying to avoid pregnancy, they might have engaged in vaginal intercourse less often, but they would have incorporated many more non-reproductive sexual activities in their lovemaking simply because sexual pleasure feels good.

For men and women, intense sexual activity and orgasm feel good because they are accompanied by the release of muscle tension as well as endorphins, dopamine, and oxytocin (Fletcher, Simpson, Campbell, & Overall, 2015; Love, 2014). Endorphins block pain and trigger a euphoric feeling, while dopamine activates the brain's reward and motivation system, contributing to feelings of pleasure and the desire for more pleasure-producing sex. Oxytocin is a hormone that also functions as a neurotransmitter (Love, 2014; Magon & Kalra, 2011). Oxytocin facilitates feelings of relaxation, safety, contentment, empathy, and happiness and promotes social bonding in humans (MacGill, 2017). Oxytocin-induced post-orgasmic feelings of closeness and contentment increase the likelihood of a continued intimate relationship, and more orgasms in the future! Evolutionary psychologist David Buss (2003) reported that women in lengthy relationships are more likely to orgasm during sexual activity, unlike men who nearly always orgasm during sex. Women in longer relationships also experience increased levels of oxytocin. Women may need more time to feel comfortable with a sexual partner and need a sexual partner who attends to her pleasure. These findings also support the notion that the quality of the relationship— the sexual context—is critical to female sexuality. In addition, oxytocin is tightly connected with other aspects of female reproduction (MacGill, 2017). Oxytocin is released in large amounts during uterine contractions and has long been used as a stimulant to induce or facilitate labor (Magon & Kalra, 2011). Oxytocin is also released in large amounts following stimulation of the nipple to induce milk excretion, which suggests that oxytocin is strongly associated with mother-child attachment. It is not surprising that oxytocin facilitates both post-orgasmic pair-bonding and maternal attachment. When needed, natural selection exploits available resources for different functions.

Furthermore, oxytocin is implicated in the way socially monogamous animals manage prolonged close contact with a mate. The role of oxytocin and vasopressin, a closely related hormone, in promoting monogamous pair-bonding was first described between two closely related species—the socially monogamous prairie vole and the promiscuous montane vole (Insel, 2010). Voles are small rodents. Prairie voles (*Microtus ochrogaster*) pair-bond for life and live in burrows with extended family, while montane voles (*Microtus montanus*) mate promiscuously and tend to live alone. Male and female voles of both species experience high levels of oxytocin and vasopressin after mating, but males evidence greater concentrations of vasopressin than females. Post-mating, female voles begin to exhibit maternal behavior, and male montane voles disappear. However, post-mating, male prairie voles quickly show a preference for affiliation with their mate (Insel, 2010). They also demonstrate increased parental behavior and become aggressive toward the presence of other males (mate guarding) after mating. Laboratory research has found that male prairie voles have a dense set of brain receptors for oxytocin and vasopressin compared to montane voles. Oxytocin and vasopressin also activate different neural pathways in the two species. Thus, pair-bonding among prairie voles appears to be a result of changes in male behavior that are facilitated by oxytocin and vasopressin.

Oxytocin and vasopressin differ by only two amino acids (Carter, 2014). They affect each other by bonding to the other's receptors. Oxytocin slows brain growth by influencing cell growth and death, allowing for an extended period of social and cognitive development well into adulthood for humans. Vasopressin also plays a role in selective sociality but in a less clear way (Carter, 2014). Vasopressin is linked to increased anxiety, arousal, and defensive aggression in both sexes. Because oxytocin and vasopressin interact, it is difficult to tease apart their individual effects. Predictably, people differ in their levels of oxytocin and vasopressin, which may explain in part why different-sex mating pair-bonds differ in quality and strength of their connection.

The role of oxytocin and to a lesser degree, vasopressin, on social affiliation has earned them reputations as "love drugs". While both hormones are important pieces of the love and bonding puzzle, they are not the whole picture. There is no evidence yet that exposure to oxytocin causes anyone to fall in love, or become infatuated with another person, or find someone attractive. In a provocative study, researchers attempted to induce partner preferences in participants by exposing them to oxytocin (Liu, Guastella, & Dadds, 2013). First, male and female participants were exposed to oxytocin, then they were shown video clips of a man and then a woman. One day later, the participants were shown videos of an additional man and woman, then they were asked which of the four individuals they were interested in learning more about and spending time with. As expected, participants showed a preference for the people who immediately followed their oxytocin exposure. However, quite unexpectedly, the majority chose same-sex individuals to get to know better! The participants had not been directed to think about the men and women in the videos as potential romantic or sexual partners, but that kind of instruction should be unnecessary if oxytocin induces affection. Why would oxytocin produce a social preference for same-sex individuals? It is entirely possible that oxytocin and vasopressin are also associated with bonding between same-sex friends.

Consistent evidence has shown that oxytocin and vasopressin facilitate feelings of trust and cooperation, critical to liking and loving. In a laboratory study, 91 college-age men self-administered a nasal spray of oxytocin, vasopressin, or a placebo and then played the Prisoner's Dilemma game with a confederate (Rilling, DeMarco, Hackett, Thompson, Ditzen, Patel, & Pagnoni, 2012). In sequential moves, each player could choose to cooperate with their partner for a small shared reward or defect and receive a larger reward, while the other player gets nothing. As anticipated, oxytocin exposure increased cooperative behavior of participants, even after unreciprocated cooperation. However, vasopressin exposure, which is associated with increased anxious arousal, strongly increased cooperation only *after* a partner's cooperative action. In a meta-analysis of 23 studies that examined the effects of nasal oxytocin, investigators found consistent evidence that oxytocin exposure enhanced the recognition of facial expressions of emotion and increased the level of in-group trust (Van IJzendoorn & Bakermans-Kranenburg, 2012). Out-group trust was unaffected by hormone exposure. The investigators concluded that oxytocin exposure positively affects emotional perception and accentuates existing positive feelings in trusting relationships. However, oxytocin does not cause liking.

In brief, oxytocin and endorphins are associated with sexual desire, attachment, and orgasm. However, neither oxytocin nor vasopressin are love drugs, although they are important components of love and attachment. Oxytocin and vasopressin increase positive emotional perceptions, heighten feelings of empathy and trust, and promote cooperation in favored relationships. While oxytocin and vasopressin can enhance existing positive feelings about someone, this is not attachment. This is not the whole puzzle. What explains continued intimate contact between different-sex couples and feelings of deep affection and devotion, if not oxytocin? What keeps different-sex couples together when infatuation and excitement diminish? We will not find the answer in hormones and endorphins, or cognitions, or conditioned associations, or comfort with the familiar. The answer is more complicated. The larger, more complex phenomenon that holds different-sex mating pair-bonds together is romantic love.

Romantic Love and Different-Sex Mating Pair-Bonds

By at least two million years ago, our early human ancestors were exhibiting physical features that suggest they often formed relatively long-term different-sex mating pair-bonds. Differences in physical size between early archaic human males and females were moderate and reduced compared to their ancestors. This trend continued up to modern humans. These findings strongly suggest that socially monogamous pair-bonding was increasingly frequent among early humans. Romantic love is hypothesized to be the emotional mechanism that facilitated long-term different-sex mating pair-bonds among our early human ancestors and contributed to the modern physical appearance of humans (Fletcher, Simpson, Campbell, & Overall, 2015). Biologist Enrique Burunat (2014) went even further to claim that romantic love is *the* cause of human evolution. Quite probably, pair-bonding facilitated the birth of romantic love. Pair-bonding, love, managing kin networks, and cultivating social alliances and friendships also necessitated a large social brain.

In the literature, the terms "social monogamy" and "mating pair-bonds" are often used interchangeably. Across species, social monogamy generally refers to mating pair-bonds who live together, affiliate closely, and care for their young during their reproductive period. That is, males stick around and contribute something to raising their young. When their offspring reach self-sufficiency, the pair may split. A few species mate for life, but many do not. At the next reproductive period, a different combination of mates may bond. Because the term "monogamy" often evokes the idea of sexual exclusivity for life, I prefer the term "pair-bonding". Human mating pair-bonds are socially monogamous in that the male-female pair live together (display attachment) and direct resources to raising their children to self-sufficiency. The two generally have a close affectionate bond. Human pair-bonds are also often formal relationships that are recognized by the community. While modern pair-bonds usually include an expectation of emotional and sexual exclusivity, it is unclear to what extent exclusivity was expected among early human couples. Pair-bonding is quite prevalent among contemporary hunter-gatherers, but social monogamy is not the only mating strategy employed in these societies. At least since the advent of farming, partnered/married women have generally been socially prohibited from having extrapair sexual partners, while partnered/married men have been allowed additional sexual partners (e.g., prostitutes, concubines, slaves, mistresses) without necessarily violating their commitment to the pair-bond.

As the emotional glue that holds different-sex mating pair-bonds together, romantic love solved several reproductive problems faced by our early ancestors (Fletcher, Simpson, Campbell, & Overall, 2015). Romantic love produced more than simple cooperation and mutual reciprocity. Romantic (and companionate) love motivated mating couples to focus on each other's needs (and the needs of their children) after the excitement of novel sexual attraction dimmed. The initial obsessive focus of romantic love allowed couples time to develop strong emotional bonds. With such bonds, partners felt a desire to benefit their mate even at their own expense, because they loved them, and not because of an obligation of exchange. Such strong bonds may have been particularly important when resources were scarce and survival difficult. Romantic (and companionate) love helped to ensure that the couple directed resources to their family unit and their offspring, which increased the likelihood that their children reached reproductive age. Although not a perfect solution, romantic love has likely aided hominin reproductive success for at least two million years. As a result, most of us today desire to fall in love with a mate and form a family.

For early human females, romantic love and pair-bonds facilitated securing committed male mates and ensuring that their mates directed efforts and resources to the females and their children (Fletcher, Simpson, Campbell, & Overall, 2015). A male who was not in love and lacked emotional commitment to his mate could divert resources to other female partners or, worse, fall in love with another female and invest in their children. For females, a male mate's emotional infidelity carried a higher reproductive cost than sexual infidelity. A large body of literature has shown that contemporary women as a group are more intensely upset by a male partner falling in love with someone else (emotional infidelity) than by sexual infidelity (Buss, 2006). Romantic love has functioned in part to disrupt the continued search for a mate (for both individuals) and perceive other potential partners as less attractive, at least for a while (Fletcher, Simpson, Campbell, & Overall, 2015). In fact, couples in love tend to perceive *each other* as more attractive and view potential partners as less attractive compared to uncommitted individuals (Fletcher & Kerr, 2010).

For early human males, romantic love and monogamous pair-bonds addressed the nagging problems of sexual infidelity by female mates and uncertain paternity, at least for a while (Fletcher, Simpson, Campbell, & Overall, 2015). Romantic love may have provided males some assurance that their female mates were sexually faithful. A sizable literature has demonstrated that contemporary men as a group are more upset by a female partner's sexual infidelity than by her falling in love with someone else (emotional infidelity) (Buss, 2006). Of course, love does not guarantee exclusivity, and males have employed other strategies such as mate-guarding and aggression to ensure their mate's sexual fidelity.

Romantic love and pair-bonding also likely benefited health, perhaps by increasing social ties and resilience, as well as available nutritional resources (Fletcher, Simpson, Campbell, & Overall, 2015). Contemporary researchers have found that married people experience significantly better overall health and well-being than unmarried people (Case, Moses, Case, McDermott, & Eberly, 1992; Goodwin, Hunt, Key, & Samet, 1987; Myers & Diener, 1995). In a large study of more than 22,000 people across 19 countries using four separate psychological measures of well-being, married men and women reported greater happiness and satisfaction with life than widowed, divorced, and never-married, single individuals (Mastekaasa, 1994). Married men derived the greatest health benefits from marriage. This may be due to increased social support and a wife's attention to her husband's health. While women benefit from marriage, married women bear more of the cost of marital conflict and generally have primary responsibility for childcare and household maintenance (Monin & Clark, 2011). While both men and women experience benefits from marriage, love relationships are work that involve compromises. No one gets exactly what they want in a love relationship, and making it work requires a good amount of effort from both parties. Some researchers have suggested that married men rate their happiness and satisfaction higher when comparing themselves to their unmarried male friends (Monin & Clark, 2011). That is, married men may feel they do pretty well compared to single men. On the other hand, married women may rate themselves less happy than married men when comparing their marriage to their satisfaction with their female friendships.

An Origin of Romantic Love

How did romantic love develop? Evolved traits are either helpful mutations or existing characteristics exploited to serve new functions (e.g., exaptations). Over time, selection favors the new function. Sexual activity is a good example, as we have seen. While critical to reproduction, humans (and other animals) engage in a great deal of sexual activity that cannot or will not result in conception. It is not that humans are inefficient reproducers. Rather, sexual activity has multiple functions. One function is to provide pleasure to promote short-term bonding. Admittedly, by focusing mainly on reproductive sexuality, evolutionists miss the bigger picture and give the impression that non-reproductive sexual activities are unimportant or even meaningless. Not so.

Romantic love evolved. Freud (1905/1953) noted the similarity between romantic love and maternal love, as have contemporary researchers. In his book, *Affective Neuroscience*, psychobiologist Jaak Panksepp (1998) argued that natural selection exploited the mother-child emotional bond and modified it into romantic love to facilitate long-term mating pair-bonds. Consistent with this hypothesis, romantic and maternal love has been shown to activate overlapping regions of the brain's reward system (Bartels & Zeki, 2004). Unsurprisingly, these regions are rich in oxytocin and vasopressin receptors. Both romantic and maternal love also deactivate similar brain regions related to negative emotions and social judgments. Neuroscientists Andreas Bartels and Semir Zeki (2004) have described human attachment, like romantic and maternal love, as employing a push-pull mechanism to overcome fear and social judgement in order to experience the positive emotions of intimacy and bonding. However, romantic love differs from maternal love in activating hypothalamic regions related to sexual arousal (Bartels & Zeki, 2004). Even so, there is some overlap here. Nursing mothers sometimes experience sexual arousal while breastfeeding because of non-sexual nipple stimulation.

Some scientists have viewed romantic love, but not maternal love, as an addiction-like process (Bartels & Zeki, 2004; Fisher, Brown, Aron, Strong, & Mashek, 2010). They have noted that romantic love activates the same dopaminergic system and produces a similar sense of euphoria as drugs and gambling. However, unlike addictions, romantic love promotes social cooperation, sharing resources, and increased intimacy. Romantic love can also be relatively short-lived and episodic, unlike an addiction. Further, people can fall in and out of love many times, or never experience love again. While there are superficial similarities, Burunat (2014) has argued that addictions and romantic love involve different behavioral components and mental states. Burunat describes romantic love as a physiological motivation, more like hunger or thirst.

The Downside of Romantic Love

While romantic love has many benefits, including aiding reproductive success, there are downsides to romantic love and being engineered to pursue love. Being adapted to want a loving romantic relationship may result in loneliness and depression when that desire is not fulfilled. The flipside of desiring love and bonding is loneliness. While humans are highly social creatures, in the United States, depression is the most common mental health condition, affecting one-fifth of adults (May 2018). Pooling results from 91 studies across 30 countries, nearly 11% of people report experiencing major depression in their lifetime (Lim, Tam, Lu, Ho, Zhang, & Ho, 2018).

Romantic love is also unstable and frequently brief. Romantic love is often one-sided and not returned, which is painful. Choosing a stable, loving partner involves considerable trial-and-error. Even when romantic love is mutual, love may not last for a variety of reasons. As noted earlier, romantic love involves an intense focus on the beloved, who is perceived as special. The relationship itself is experienced as special. This feeling of specialness by people in love may contribute to the expectation that their beloved loves no other. When partners give attention to others (or receive attention from others), jealousy, accusations, and distrust can erupt and interfere with romantic relationships. People also can change over time and fall out of love, which is devastating. Break-ups may trigger depression (Mastekaasa, 1994). The instability of romantic love may be one reason that parents in many cultures have arranged their children's marriages. Parents may believe that arranged marriages better ensure a stable family unit for their grandchildren than love marriages. However, it seems more likely that parents favor arranged marriages to create useful alliances with other families and control the inheritance of wealth.

Challenges to Romantic Love in Different-Sex Mating Pair-Bonds

In their review of the literature, evolutionary psychologists Fletcher, Simpson, Campbell, and Overall (2015) cited four challenges to the idea that romantic love is an adaptive trait that functions to promote different-sex mating pair-bonds. These challenges include 1) arranged marriages, 2) polygyny (I include polyandry too), 3) infidelity, and 4) divorce. Below I briefly review these four challenges and note a fifth challenge from my reading of the literature: Commitment without love. All five arguments suppose that romantic love is too weak a force to promote successful different-sex mating pair-bonds among humans. Consistent with Fletcher, Simpson, Campbell and Overall, I will show that these arguments are not convincing.

Arranged Marriages

If romantic love was so important for the maintenance of different-sex mating pair-bonds among our early ancestors, then why have arranged marriages been so prevalent? Arranged marriages have been common in many traditional cultures, including those of Africa, India, Pakistan, Japan, China, Kenya, the Middle East, and China, to name a few (Buunk, Park, & Duncan, 2010; Fisher, 1992; Gupta, 1976; Hatfield & Rapson, 2006; Mehndiratta, Paul, & Mehndiratta, 2007; Symons, 1979). Arranged marriages were also quite common in the ancient world of Rome, Greece, and Egypt (Cantarella, 2002; Foucault, 1980/1986; Gregersen, 1996). In these cultures, marriage was viewed mainly as a kind of property exchange, with the bride as property (Goodwin, 1999). The father of the bride literally transferred ownership of his daughter to the bridegroom, her husband. In traditional cultures, women are not viewed as equal to men; women are not independent and are overseen by their father or other male relatives.

In arranged marriages, the parents, or just the father, select a suitable (or acceptable) spouse for their children. Arranged marriages are particularly common in sex-segregated cultures where young boys and girls (and even adult women) have little opportunity to interact (Mehndiratta, Paul, & Mehndiratta, 2007). It is uncertain when arranged marriages began. However, with the rise of permanent settlements, agriculture, and the accumulation of wealth a few thousand years ago, parents had strong incentives to keep property within the family or clan (Taylor, 1996). Through arranged marriages, parents could maintain some control over property and wealth by ensuring paternity and by creating alliances between families. Consistent with this argument, arranged in-marriages, or cousin or sister-brother marriages, have been common among agriculturalists. Even so, arranged marriages are also common among contemporary hunter-gatherer cultures, who have little tangible "property" except their daughters (Walker, Hill, Flinn, & Ellsworth, 2011; Symons, 1979). Many hunter-gatherer and agriculturalist cultures practice *exogamy*, whereby a young girl is betrothed to a man in another community. The girl leaves her natal kin to live with her husband and his female relatives (sisters, mother, grandmother). Clan exogamy has been hypothesized to have originated to avoid incest, as well as to establish alliances across clans or distant groups, which would make it a very old practice (Kang, 1979).

Early human parents had a strong interest in who their children married, and they were in positions to impose their choice. No doubt, the parents' choice of marriage partners for their children reflected their own values. Yet from a natural selection perspective, reproductive success for parents means their children successfully mate and produce children who later produce their own children. Because parents and children share genes and likely share many of the same values, parents and their children's preferences for qualities in a good mate may be similar, although personal choices might vary considerably (Fletcher, Simpson, Campbell, & Overall, 2015). For readers in countries where love marriage and personal choice are common, the idea that parents and their child might agree on the child's spouse may seem bizarre. However, a recent study found remarkable agreement between parents and their children on this issue. Investigators asked heterosexual adults and their parents to separately rank the importance of 13 traits in a romantic partner for a long-term relationship (Perilloux, Fleischman, & Buss, 2011). Daughters and sons ranked partner traits quite similar to their parents, with correlations of .82 and .83, respectively.

While arranged marriages directly reflect parents' interests, arranged marriages do not necessarily eliminate the young girl or boy's choice. Arranged marriages vary in how dictatorial the parents are and how much choice the youth has in the decision. Some young brides (and grooms) have little or no choice in who they marry. However, in many recent traditional cultures with arranged marriages, brides and groom-to-be have some say, even though the final decision is not theirs (Fletcher, Simpson, Campbell, & Overall, 2015). Female and male youths can communicate their choice in a variety of direct and indirect ways. While parents may be motivated by securing family alliances and maintaining wealth, they also want their children to have a successful marriage. Parents want their children's cooperation and satisfaction. They want a stable family environment and healthy grandchildren. Prospective partners who dislike each other or who are opposed to marrying predict big problems ahead, including acrimony, infidelity, and potentially break-up of the marriage (Scelza, 2013). An unhappy marriage or divorce do not meet the parents' goals. Failing to account for their children's wishes has negative consequences. Among the semi-nomadic Himba of Namibia, for example, women who have no choice in their arranged marriages are much less sexually faithful than women who have some choice (Scelza, 2011). Among the Ju/'Hoansi bushmen in southern Africa, more than 60% of brides report being mildly or strongly reluctant about their arranged first marriage (Scelza, 2013). While only about one-quarter of first marriages end in divorce within five years, Ju/'Hoansi wives initiate divorce 90% of the time, suggesting a bad match. Ju/'Hoansi women have more partner choice in their second marriages.

Cultures with arranged marriages tend to emphasize obedience to parental wishes (Apostolou, 2010). In such cultures, parents focus on the good investment characteristics of a potential marriage partner (e.g., social status, wealth) over the sexual attractiveness of a partner or romantic love, which are viewed as brief and unstable. However, an arranged marriage does not necessarily mean a love-less marriage. In many traditional cultures, the mating pair are expected to like each other at minimum and even grow to love each other over time, although love is not the goal of marriage (Allendorf, 2013; Goodwin, 1999). In *Anatomy of Love*, anthropologist Helen Fisher (1992) quotes a Hindu saying that illustrates this value: "First we marry, then we fall in love" (p. 73). To better ensure a successful arranged marriage, some parents first introduce their children to see if an attraction is possible or at least know that the two do not strongly dislike each other (Fisher, 1992: Patel, 2018). Some contemporary arranged marriages are preceded by a period of dating or courtship that help the couple develop positive feelings for their soon-to-be spouse (7 couples in arranged marriages, 2017). There are many examples of couples in contemporary arranged marriages who have fallen in love (e.g., Patel, 2018). Their testimonials reveal a variety of ways that romantic love develops in the marriage. Sometimes, love sprouts quickly from a spouse's selfless concern. In other cases, love grows slowly over several years. Among contemporary cultures with arranged marriages, advice books on how to fall in love with one's spouse are plentiful, perhaps in part due to the growing popularity of love marriages around the world (Allendorf, 2013; Levine, Sato, Hashimoto, & Verma, 1995; Goodwin, 1999).

It is unclear to how often romantic love develops in arranged marriages. It is also difficult to draw generalizations about arranged marriages in traditional cultures because the cultures are quite varied. Obviously, couples in arranged marriages—all marriages really—stay together for a variety of reasons unrelated to love. In traditional collective cultures, the needs of the family outweigh the needs or desires of the individual, so some unhappy spouses may stay together for the perceived good of the family. Further, in traditional cultures, women often have little power to change their life circumstances and potentially have much to lose if their marriage ends, even if the relationship is unhappy or abusive. Even so, remaining together does not equal reproductive success. It seems unlikely that abusive or acrimonious marriages have been more reproductively successful than cooperative, agreeable marriages.

While arranged marriages are not based on love, evidence suggests that romantic love played an important role in arranged marriages in traditional cultures. For the most part, love is expected to develop over time. Even though parents have the final decision in prospective spouses, research shows that parents and their children share similar preferences in marriage partners. Among cultures with arranged marriages, parents often allow some input from the bride- and groom-to-be, including an opportunity to get to know each other to better ensure a successful marriage. Anecdotes from people in contemporary arranged marriages demonstrate that falling in love with one's spouse is a strong value. In short, the value of love in arranged marriages supports the idea that romantic love is central to maintaining long-term, different-sex mating pair-bonds.

Polygyny (and Polyandry)

A second challenge to the role of romantic love in maintaining long-term different-sex mating pair-bonds is the prevalence of alternative mating strategies such as *polygyny* and *polyandry*. If romantic love and pair-bonds are adaptations that optimize reproductive success, then polygyny and polyandry should be rare. In general, polygyny refers to a man mating with several women concurrently or having more than one wife. Approximately 84% of world cultures allow polygynous marriages, so the practice is accepted and not unusual (Fisher, 1992). However, only 5%–10% of men in cultures that allow polygyny have more than one wife. The few men who have multiple wives tend to be in positions of power. Having additional wives may even function to demonstrate personal power. For example, Genghis Khan (c. 1162–1227), the first Great Khan of the Mongol Empire, had one primary wife and at least 500 secondary wives and numerous children (Genghis Khan, 2019). His reproductive success is responsible in part for the high proportion of identical Y-chromosome sequences among living men in Asia today, although Genghis Khan himself may not be the only source for that

Y-chromosome (Callaway, 2015). In addition, the second Shah of Iran, Fath-Ali Shah Qajar (1772–1834), allegedly had more than 1,000 wives and at least 100 children (Fath-Ali Shah Qajar, 2019). Brigham Young (1801–1877), second President of The Church of Jesus Christ of Latter-Day Saints and founder of Salt Lake City, married 55 women and had 56 children (List of Brigham Young's wives, 2019). While polygyny worked for these powerful men, they are exceptions. Few men can afford to have more than one wife. While men in polygynous marriages may be in love with multiple women at the same time, having multiple wives is costly to support, difficult to maintain, and contentious (Schacht & Kramer, 2019). In one study of polygyny across 69 cultures, wives reported that the threat of limited sexual access to her husband and emotional jealousy were major sources of conflict in their marriages, consistent with the idea that romantic love promotes a desire for exclusivity (Jankowiak, Sudakov, & Wilreker, 2005). First-wives experienced a strong sense of loss, sadness, and anger when the second wife entered the family.

By far, monogamous pair-bonding, including serial pair-bonds, is the most common human mating practice across cultures and throughout history (Schacht & Kramer, 2019; Walker, Hill, Flinn & Ellsworth, 2011). As noted previously, early human hunter-gatherers exhibited low-to-moderate sexual dimorphism that strongly suggests they formed mostly socially monogamous mating pair-bonds. While among contemporary hunter-gatherer societies, arranged marriages are common, so are divorce and remarriage. Given that many first marriages are arranged, quite possibly, men and women have more choice (for love?) in their second marriages. Thus, over a lifetime, many hunter-gatherer men have more than one wife and children by different wives and have also likely married for love. If contemporary hunter-gatherers are any indication of mating practices in the distant past, some ancient hunter-gatherers may have had polygynous relationships, but many more men likely had serial pair-bonds. While it is difficult to know what happened that far in the past, anthropologists Robert Walker, Kim Hill, Mark Flinn, and Ryan Ellsworth (2011) reconstructed ancestral marriage practices using mitochondrial DNA phylogenies from 15 contemporary hunter-gatherer cultures. The results reflected low levels of polygyny and frequent bride exchanges between family groups. In short, they found no evidence that polygyny was the dominant mating strategy in our ancient human past. Monogamous mating pair-bonds appear to be more stable than polygynous relationships across a variety of ecologies. Furthermore, polygynous relationships fail to refute the role of romantic love in maintaining long-term mating relationships.

Polyandry refers to a woman mating with several men or having more than one husband. Again, if romantic love and pair-bonds are adaptations that optimize reproductive success, then polyandry should be rare and, indeed, it is quite rare but more common than once thought (Starkweather & Hames, 2012). Past reviews of the literature often refer to less than 10 such cultures, although scholars have claimed there are as many as 28 classical polyandrous cultures, mostly in the Himalaya mountains and the Marquesas Islands in the South Pacific. As in polygynous cultures, few marriages in these cultures are polyandrous. Prevalence estimates vary wildly from 3% to more than 50% of all marriages. Through a variety of sources, anthropologists Katherine Starkweather and Raymond Hames (2012) identified an additional 53 polyandrous cultures that do not fit the classical Himalayan-Marquesan pattern. Classical polyandry occurs in cultures where the sex ratio is male-biased, land is scarce and essential for status in the community, and division of family land is strongly avoided. Among non-classical polyandrous cultures, the most common form is fraternal (brothers marry the same wife). Non-classical polyandrous cultures are more typical of egalitarian societies and common among contemporary hunter-gatherers and foraging horticulturalists. However, belief in partible paternity is unrelated to non-classical polyandry. Starkweather and Hames (2012) concluded that polyandry is a coordinated response among cultures where generally land is scarce, difficult to cultivate, and essential for survival and where men greatly outnumber women. Polyandrous cultures may be more egalitarian because the skewed sex ratio favors women, giving them more power in the community. However, polyandry is less stable as a mating strategy than either polygyny or serial monogamy due to male sexual jealousy and violence around sharing a spouse. As well, polyandrous relationships fail to refute the role of romantic love in maintaining long-term mating pair-bonds.

Infidelity

A third challenge to the role of romantic love in long-term different-sex mating pair-bonds is sexual infidelity. If romantic love is so powerful, then why does infidelity occur so frequently? Cheating or extra-marital sex is a major reason for relationship breakup and divorce. In nationally representative surveys in the United States, 20–25% of men and 10–15% of women acknowledge having had sex with someone other than their spouse some time during their marriage (Munsch, 2012). While that seems like a high rate of infidelity, it is far from most marriages. Other cultures report different rates of infidelity, but men consistently report higher rates of sexual infidelity than women. In Hong Kong, for example, only 8% of men and just 1% of women report having engaged in extra-marital sex in the past year (Caraël, Cleland, Deheneffe, Ferry, & Ingham, 1995). However, in one hunter-gatherer culture in Guinea Bissau, Africa, 38% of men and 19% of women reported having extra-marital sex in just the past year (Caraël, Cleland, Deheneffe, Ferry, & Ingham, 1995).

Numerous studies on sexual infidelity and jealousy have demonstrated that men are far more likely than women to engage in extra-marital sex (Buss, 2003). Much of this work has focused on differences between different-sex attracted men and women and their distress over sexual or emotional infidelity. A meta-analysis of 40 published and unpublished papers from 47 independent samples reconfirmed expected sex differences in reaction to hypothetical and actual sexual and emotional infidelities (Sagarin, Martin, Coutinho, Edlund, Patel, Skowronski, & Zengel, 2012). That is, different-sex attracted men were more upset by sexual infidelity than women, while women were more distressed by emotional infidelity. However, a different meta-analysis of 54 published studies found that both different-sex attracted men and women rated emotional infidelity as more distressing than sexual infidelity, when forced to choose (Carpenter, 2012). Oddly enough, when continuous measure responses were examined, both men and women rated sexual infidelity as more distressing than emotional infidelity! Differences based on response formats are hard to explain because the earlier meta-analysis did not find differences between forced-choice and continuous measure formats (Sagarin et al., 2012). The two meta-analyses included different samples, although across studies participants were mostly Americans and college students. A recent study on infidelity in a traditional culture supported expected sex differences (Urooj, Anis-ul-Haque, & Anjum, 2015). Among 300 married participants (aged 24–37) in Pakistan, men viewed sexual infidelity by their female mate as more distressing than emotional infidelity and more difficult to forgive. Women viewed emotional infidelity by their male mate as most distressing and difficult to forgive. Men identified loss of affection and sexual dissatisfaction as the primary reasons for infidelity in a relationship. Women also believed that loss of love and affection were the main causes of affairs. Of course, loss of love and affection is not the only reason why married people have affairs. In addition, immaturity, poor impulse control, faulty moral reasoning, boredom, alcohol, believing that no one will find out, or excitement related to risk-taking contribute to infidelity. Romantic (and companionate) love requires regular effort by both parties to keep it alive. When efforts slacken and love is taken for granted and abused, feelings change. When the affair is discovered, loss of love is a probable consequence.

Stepping back for a moment, it is important to remember that most married couples do not have affairs, whatever the circumstances of their relationship. Love may minimize, but not eliminate, the risk of extra-pair sexual relationships. Romantic love may convey some assurance of emotional fidelity through a sense of affection, trust, and commitment (Miller, 2000). *Life History Theory* predicts that individuals will employ a mix of short-term and long-term mating strategies based on opportunities or restrictions specific to their life circumstances and the environment and culture (Del Giudice, Gangestad & Kaplan, 2015). That is, an individual's mating strategy(ies) will vary because of a number of variables: their development history, social status (or their partner's), social customs and rules, enforcement of those customs, size of the living group, access to quality nutrition and resources in the environment, and access to high quality potential partners. Real life has trade-offs and consequences. If infidelity is a good, but risky, reproductive strategy, then it should be effective but occur at a low rate. As a mating strategy, infidelity differs from polygyny and polyandry in that infidelity is secretive, not public knowledge, and not a formal union. While polygyny and polyandry are social customs, infidelity is a violation of trust. Therefore, extra-pair sexual relationships should have a pretty big reproductive pay-off to make it worth risking one's current situation or the risk of discovery should be quite small. Discovery could be minimized if an extra-pair sexual encounter is quick and highly likely to result in conception, thereby not necessitating repeated sexual encounters. However, it seems unlikely that most infidelities meet these conditions.

Based on a national survey in Britain, biologists Robin Baker and Mark Bellis (1995) in their book, *Human Sperm Competition*, reported that 6%–9% of women had sex with an extra-marital partner within five days of having sex with their primary male partner. However, the probability of conception in any given act of sexual intercourse was remarkably low at about 3%. Even if the goal of an affair is to get pregnant, the likelihood that a single sexual encounter will result in conception is quite low. In a review of extra-pair paternity across 67 studies, the median rate of children fathered by a man who is not the mother's primary partner was only 3.3% (Anderson, 2006). By comparison, among monogamous birds, the average rate of extra-pair paternity is about 11% (Griffith, Owens, & Thuman, 2002). For 22 species of monogamous mammals, the average rate of extra-pair paternity is 38% (Cohas & Allainé, 2009). However, a recently published study of Himba pastoralists in Namibia found an extra-pair paternity rate of 48%, with 70% of couples having at least one child from an extra-pair encounter (Scelza, Prall, Swinford, Gopalan, Atkinson, McElreath, Sheehama, & Henn, 2020). That is quite remarkable. Even more so, Himba men were better than 70% accurate in identifying extra-pair conceived children. Further, extra-pair sexual encounters and conception were not stigmatized. Given the Himba's acceptance of extra-pair sexual relationships, this practice cannot be called infidelity. The Himba appear to have an informal polyandrous society, where secondary fathers or social fathers provide support to a shared female mate and her children. The study authors noted that arranged marriages are common among the Himba, and so is divorce and remarriage. Love marriages are more typical for second marriages. Therefore, over a lifetime, many Himba women have multiple husbands and children from multiple male partners. The authors do not report whether the Himba hold beliefs about partible paternity.

In sum, infidelity presents a weak challenge against romantic love for maintaining human mating pair-bonds. Romantic love may minimize infidelity but not prevent it. Nevertheless, most contemporary married men and women do not have extra-pair sexual affairs. When they do, even if pregnancy is the goal, extra-pair conception is quite low. Given the risk associated with infidelity and the low rate of conception, infidelity appears to be a poor mating strategy. At least one pastoral culture has a high rate of extra-pair paternity, but their mating pattern is more consistent with a polyandrous culture (Scelza et al., 2020). It is possible that infidelity was a more effective mating strategy in the distant past. In many cultures, married men, but not women, have been allowed extra-pair sexual partners, without being perceiving as violating their marriage vows, but these relationships were generally for pleasure, not reproduction.

Divorce

A fourth challenge to romantic love's role in maintaining long-term, different-sex mating pair-bonds is divorce. If romantic love is a powerful force in maintaining human pair-bonds, then why do so many relationships end after a few years? This is an interesting argument which assumes that love should last forever and that we mainly fall in love with people who are good for us! Readers who have experienced love know that people can fall in love quickly and cannot control who they love. Clearly, love is not rational. Love is emotional. The seventeenth-century French philosopher and mathematician, Blaise Pascal famously said, "The heart has its reasons of which reason knows nothing" (1660/1995, p. 127). Probably most of us have fallen in love with someone who did not feel the same. Unrequited love is a difficult reality to accept. As well, probably many of us have fallen in love with someone who seemed fascinating at first, but who later became intolerable. There are numerous personal, interpersonal, and social variables involved in whether a love relationship works or not. Even though many love relationships end after a short time because the match is not right, many other love relationships have lasted a lifetime. If the relationship works, love grows as the two individuals become more intimate and invested in each other, and when the passion fades, what remains is mutual affection, respect, and devotion.

Helen Fisher (1992) hypothesized that romantic love (sexual attraction, emotional intimacy, and commitment) evolved in hunter-gatherer societies to support pair-bonds for about four years. That is about the time when the first-born child is weaned and becomes more self-sufficient. Four years is a common duration of birth spacing in contemporary hunter-gatherer societies (Fisher, 1992). Whether or not love lasts four years or some other duration, a charitable way to characterize Fisher's hypothesis is that romantic love evolved to last at least as long as necessary for human children to become somewhat self-sufficient. This idea may help explain the so-called "seven-year itch" which characterizes the peak in divorce rates in Western and Chinese societies (Kulu, 2014; Xu, Qiu, & Li, 2016). Sequential births could potentially lengthen the duration of love and the pair-bond. Studies find that the presence of young children reduces the probability of divorce (Heaton, 1990; Waite & Lillard, 1991; Xu, Yu, & Qiu, 2015). However, the idea that romantic love is engineered to last only four or seven years is improbable. Most married couples in the West, who presumably marry for love, stay together for more than four or seven years. Most stay together for the rest of their lives.

Many people believe the divorce rate is around 50%. In Western countries, like the United States, Australia, and New Zealand, where love marriages are the norm, only about one-third of first marriages end in divorce (Australian statistics on divorce, 2016; Bramlett & Moser, 2002; McPherson, 2017). In the United States, about one-fifth of marriages end in the first five years (Bramlett & Moser, 2002). By contrast, in contemporary hunter-gatherer cultures, where arranged marriages are common, divorce rates are only slightly higher. Among the !Kung of the Kalahari Desert, about 37% of marriages end in the first five years (Howell, 1979). Among the Hadza in north-central Tanzania, almost 40% of marriages break up within five years (Blurton-Jones, Marlowe, Hawkes, & O'Connell, 2000). As previously noted, second marriages are more likely to be based on love, although there is little data about the duration of second marriages in contemporary hunter-gatherer societies. In short, modern love marriages in Western cultures actually have a pretty good success rate.

As noted earlier, couples remain together or break up for a variety of reasons, which makes it difficult to compare divorce rates. We do not know why most marriages end. To further complicate the issue, in Western countries, young couples increasingly live together for lengthy periods of time before deciding to marry. Consequently, when they marry, these couples are older and perhaps more mature and committed to each other than earlier married couples who did not live together first. In the United States, about 73% of young women, aged 25–29, live with a romantic partner (Lamidi & Manning, 2016), and in Sweden, Norway, and France, nearly 90% of young people, aged 15–24, live with a romantic partner (Gassen & Perelli-Harris, 2015). Some couples who live together for a long time choose not to marry. Fletcher, Simpson, Campbell, and Overall (2015) argued that the kind of cohabitation we see in contemporary Western countries may be very similar to early forms of marriage in ancient hunter-gatherer cultures. They would be very, very early forms of marriage. Evidence from contemporary hunter-gatherers suggests that long-ago parents began arranging marriages to create ties and alliances between family groups and communities (Walker, Hill, Flinn & Ellsworth, 2011).

Consistent with the idea that romantic love is central to long-term different-sex mating pair-bonds, most marriages do not end in divorce. Many last a lifetime. Across modern Western cultures where love marriages are common, divorce rates are relatively low. While young people today may be wary of marriage, many still form different-sex pair-bonds and live together. Whether married or not, these couples have formed a mating pair-bond because they love each other. Nevertheless, many young-love couplings go awry early, because love is not returned or because of mismatched personalities. Romantic love is an emotional experience, not a rational decision, and love cannot overcome every problem faced by young couples.

Commitment Without Love

A fifth challenge to romantic love's role in long-term different-sex mating pair-bonds is whether commitment requires love at all. This argument extends the assertion that romantic love is too weak to be an adaptive trait. As noted, arranged marriages have been quite common throughout human history. While there is an expectation in many cultures that spouses in arranged marriages will grow to love each other eventually (Allendorf, 2013; Goodwin, 1999), it is unclear how frequently this happens. Do couples fall in love most of the time? Sometimes? Presumably, some proportion of couples in arranged marriages do not fall in love yet remain married. For these couples, commitment to the relationship, adherence to social customs, and obedience to the wishes of their parents may be the essential components of a lasting marriage.

Arranged or not, divorce may take care of several unhappy marriages in the first few years. Among the marriages that remain, some couples may not be in love but also not unhappy, or at least not sufficiently unhappy to press for divorce. Married couples may remain together because of their commitment to the marriage, family honor, status as a married couple, a stable environment for the children, financial security, fear of embarrassment and shame over the end of their marriage, or the lack of good alternatives (c.f., Apostolou, 2010; Previti & Amato, 2004). Especially in traditional cultures, women have few good alternatives when leaving their marriages (cf., Pande, 2015). Researchers examining contemporary Western couples have reported that perceiving more rewards than barriers in marriage is critical to staying married (Previti & Amato, 2004). Among couples who stay together after an infidelity, for example, the major motivations for remaining together include a strong determination to make the marriage work and fear of a failed marriage (Abrahamson, Hussain, Khan, & Schofield, 2012). Parents and the community impose social pressures that make it difficult for marriages to end.

Commitment to the relationship is critical to making a marriage last. Mutual commitment may be enough to hold-together a loveless marriage because the benefits of staying together outweigh the costs of ending the marriage. However, commitment without love is unlikely to be a better reproductive strategy than commitment with love. This is an empirical question, and I am unaware of research that has examined this issue. I suspect that commitment without love is not a better reproductive strategy because if it was love marriages would be less prevalent. If commitment without love was effective and efficient, pairing to reproduce would be more like a business arrangement with obligations and expected outcomes: children. In marriages based on commitment without love, spouses might function more like teammates or work colleagues. Parenting would be very formal. Unproductive marriages (no children) would be ended quickly. As a business arrangement, there would be no reason for jealousies in a marriage based on commitment without love. Reproductive relationships would be separate from emotional, meaningful love relationships, and people who had no interest in having children or who were infertile would not (or could not) get married. Obviously, this is not the world we live in. As a competitive reproductive strategy, long-term different-sex mating pair-bonds with love have edged out other strategies and become predominant in the population.

To summarize this section on challenges to romantic love, I have argued that romantic love is an ancient adaptation to sustain different-sex, mating pair-bonds at least long enough for couples to raise their children to relative self-sufficiency. Romantic love functions like a glue to hold couples together. Polygynous and polyandrous relationships may involve romantic love, but these mating strategies have been more difficult to maintain across a variety of ecologies than monogamous pair-bonds. However, under limited conditions, polygynous and polyandrous relationships can work. Consistent with Life History Theory, humans employ a variety of mating strategies based on their individual characteristics, social circumstances, and the ecologies in which they live. However, socially monogamous pair-bonding has been the most common mating strategy across cultures and throughout history. Reduced sexual dimorphism among early humans is consistent with monogamous (even serial) pair-bonding. Several challenges to the idea that romantic love is central to long-term, different-sex mating pair-bonds have little support. Contemporary arranged marriages are expected to result in love. Romantic love may minimize infidelity, which is a risky and ineffective reproductive strategy. In contemporary Western cultures, most married couples who marry for love stay together for the rest of their lives. Lastly, if commitment without love was a more effective reproductive strategy, marriage and family would look very different than it does today. While often misplaced and an effort to sustain, romantic love is nevertheless a powerful force that has fueled human evolution by supporting long-term mating pair-bonds.

Summary

In this chapter, I described the role of different-sex (male-female) sexual attraction and romantic love in promoting long-term male-female mating pair-bonds and reproductive success. Surprisingly, scientists have shown little interest in understanding the etiology of different-sex sexual attraction, as opposed to same-sex attraction. Different-sex sexual attraction functions in part to draw two individuals together and facilitate sexual activities that eventually will lead to conception. Different-sex attraction and romantic love function to deepen attachment to keep the couple interested in each other in order to conceive children and raise them to relative self-sufficiency. As early human relationships became more complex, social customs developed to further support long-term pair-bonds as marriage. Romantic love and marriage appear to be universal human phenomena, although not invariably linked together.

Human mating strategies are driven by differential male and female reproductive investments across ecological and cultural contexts. Reduced sexual dimorphism among early humans strongly suggests that many formed relatively long-term different-sex mating pair-bonds (or serial pair-bonds). Romantic love is the probable mechanism that bonded couples together. For early humans, long-term different-sex loving pair-bonds addressed the demand for greater parental investment to raise children with larger, slow growing brains. In choosing male mates who remained committed to them and their children by supplying food and providing protection, ancestral human females out-reproduced females who employed other mating strategies. Different-sex romantic love and pair-bonding may have first emerged by ancestral females selecting (falling in love with) males who loved them back and who demonstrated their love through courtship, gifts, affection, sexual pleasure, and provisioning the family.

By creating a long-term emotional bond with their female reproductive mate, ancestral human males experienced greater reproductive success than males who employed other mating strategies. While sexual attraction and sexual activity bonded the couple initially, romantic (and companionate) love became important when the novelty of sex with the same partner faded and the partner's attention shifted to a newborn child. Romantic love and devotion from their mate provided males greater certainty regarding paternity. Thus, ancestral human males benefited by choosing (falling in love with) female mates who loved them back and demonstrated their love through sexual fidelity and emotional commitment.

Romantic love and male-female pair-bonding are not perfect reproductive solutions. However, they only needed to be slightly better than alternatives, such as polygyny or polyandry, infidelity, or commitment without love. While some men and women fall in love easily with others who are poor matches, many couples form loving relationships that last a lifetime. The strength, endurance, and effectiveness of romantic love is why men and women today long to fall in love with someone who will love them too. It goes without saying that men and women who are same-sex attracted also fall in love, but this topic is addressed in later chapters.

Because natural selection is conservative and exploits existing characteristics for other functions, it is possible that erotic/sexual attraction and romantic love are also central to devoted same-sex friendships. Devoted friendships addressed another survival and reproductive problem faced by our early human ancestors—navigating same-sex social environments. Attraction, love, and devoted same-sex friendship are the subjects of the next two chapters.

Take home points

- Human males and females have different reproductive investments and, consequently, take different mating strategies.
- Since they first appeared, early humans have often formed different-sex mating pair-bonds. Alternative mating strategies, such as polygyny and polyandry, while not uncommon, have been less stable across ecologies than monogamous pair-bonding.
- Romantic love functioned to ensure that male mates directed resources to their families and that females remained mostly sexually faithful for paternity certainty.
- Romantic love evolved to maintain long-term different-sex mating pair-bonds. Romantic love and marriage appear to be universal across human cultures, although not always linked together.

References

Abrahamson, I., Hussain, R., Khan, A., & Schofield, M. J. (2012). What helps couples rebuild their relationships after infidelity? *Journal of Family Issues*, 33(11), 1494–1519.

Allendorf, K. (2013). Schemas of marital change: From arranged marriages to eloping for love. *Journal of Marriage and Family*, 72(2), 453–469.

Anderson, K. G. (2006). How well does paternity confidence match actual paternity? Evidence from worldwide nonpaternity rates. *Current Anthropology*, 47(3), 513–520.

Apostolou, M. (2010). Parental choice: What parents want in a son-in-law and a daughter-in-law across 67 preindustrial societies. *British Journal of Psychology*, 101(4), 695–704.

Ard, B. N. (1977). Sex in lasting marriages: A longitudinal study. *Journal of Sex Research*, 13(4), 274–285.

Arsenault, A. (2017). Here's how much sex couples are having to get pregnant. *The Bump*. https://www.thebump.com/news/how-much-sex-getting-pregnant

Australian statistics on divorce (2016). CMLawyers. https://www.cmlaw.com.au/blog/post/australian-statistics-divorce/

Baer, D. (2017). There's a word for the assumption that everybody should be in a relationship. *The Cut*. https://www.thecut.com/2017/03/amatonormativity-everybody-should-be-coupled-up.html

Baker, R. R., & Bellis, M. A. (1995). *Human sperm competition: Copulation, masturbation and infidelity*. London, UK: Chapman and Hall.

Bartels, A., & Zeki, S. (2004). The neural correlates of romantic and maternal love. *NeuroImage*, *21*(3), 1155–1166.

Baumeister, R. F., Catanese, K. R., & Vohs, K. D. (2001). Is there a gender difference in strength of sex drive? Theoretical views, conceptual distinctions, and a review of relevant evidence. *Personality and Social Psychology Review*, *5*(3), 242–273.

Beckerman, S., Lizzaralde, R., Ballew, C., Schroeder, S., Fingelton, C., Garrison, A., & Smith, H. (1998). The Barí partible paternity project: Preliminary results. *Current Anthropology*, *39*(1), 164–167.

Benenson, J. F. (2013). The development of human female competition: Allies and adversaries. *Philosophical Transactions of the Royal Society of London Series B*, *368*(1631). https://royalsocietypublishing.org/doi/full/10.1098/rstb.2013.0079

Bergström-Walan, M. B., & Nielsen, H. H. (1990). Sexual expression among 60–80-year-old men and women: A sample from Stockholm, Sweden. *Journal of Sex Research*, *27*(2), 289–295.

Blumstein, P., & Schwartz, P. (1983). *American couples*. New York: Simon & Schuster.

Blurton-Jones, N. G., Marlowe, F. W., Hawkes, K., & O'Connell, J. F. (2000). Paternal investment and hunter-gatherer divorce rates. In L. Cronk, N. Chagnon, & W. Irons (Eds.), *Adaptation in human behavior: An anthropological perspective* (pp. 69–90). Chicago, IL: Aldine Transaction.

Bramlett, M. D., & Mosher, W. D. (2002). *Cohabitation, marriage, divorce, and remarriage in the United States (Vital and Health Statistics, Series 23, Number 22)*. Washington, DC: U.S. Government Printing Office.

Broad, K. D., Curley, J. P., & Keverne, E. B. (2007). Mother–infant bonding and the evolution of mammalian social relationships. *Philosophical Transactions of the Royal Society of London Series B*, *361*(1476), 2199–2214.

Burunat, E. (2014). Love is the cause of human evolution. *Advances in Anthropology*, *4*(2), 99–116.

Buss, D. M. (2003). *The evolution of desire: Strategies of human mating – Revised and expanded*. New York: Basic Books.

Buss, D. M. (2006). Strategies of human mating. *American Scientist*, *15*(2), 239–260.

Buss, D. M., Abbott, M., Angleitner, A., Asherian, A., Biaggio, A., Blanco-Villasenor, A., … Yang, K. (1990). International preferences in selecting mates: A study of 37 cultures. *Journal of Cross-Cultural Psychology*, *27*(1), 5–47.

Buunk, A. P., Park, J. H., & Duncan, L. A. (2010). Cultural variation in parental influence on mate choice. *Cross-Cultural Research*, *44*(1), 23–40.

Callaway, E. (2015). Genghis Khan's genetic legacy has competition. *Nature.com*. https://www.nature.com/news/genghis-khan-s-genetic-legacy-has-competition-1.16767

Cantarella, E. (2002). Marriage and sexuality in Republican Rome: A Roman conjugal love story. In M. C. Nussbaum & J. Sihvola (Eds.), *The sleep of reason: Erotic experience and sexual ethics in ancient Greece and Rome* (pp. 269–282). Chicago, IL: University of Chicago Press.

Caraël, M., Cleland, J., Deheneffe, J., Ferry, B., & Ingham, R. (1995). Sexual behavior in developing countries: Implications for HIV control. *AIDS, 9*(10), 1171–1175.

Carpenter, C. J. (2012). Meta-analyses of sex differences in responses to sexual versus emotional infidelity: Men and women are more similar than different. *Psychology of Women Quarterly, 36*(1), 25–37.

Carter, C. S. (2014). Oxytocin pathways and the evolution of human behavior. *The Annual Review of Psychology, 65*, 17–39.

Case, R. B., Moses, A. J., Case, N., McDermott, M., & Eberly, S. (1992). Living alone after myocardial infarction: Impact on prognosis. *JAMA, 267*(4), 515–519.

Chivers, M. L. (2005). A brief review and discussion of sex differences in the specificity of sexual arousal. *Sexual and Relationship Therapy, 20*(4), 377–390.

Chivers, M. L., Seto, M. C., & Blanchard, R. (2007). Gender and sexual orientation differences in sexual response to sexual activities versus gender of actors in sexual films. *Journal of Personality and Social Psychology, 93*(6), 1108–1121.

Cohas, A., & Allainé, D. (2009). Social structure influences extra-pair paternity in socially monogamous mammals. *Biology Letters, 5*(3), 313–316.

Curry, A. (2013). Archaeology: The milk revolution. *Nature, 500*(7460), 20–22.

Damrosch, D. (2003). *What is world literature?* Princeton, NJ: Princeton University Press.

Darwin, C. (1871/1981). *The descent of man and selection in relation to sex.* Princeton, NJ: Princeton University Press.

Del Giudice, M., Gangestad, S. W., & Kaplan, H. S. (2015). Life history theory and evolutionary psychology. In D. Buss (Ed.), *The handbook of evolutionary psychology, volume 1: Foundations*, 2nd ed. (pp. 88–114). New York: John Wiley & Sons.

Drea, C. M. (2015). D'scent of man: A comparative study of primate chemosignaling in relation to sex. *Hormones and Behavior, 68*, 117–133.

Fath-Ali Shah Qajar. (2019). *Wikipedia.* https://en.wikipedia.org/wiki/Fath-Ali_S hah_Qajar

Figueiredo, B., Costa, R., Pacheco, A., & Pais, A. (2007). Mother-to-infant and father-to-infant initial emotional involvement. *Early Child Development and Care, 177*(5), 521–532.

Fisher, H. E. (1992). *Anatomy of love.* New York: W.W. Norton.

Fisher, H. E., Brown, L. L., Aron, A., Strong, G., & Mashek, D. (2010). Reward, addiction, and emotion regulation systems associated with rejection in love. *Journal of Neurophysiology, 104*(1), 51–60.

Fletcher, G. J. O., & Kerr, P. S. G. (2010). Through the eyes of love: Reality and illusion in intimate relationships. *Psychological Bulletin, 136*(4), 627–658.

Fletcher, G. J. O., Simpson, J. A., Campbell, L., & Overall, N. C. (2015). Pair-bonding, romantic love, and evolution: The curious case of *Homo sapiens. Perspectives on Psychological Science, 10*(1), 20–36.

Foucault, M. (1980/1986). *The care of the self: Volume 3 of the history of sexuality* (R. Hurley, trans.). New York: Vintage Books.

Freud, S. (1905/1953). Three essays on the theory of sexuality. In J. Strachey (Ed.), *The standard edition of the complete psychological works of Sigmund Freud (Vol. 7)*, (pp. 123–246). London: Hogarth.

Gassen, N. S., & Perelli-Harris, B. (2015). The increase in cohabitation and the role of union status in family policies: A comparison of 12 European countries. *Journal of European Social Policy, 25*(4), 431–449.

Genghis Khan. (2019). *Wikipedia*. https://en.wikipedia.org/wiki/Genghis_Khan

Goodwin, J. S., Hunt, W. C., Key, C. R., & Samet, J. M. (1987). The effect of marital status on stage, treatment, and survival of cancer patients. *JAMA, 258*(21), 3125–3130.

Goodwin, R. (1999). *Personal relationships across cultures*. London: Routledge.

Gregersen, E. (1996). *The world of human sexuality: Behaviors, customs, and beliefs*. New York: Irvington Publishers.

Griffith, S. C., Owens, I. P. F., & Thuman, K. A. (2002). Extra pair paternity in birds: A review of interspecific variation and adaptive function. *Molecular Ecology, 11*(11), 2195–2212.

Grueter, C. C., Chapais, B., & Zinner, D. (2012). Evolution of multilevel social systems in nonhuman primates and humans. *International Journal of Primatology, 33*(5), 1002–1037.

Gupta, G. R. (1976). Love, arranged marriage, and the Indian social structure. *Journal of Comparative Family Studies, 7*(1), 75–85.

Haas, W. R., Klink, C. J., Maggard, G. J., & Aldenderfer, M. S. (2015). Settlement-size scaling among prehistoric hunter-gatherer settlement systems in the new world. *PLOS ONE, 10*(11), e0140127.

Hatfield, E., & Rapson, R. L. (1993). *Love, sex, and intimacy: Their psychology, biology, and history*. New York: Harper & Collins.

Hatfield, E., & Rapson, R. I. (2006). Passionate love, sexual desire, and mate selection: Cross-cultural and historical perspectives. In P. Noller & J. Feeney (Eds.), *Close relationships: Functions, forms and processes* (pp. 227–243). London: Psychology Press.

Heaton, T. B. (1990). Marital stability throughout the child-rearing years. *Demography, 27*(1), 55–63.

Howell, N. (1979). *Demography of the Dobe !Kung*. New York: Walter de Gruyter.

Hrdy, S. B. (2000). The optimal number of fathers: Evolution, demography, and history in the shaping of female mate preferences. *Annals of the New York Academy of Sciences, 907*(1), 75–96.

Hrdy, S. B. (2009). *Mothers and others: The evolutionary origins of mutual understanding*. Cambridge, MA: Belknap Press.

Insel, T. R. (2010). The challenge of translation in social neuroscience: A review of oxytocin, vasopressin, and affiliative behavior. *Neuron, 65*(6), 768–779.

Jankowiak, W. R., & Fischer, E. F. (1992). A cross-cultural perspective on romantic love. *Ethnology, 31*(2), 149–155.

Jankowiak, W. R., Sudakov, M., & Wilreker, B. C. (2005). Co-wife conflict and co-operation. *Ethnology, 44*(1), 81–98.

Kang, G. E. (1979). Exogamy and peace relations of social units: A cross-cultural test. *Ethnology, 18*(1), 85–99.

Kaplan, H., Hill, K., Lancaster, J. B., & Hurtado, A. M. (2000). A theory of human life history evolution: Diet, intelligence, and longevity. *Evolutionary Anthropology, 9*(4), 156–185.

Karandashev, V. (2015). A cultural perspective on romantic love. *Online Readings in Psychology and Culture, 5*(4), 1–21. doi: 10.9707/2307-0919.1135.

Keverne, E. B. (1983). Chemical communication in primate reproduction. In J. Vanderbergh (Ed.), *Pheromones and reproduction in mammals* (pp. 79–92). Orlando, FL: Academic Press.

Knapp, R. (2013). *Invisible Romans: Prostitutes, outlaws, slaves, gladiators, ordinary men and women... the Romans that history forgot.* London: Profile Books.

Kramer, K. L. (2010). Cooperative breeding and its significance to the demographic success of humans. *Annual Review of Anthropology, 39*(1), 417–436.

Kulu, H. (2014). Marriage duration and divorce: The seven-year itch or a lifelong itch? *Demography, 51*(3), 881–893.

Lamidi, E., & Manning, W. D. (2016). FP-16-17 marriage and cohabitation experiences among young adults. National Center for Family and Marriage Research Family Profiles, 60. https://scholarworks.bgsu.edu/ncfmr_family_profiles/60

Laumann, E. O., Gagnon, J. H., Michael, R. T., & Michaels, S. (1994). *The social organization of sexuality: Sexual practices in the United States.* Chicago: University of Chicago Press.

Lehmann, J., Lee, P. C., & Dunbar, R. I. M. (2014). Unravelling the evolutionary function of communities. In R. I. M. Dunbar, C. Gamble, & J. A. J. Gowlett (Eds.), *Lucy to language: The benchmark papers* (pp. 245–276). Oxford: Oxford University Press.

Levine, R., Sato, S., Hashimoto, T., & Verma, J. (1995). Love and marriage in eleven cultures. *Journal of Cross-Cultural Psychology, 26*(5), 554–571.

Lieberman, D., & Hatfield, E. (2006). Passionate love: Cross cultural and evolutionary perspectives. In R. J. Sternberg & K. Weis (Eds.), *The new psychology of love* (pp. 274–297). New Haven: Yale University Press.

Lim, G. Y., Tam, W. W., Lu, Y., Ho, C. S., Zhang, M. W., & Ho, R. C. (2018). Prevalence of depression in the community from 30 countries between 1994 and 2014. *Scientific Reports, 8*(2861), 1–10. doi: 10.1038/s41598-018-21243-x.

List of Brigham Young's wives. (2019). *Wikipedia.* https://en.wikipedia.org/wiki/List_of_Brigham_Young%27s_wives

Liu, J. C., Guastella, A. J., & Dadds, M. R. (2013). Exploring the role of intra-nasal oxytocin on the partner preference effect in humans. *Psychoneuroendocrinology, 38*(4), 587–591.

Love, T. M. (2014). Oxytocin, motivation and the role of dopamine. *Pharmacology, Biochemistry and Behavior, 119,* 49–60.

MacGill, M. (2017). What is the link between love and oxytocin? *Medical News Today.* https://www.medicalnewstoday.com/articles/275795.php

Magon, N., & Kalra, S. (2011). The orgasmic history of oxytocin: Love, lust, and labor. *Indian Journal of Endocrinology and Metabolism, 15*(Suppl. 3), S156–S161.

Mastekaasa, A. (1994). Marital status, distress, and well-being: An international comparison. *Journal of Comparative Family Studies, 25*(2), 183–206.

McCabe, P. (1987). Desired and experienced levels of premarital affection and sexual intercourse during dating. *Journal of Sex Research, 23*(1), 23–33.

McPherson, L. (2017). Marriages, civil unions, and divorces: Year ended December 2016. *Stats.NZ.* http://archive.stats.govt.nz/~/media/Statistics/Browse%20for%20stats/MarriagesCivilUnionsandDivorces/HOTPYeDec16/MarriagesCivilUnionsandDivorcesYeDec16HOTP.pdf

Mehndiratta, M. M., Paul, B., & Mehndiratta, P. (2007). Arranged marriage, consanguinity and epilepsy. *Neurology Asia, 12*(1), 15–17.

Miller, G. (2000). *The mating mind: How sexual choice shaped the evolution of human nature.* New York: Anchor Books.

Mitchell, S. (2004). *Gilgamesh: A new English version*. New York: Free Press.

Monin, J. K., & Clark, M. S. (2011). Why do men *benefit* more from marriage than do women? Thinking more broadly about interpersonal processes that occur within *and* outside of marriage. *Sex Roles, 65*(5), 320–326.

Munsch, C. L. (2012). The science of two-timing: The state of infidelity research. *Sociology Compass, 6*(1), 46–59.

Myers, D. G., & Diener, E. (1995). Who is happy? *Psychological Science, 6*(1), 10–19.

Oliver, M. B., & Hyde, J. S. (1993). Gender differences in sexuality: A meta-analysis. *Psychological Bulletin, 114*(1), 29–51.

Opie, C., Atkinson, Q. D., Dunbar, R. I. M., & Shultz, S. (2013). Male infanticide leads to social monogamy in primates. *Proceedings of the National Academy of Sciences, United States of America, 110*(33), 13328–13332.

Pande, R. (2015). "I arranged my own marriage": Arranged marriages and post-colonial feminism. *Gender, Place and Culture: A Journal of Feminist Geography, 22*(2), 172–187.

Panksepp, J. (1998). *Affective neuroscience: The foundations of human and animal emotions*. New York: Oxford University Press.

Pascal, B. (1660/1995). *Pensées* (A. J. Krailsheimer, trans.). London: Penguin Books.

Patel, A. (2018). Marriage, then love – Why arranged marriages still work today. *Global News*. https://globalnews.ca/news/4320972/arranged-marriage/

Perilloux, C., Fleischman, D. S., & Buss, D. M. (2011). Meet the parents: Parent-offspring convergence and divergence in mate preferences. *Personality and Individual Differences, 50*(2), 253–258.

Porn tube sites are free, so how does the porn industry make money today? (2018). *Fight the New Drug*. https://fightthenewdrug.org/how-does-the-porn-industry-actually-make-money-today/

Previti, D., & Amato, P. R. (2004). Why stay married? Rewards, barriers, and marital stability. *Journal of Marriage and Family, 65*(3), 561–573.

Prostitution revenue by country. (2018). *Havoscope Black Market Information*. https://www.havocscope.com/prostitution-revenue-by-country/

Prum, R. O. (2017). *The evolution of beauty: How Darwin's forgotten theory of mate choice shapes the animal world—And us*. New York: Doubleday.

Ridley, M. (1993). *The red queen: Sex and the evolution of human nature*. New York: Penguin.

Rilling, J. K., DeMarco, A. C., Hackett, P. D., Thompson, R., Ditzen, D., Patel, R., & Pagnoni, G. (2012). Effects of intranasal oxytocin and vasopressin on cooperative behavior and associated brain activity in men. *Psychoneuroendocrinology, 37*(4), 447–461.

Saey, T. H. (2018). Ancient DNA suggests that people settled in South America in at least 3 waves. *Science News*. https://www.sciencenews.org/article/ancient-dna-fossils-south-america-populated

Sagarin, B. J., Martin, A. L., Coutinho, S. A., Edlund, J. E., Patel, L., Skowronski, J. J., & Zengel, B. (2012). Sex differences in jealousy: A meta-analytic examination. *Evolution and Human Behavior, 33*(6), 595–614.

Scelza, B. A. (2011). Female choice and extra-pair paternity in a traditional human population. *Biological Letters, 7*(6), 889–891.

Scelza, B. A. (2013). Choosy but not chaste: Multiple mating in human females. *Evolutionary Anthropology, 22*(5), 259–269.

Scelza, B. A., Prall, S. P., Swinford, N., Gopalan, S., Atkinson, E. G., McElreath, R., … Henn, B. M. (2020). High rate of extrapair paternity in a human population demonstrates diversity in human reproductive strategies. *Science Advances, 6*(8), eaay6195.

Schacht, R., & Kramer, K. L. (2019). Are we monogamous? A review of the evolution of pair-bonding and its contemporary variation cross-culturally. *Frontiers in Ecology and Evolution, 7*(23). doi: 10.3389/fevo.2019.00230.

Sear, R., & Mace, R. (2008). Who keeps children alive? A review of the effects of kin on child survival. *Evolution of Human Behavior, 29*(1), 1–18.

Shaver, P. R., & Hazan, C. (1988). A biased overview of the study of love. *Journal of Social and Personal Relationships, 5*(4), 473–501.

Sprecher, S., Aron, A., Hatfield, E., Cortese, A., Potapova, E., & Levitskaya, A. (1994). Love: American style, Russian style, and Japanese style. *Personal Relationships, 1*(4), 349–369.

Starkweather, K. E., & Hames, R. (2012). A survey of non-classical polyandry. *Human Nature, 23*(2), 149–172.

Symons, D. (1979). *The evolution of human sexuality.* Oxford: Oxford University Press.

Taylor, T. (1996). *The prehistory of sex: Four million years of human sexual culture.* New York: Bantam Press Books.

Urooj, A., Anis-ul-Haque, & Anjum, G. (2015). Perception of sexual and emotional infidelity among married men and women. *Pakistan Journal of Psychological Research, 30*(2), 421–429.

Van IJzendoorn, M. H., & Bakermans-Kranenburg, M. J. (2012). A sniff of trust: Meta-analysis of the effects of intranasal oxytocin administration on face recognition, trust to in-group, and trust to out-group. *Psychoneuroendocrinology, 37*(3), 438–443.

Waite, L. J., & Lillard, L. A. (1991). Children and marital disruption. *American Journal of Sociology, 96*(4), 930–953.

Walker, R. S., Hill, K. R., Flinn, M. V., & Ellsworth, R. M. (2011). Evolutionary history of hunter-gatherer marriage practices. *PLOS ONE, 6*(4), 1–6.

Xu, Q., Qiu, Z., & Li, J. (2016). Is the "seven-year itch" real?—A study on the changing divorce pattern in Chinese marriages. *Journal of Chinese Sociology, 3*(17). Doi: 10.1186/s40711-016-0038-x

Xu, Q., Yu, J., & Qiu, Z. (2015). The impact of children on divorce risk. *Journal of Chinese Sociology, 2*(1). https://link.springer.com/article/10.1186/s40711-015-00 03-0#citeas

Chapter 3

Friends with Benefits
Devoted Same-Sex Friendship as an Adaptation

Do friends matter? The Ancients thought so, according to Christian philosopher C. S. Lewis (1960), who stated: "To the Ancients, Friendship seemed the happiest and most fully human of all loves; The crown of life and the school of virtue. The modern world, in comparison, ignores it" (p. 69). Lewis believed that modern people no longer valued the deeply emotional love of true friendship exemplified by David and Jonathan and Orestes and Pylades. Life is difficult, and having a true friend makes it easier. A true friend is always there. A true friend has your back. A true friend understands. A true friend likes you, even when you are at fault. A true friend is trustworthy and loyal when others cannot be bothered. Yet Lewis (1960) viewed true friendship as "the least natural of loves" because it is freely chosen, unlike empathy, charity, and romantic love, which are innate in his view (p. 70). Further, *true* friends are inherently male. His examples of true friendships only included men. While I doubt that Lewis believed that women could not be friends, women's relationships did not enter his mind. Lewis conceptualized true, ideal friendship as male friendship. Historically, friendship has been presented as a male relationship, which no doubt reflects male bias. Lewis also poetically asserted that friendship had no survival value although it added value to survival! A major claim of this chapter is that same-sex alliances and devoted same-sex friendships indeed have survival value, or at least they did in the past.

Friendship is not as valued today and does not mean quite what it did to ancient cultures, yet friendship is ubiquitous. The concept of "friend" and "friendship" is readily recognized among contemporary cultures as *ami/relation amicale* (French), *amico/amicizia* (Italian), *amigo/amistad* (Spanish), *freund/freundschaft* (German), *venn/vennskap* (Norwegian), *vän/vänskap* (Swedish), *drug/druzhba* (Russian), *odyn/druzhba* (Ukranian), *dost/dostluq* (Azerbaijani), *péngyǒu/yǒuyì* (Chinese), *chingu/ujeong* (Korean), *do'st/do'stlik* (Uzbek), *sadiq/sadaqa* (Arabic), *arkadaş/dostluk* (Turkish), *saaxiib/saaxiibtinimo* (Somali), *rafiki/urafiki* (Swahili), *umngane/ubungani* (Zulu), *teman/persahabatan* (Indonesian), and *rakan/persahabatan* (Malay), to name a few (How to Say Friendship, 2019). While these terms are not exact equivalents, as we will see later, it is easy to spot common roots across language groups.

Friendship may not be as valued today as in the past, but it is still viewed as important. Friends matter. People are pretty good at knowing who in their social network is loyal and supportive. Psychologists Peter DeScioli and Robert Kurzban (2009) have suggested that people today strongly value and invest in a few close friends but maintain a large network of allies who may be potentially helpful in the future. Close friendship is special and celebrated in many parts of the world. Bracelets, jewelry, or other small gifts are exchanged by friends to recognize their close relationships. Colorful, patterned bands of knotted embroidery floss or thread are worn around the wrist or ankle by both men and women as a symbol of a close friendship and can be traced back several hundred years to the indigenous people of Central and South America and even earlier to regions of China (Friendship Bracelets, 2020). Today friendship bracelets can be purchased at gift shops, local festivals, and tourist shops as souvenirs. Friends may also exchange jewelry, like a ring or chain worn around the neck to symbolize their close relationship. The Claddagh symbol, for example, thought to be of Celtic origin, of two hands holding a crowned heart is a common friendship sign (Angers, 2020). Currently, tattoos of matching images are popular symbols of friendship. Common friendship tattoos include the infinity symbol, interlocking hearts, a Chinese or Japanese logogram for friendship, or two crossed arrows from Native American tradition representing two people or two clans. In some countries, friendship is a special observance. World Friendship Day, an unofficial holiday, is especially popular in Asian countries (Friendship Day, 2020). On this day, friends exchange cards, flowers, or small gifts like friendship bracelets. World Friendship Day began in 1958 in Paraguay as an activity of the World Friendship Campaign, an international organization working to promote peace. In 2011, the United Nations General Assembly proclaimed July 30 as the International Day of Friendship.

Close same-sex friendships are popular themes in modern literature and plays. Famous fictional best friends include Sancho Panza and Don Quixote (*Don Quixote*, de Cervantes); Celie and Shug in *The Color Purple* (Walker); Tom Sawyer and Huck Finn (*The Adventures of Tom Sawyer*, Twain); and Vladimir and Estragon in *Waiting for Godot* (Beckett). Buddy movies, featuring close male friends, are extremely popular today. Famous buddies in film include Felix and Oscar (*The Odd Couple*, 1968, Paramount Pictures), Butch Cassidy and the Sundance Kid in the movie of the same name (1969, 20th Century Fox), Harold and Kumar (*Harold & Kumar Go to White Castle*, 2004, Endgame Entertainment), and Phil, Stu, Alan, and Doug in *The Hangover* (2009, Warner Bros). Female buddy movies are less common, but two good examples are CC and Hillary in *Beaches* (1988, All Girls

Productions) and Thelma and Louise in the movie of the same name (1991, Pathé Entertainment). In the United States, *The Golden Girls* (1985–1992, Touchstone Television), *Friends* (1994–2004, Warner Bros. Television), and *Living Single* (1993–1998, Fox) are quintessential television series about friendship. Although these shows ended 15 or more years ago, through cable television, audiences continue to follow and identify with the friendships of Dorothy, Blanche, Rose, and Sophia; Rachel, Monica, Phoebe, Joey, Chandler, and Ross; as well as Khadijah, Synclaire, Regine, Max, Kyle, and Obie. Just reading these familiar names evokes warm feelings!

These days, the Internet and social media have made it easy to stay connected with friends. In the 1990s, with the introduction of Internet Service Providers like AOL, Prodigy, and CompuServe, friends and family could stay in touch through email. In the 2000s, social platforms like Myspace, Friendster, LinkedIn, and Flickr emerged to provide virtual space for people to share news and photos with their social networks. Today nearly three billion people actively use Facebook, Instagram, Pinterest, Tumblr, Twitter, and YouTube to communicate with friends and followers (Number of Social Media Users, 2019). Facebook alone has nearly 2 billion users.

Friendship is ubiquitous. The persistence of friendship across cultures and the contemporary social emphasis on friendship strongly suggests that friends are important. Friendships today are more casual in many ways than in the past, but they remain valued. Further, as I will argue, friendships are necessary.

Friendship and Interpersonal Relationships

As noted above, the word for friend has slightly different meanings and different obligations depending on the language and culture. In general, a friend is a close intimate and not an enemy, although the term can be used ironically to mean someone who is not at all a friend. Friendship is voluntary. Friendship is more intimate and affectionate than most other voluntary interpersonal relationships with unrelated individuals. (See Table 3.1). At a basic level, acquaintanceships are polite but impersonal and transitory interactions. For example, an acquaintance is someone you see daily on the way to work but to whom you rarely say more than "Good morning!" and comment on the weather. In the previous chapter, I defined coalitions, another kind of personal cooperative relationship, as temporary task-specific associations. Coalition partners are people with whom you are briefly linked in order to engage in some immediate action, like building a shelter, completing a work-related assignment, participating in a pick-up game of basketball, or marching in protest against some political issue. Coalitions in the form of mobs can be quite effective and powerful, but also dangerous and unmanageable. Coalitions are generally short-lived and involve little intimacy or personal sharing and no further obligation to each other.

Table 3.1 Voluntary Interpersonal Relationships Among Unrelated Individuals by Level of Intimacy and Duration

Type	Description	Examples
Devoted friendship	Same-sex individuals Passionate, intimate, affectionate, sometimes sexual May involve formal ceremony and exchange of vows Long-term	Blood brothers, bond brothers, adoptive brothers, sworn brothers, second self
Marriage	Different-sex individuals[1] Passionate, intimate, affectionate, sexual Formal ceremony and exchange of vows Long-term	Spouse, husband, wife
Close friendship	Same-sex individuals[2] Personal, warm, platonic, committed Long-term	Best friend, good friend, buddy
Alliance	Same-sex individuals[2] Situation-specific, transactional, cooperative, friendly Variable duration, but can be lengthy	Employer-employee, business partners, indentureship, mentor-mentee, work colleagues, soldiers, sports teammates, club members, guest-friends
Coalition	Same-sex or different-sex individuals[2] Task-specific, transactional, cooperative, low intimacy Brief	Work group members, search parties, pick-up games, mob
Acquaintanceship	Same-sex or different-sex individuals[2] Situation-specific, low commitment, polite, impersonal Brief, transitory	Neighbors known by sight, someone met at a party, person seen daily on the commute to work, waiter at a restaurant

[1] While formal same-sex unions have been recognized in some past cultures, these unions were generally not called "marriage". Recently, Western European countries and the United States have legalized same-sex marriage.

[2] As social segregation by sex has decreased in Western cultures, men and women have experienced greater public and private social contact, permitting casual interaction, work relationships, and even personal friendships.

Alliances differ from friendships in my view, although some writers treat alliances as a behavioral form of friendship. However, I see alliances as enduring working relationships that last as long as the partnership is beneficial to both parties. Alliances come in various forms but are voluntary, situation-specific, cooperative, and transactional. Cooperative alliances are critically important in explaining major human social advancements.

There is an expectation of mutual support and benefit with alliances, but the benefits may be uneven. Alliances include employer-employees, business partners, and even indentured servitude. One can argue whether indentured servitude is ever voluntary. In many cultures, individuals have contractually given up their liberty to someone else for a (sometimes lengthy) period of time to pay off debts. Certainly, some people have been forced into servitude. Conceptually, indentured servitude is not slavery and should end at some point (when the contract has been fulfilled), although the boundaries between servitude and slavery have often blurred.

A mentoring alliance is another situation-specific but formal relationship involving individuals of different statuses: in this case, a typically older, knowledgeable person and a young novice. Mentoring alliances may be lengthy and intimate and may evolve into friendship over time. Voluntary, situation-specific alliances between individuals with relatively equivalent status include work colleagues, military soldiers, police partners, and mates on a semi-permanent sports team. While all forms of alliances are personal in some way, they are not necessarily close or emotionally intimate. Later, I will discuss in more detail the ancient world concept of *guest-friend*, a largely antiquated personal relationship. A guest-friend is a visiting foreigner who is granted special hospitalities by the host (Konstan, 1997). The host and guest-friend may have different social statuses, although the guest-friend should have sufficient status and resources to reciprocate when their roles are reversed.

If asked to think about an important friendship, we might recall a close, personal friend whom we have known for many years—perhaps a best friend. A close, best friend is someone we look forward to seeing and miss when we are apart. Close friendships are based on common interests and shared activities and are enduring and meaningful. Close friends share a mutual respect and affection for each other. Close friends help each other. However, the relationship may not be equal; one friend may have more or different needs than the other. Close friends may differ in social status, although in modern times, people have less personal exposure to those who are ethnically and economically different so are more likely to make friends with individuals who are similar to them. In most cultures, not only those that limit socialization by sex, a close friend is nearly always someone of the same sex. In recent modern times, a close friendship is almost always non-sexual—not counting sexual experimentation among adolescents. In contemporary culture, we cannot conceive of same-sex friendships involving sexual intimacy and pleasure because having sex with a person of the same sex is a "gay" relationship, not friendship.

A close modern friendship is distinct from historical devoted friendships. As I will explore in this chapter, devoted male friendships in the past were self-chosen, passionate, intimate, deeply committed, loving relationships. What distinguishes historical devoted male friendships from modern male friendships is a public expression of love and commitment through formal vows and rituals. Devoted friends vowed loyalty and mutual support to each other. The commitment was often lifelong, and the community recognized the special relationship between the pair. As we will see, in some cultures devoted friends had similar status and equivalent roles, while in other cultures friends differed in status, age, or social role. Devoted male friends lived together or apart but greatly enjoyed each other's company. As we will see, many devoted male friends engaged in sexual activity together, but some did not. In many cases, devoted male friends were also married to women and had families. In many ways, historical devoted male friendships were comparable to male-female marriages. Both kinds of relationships involved formal ceremonies and public recognition, expressions of love and affection, an exchange of vows, a long-term commitment, and even sexual intimacy. Unfortunately, too little is known about historical devoted female friendships to speak confidently about the structure and nature of these relationships.

Historical devoted male friendships differed from male-female marriages in traditional cultures. As we will see later, in traditional cultures, wives had lower social status than their husbands, who often had governance over their wives and everyone else in the household. Owing to their inequivalent genders, husbands and wives in traditional cultures were never peers. Husbands usually found companionship with close male friends, not their wives. I suspect that wives in traditional cultures found companionship with female friends. Depending on the culture, brides and bridegrooms had varying degrees of choice in who they married, but they were free to choose a close, best friend. In traditional cultures, devoted friends were often viewed as emotionally closer than spouses.

As I will show later, some cultures have used friendship terms to denote close intimate relationships between siblings. For example, close brothers have sometimes been referred to as "friends" to highlight their special relationship. However, kinship terms have often been used to denote close intimate relationships between unrelated individuals, such as "blood brothers", "adoptive brothers", and "sworn brothers". Such terms are not common in contemporary Western culture. Finally, other cultures have simply invented new words such as *i-amo*, *mbai*, and *nanshoku* to account for the special kind of devoted friendship between two unrelated same-sex individuals.

Not only do historical devoted friendships look different from contemporary Western friendships, they "feel" different as well. It is a little odd for us to think of male friends being closer to each other than to their female spouses. It also feels strange to think of male friends expressing their love and affection for each other sexually. And it seems unusual that men from different social classes with different privileges, perhaps a warrior and apprentice or a master and slave, would ever refer to each other as a (devoted) friend. In the pages ahead, I will present a wide variety of devoted male friendships across cultures. The next chapter will explore in more detail how Western culture became uncomfortable with sexual male friendships. This chapter and the next will argue that devoted male friendships have persisted through history and across cultures because men needed loyal friends to survive. Devoted male friendships persisted because they were necessary. I will also try to show that women needed and benefited from devoted female friendships where the evidence exists.

If devoted male friendships are an adaptive trait that directly benefits survival and indirectly benefits reproductive success, then we would expect to find evidence of such relationships among contemporary hunter-gatherer societies. If this trait is older still, then we would expect to find evidence of similar preferential relationships among our closest non-human primate relatives. Evidence of friendship across species would demonstrate that this is an old conserved, adaptive trait. In the next section, I will undertake an evolutionary analysis of friendship across species, presenting evidence for how friendship developed and its potential function. With that background, I will then examine the role of close friendship among early human hunter-gatherers.

An Evolutionary Analysis of Friendship Across Species

How can we talk about friendship among non-human animals? We do not know their feelings or thoughts. They cannot tell us in words. While non-human animals cannot communicate directly about their interpersonal relationships, we can observe their behavior and make cautious inferences about their preferential relationships. Animal behaviorist, Robert Seyfarth, and zoologist, Dorothy Cheney, in their paper, "The Evolutionary Origins of Friendship" (2012), argued that it is not anthropomorphic to talk about friendships among non-human species. Seyfarth and Cheney cite evidence for preferential interpersonal relationships—possibly friendships—between individuals across several species. So how should we distinguish coalitions or alliances from friendships among non-humans? Distinguishing characteristics might include their brevity and transactional nature. Coalitions refer to temporary, task-based, cooperative associations between unrelated individuals and for the most part, that definition works across species. For example, a band of male chimpanzees who temporarily work together to patrol territorial boundaries represents a same-sex coalition. In the primatology literature, longer-term cooperative relationships between individuals, who may or may not be related, are typically called alliances. This definition of alliances is broader than for humans. Closely related chimpanzees gain reproductive advantages by cooperating. Mother-daughter kin alliances are common among chimpanzees and even among humans. However, we are interested in preferential same-sex alliances—potential friendships—between unrelated individuals. Among male chimpanzees, alliances between unrelated individuals are quite common. Male alliances among chimpanzees also tend to be hierarchical and transactional. That is, male chimpanzees usually align themselves with a higher-ranking individual. Alliances among male chimpanzees are associated with power and protection. Alliances may shift to a lower-ranking individual who challenges the ranking male or end when the ranking male loses dominance.

Seyfarth and Cheney (2012) argued that the term "friendship" should be reserved for special cooperative relationships between unrelated non-human animals that appear preferential and not strictly transactional. While Seyfarth and Cheney cite evidence for long-term friendships among horses, elephants, dolphins, and monkeys, I will limit my discussion to alliances and friendships among apes, our closest living relatives. The lesser and great apes include gibbons (genera *Hoolock, Hylobates, Symphalangus, Nomascus*; the lesser apes), orangutans (*Pongo pygmaeus, Pongo abelii*, and possibly *Pongo tapanuliensis*), gorillas (*Gorilla gorilla* and *Gorilla beringei*), chimpanzees (*Pan troglodytes* and *Pan paniscus)*, and humans (*Homo sapiens*). Humans and gibbons shared a common ancestor some 16 million years ago. Humans and chimpanzees, including bonobos, shared a common ancestor only about 6.3 million years ago.

Except for orangutans, all apes form relatively stable social groups (Watts, 2012). Orangutans tend to form single male-multifemale groups, but adults largely remain alone in their feeding territory, with the exception that female mothers tend to their immature young. Sexually mature males tend to disperse from their natal group. Mature flanged male orangutans compete with non-resident flanged males and unflanged males for territory and access to fertile females. Adult males do not associate with each other and do not form alliances. Adult flanged males are hostile to other flanged males but less hostile to unflanged males. Alliances among adult male gorillas are also rare, although solitary non-dominant males may form temporary bands or coalitions (Watts, 2012). Gorillas largely form single male-multifemale social systems, or harems, that include immature offspring. Sexually mature gorillas of both sexes disperse from their natal group. Most male mountain gorillas become solitary or join all-male bands until they acquire a female mate or harem. Among mountain and western gorillas, the strongest social bond is between the dominant male and adult females, as evidenced by time spent grooming. Mothers, daughters, and sisters also form strong social bonds. However, female gorillas spend more time near and grooming the dominant male than any other animal. Adult-adolescent female grooming is the next most common. While female mountain gorillas have a loose hierarchy, alliances between unrelated females are infrequent and aggressively discouraged by the dominant male. Unrelated female gorillas are only somewhat tolerant of each other.

The story is quite different for chimpanzees and bonobos, our closest living relatives. Male chimpanzees and female bonobos frequently form same-sex alliances with unrelated individuals. Some female chimpanzees have been observed in long-term same-sex alliances, but male bonobos have not. Both chimpanzees and bonobos form multimale-multifemale *fission-fusion* societies, meaning the size and composition of the group is dynamic (Watts, 2012). In fission-fusion societies, small groups form temporarily (e.g., foraging activities) and continually within the larger group, then disband, and form again. *Polygynandrous* mating (both males and females have multiple partners) is thought to confuse paternity and reduce the risk of infanticide. Dominant male chimpanzees may restrict lower ranking males from access to fertile females, as well as coerce ovulating females ("consorts") to separate themselves from the larger group long enough to copulate with less risk of being interrupted. Unrelated adult male and female chimpanzees spend little time together grooming. However, mother-adult son grooming is quite common, reflecting a close bond. Sexually mature female chimpanzees often immigrate to nearby communities, where they may experience aggression from other females or coalitions of females who view immigrants as competitors. Among bonobos, females are more gregarious and associate frequently, while males have weaker social bonds (Watts, 2005; 2012). Male-female alliances are common among bonobos, unlike chimpanzees. Mother-adult son alliances are also common, and mothers often support their sons in acquiring rank. Female bonobos frequently groom each other and engage in sexual behaviors. Immigrant female bonobos experience little aggression from resident females. Among bonobos, immigrant females often align themselves with resident females who can provide them some protection from others (Idani, 1991). Male bonobos form loose dominance hierarchies. Although male bonobos most frequently groom other males, they rarely form alliances.

Male common chimpanzees maintain complex relationships with each other (Watts, 2012). Male chimpanzees evidence high rates of affiliation and cooperation, while competing for status within the hierarchy. High-ranking males attract grooming from male partners and receive more grooming than low ranking males. Grooming demonstrates an alliance. Grooming is reciprocal and occurs more frequently between male chimpanzees than between males and females. Male chimpanzees often form temporary coalitions, led by a dominant male, to patrol, hunt, or defend territory against marauding nonresident males. Collaborative hunting increases their chances of success. Dominant males reward the hunting party with pieces of meat and favor allies. Long-term alliances, as opposed to temporary coalitions, facilitate male chimpanzees' acquisition and maintenance of rank. Males close in age are most likely to form long-term alliances, although age disparate alliances are not infrequent. Most male alliances are between unrelated individuals. By contrast, female chimpanzee associations are more variable. Some females groom others and maintain long-term alliances, while some avoid each other (Watts, 2012). There is debate about whether female chimpanzees form dominance hierarchies. Female chimpanzees clearly do not form linear hierarchies like males or associate as frequently. Yet top-ranking females use their status to acquire higher quality food and preferential copulations with dominant males. Alpha females also have shorter interbirth intervals and higher infant survival, suggesting their higher rank affords them greater reproductive success than lower-ranking females.

Anthropologists David Watts and John Mitani conducted an impressive 10-year study of 35 male common chimpanzees in the large Ngogo community in Uganda, which provides key details about their long-term alliances (cited in Seyfarth & Cheney, 2012). They found that social bonds varied in length from one to ten years, with the vast majority of individuals having formed at least one close male alliance lasting five years or more. Males often had multiple alliances. Among 28 males observed for at least five years, strong alliances of one year or more were evident among 66% of unrelated age mates and 48% of unrelated age-disparate mates. Similarly ranked males had equitable grooming exchanges and longer lasting alliances than males of unequal rank. While many alliances in the Ngogo community were among kin, 22 of 28 male chimpanzees formed their strongest bond with an unrelated male. Most cooperative behavior among males was observed between unrelated males. When Mitani compared reciprocal exchanges among the 22 male chimpanzees with strong alliances, the best predictor of an individual's interaction with another male was that male's rate of interaction with the subject, suggesting that male chimpanzees monitored and tracked exchanges within an alliance. Perhaps mutual reciprocity over time produced a sense of trust, confidence, or expectation of future behavior. It seems probable that close alliances that benefited both parties also felt satisfying, which promoted liking. In a study of 39 female common chimpanzees in the Ngogo community, Mitani and colleagues observed females associating with each other less often on average than males associated with other males (Seyfarth & Cheney, 2012). However, contrary to previous reports that adult female chimpanzees do not associate, Mitani and colleagues found that the strongest alliances were observed among females. What is more, most female alliances were with unrelated individuals. Apparently, unrelated female chimpanzees do form strong alliances.

In another fascinating study of two captive colonies of common chimpanzees in The Netherlands, investigators examined how personality characteristics affected social bonds among 38 individuals (Massen & Koski, 2014). The age of the chimpanzees ranged from 1.5 to 53 years across the two colonies. Previous work by one of the investigators had identified four personality factors—*Sociability*, *Positive Affect*, *Anxiety*, and *Grooming Equity*—from 15 behavioral variables observed among 75 chimpanzees at one of the colonies. Another set of studies of chimpanzee responses to novel objects and situations had identified two non-social personality factors—*Exploration Tendency-Persistence* and *Boldness*—in one colony. Using these personality factors, investigators in The Netherlands assessed individuals' personalities and measured the relationship quality between chimpanzees by how close they sat next to another individual. Contact-sitting referred to sitting close enough to touch the other individual. Across the two colonies, individuals who sat close together, whether kin or non-kin, had similar Sociability scores, when controlling for age and sex-combination of the dyad. This relationship held whether the pair were high or low in Sociability. That is, individuals, whether related or not, preferred to be in close contact with others who were most like them in social characteristics. What is more, Boldness and Grooming Equity predicted close contact between unrelated individuals, but not kin dyads. It makes sense that individuals must overcome their initial fear to approach unfamiliar chimpanzees, and close relationships among unrelated individuals depend on reciprocity. It also makes sense that individual chimpanzees would prefer close contact with those who are most like them. Their interactions are predictable and similar.

It is also interesting how these personality characteristics observed among chimpanzees are similar to the Big Five Personality factors found among humans: *Extraversion*, *Neuroticism*, *Openness*, *Conscientiousness*, and *Agreeableness*. Cooperative social living among humans and close interpersonal relationships, like friendship, are thought to have co-evolved with personality (Nettle, 2006). In particular, the Sociability characteristic observed among chimpanzees, associated with preferential physical contact with another individual, seems comparable to Extraversion in the Big Five. Extraversion is linked with positive emotion and exploration of the environment. People high in Extraversion initiate social contact more often, are more physically active, and engage in sensation-seeking behavior. Sociability among chimpanzees also seems related to Agreeableness in the Big Five. Agreeableness is associated with feeling empathy and trust. People high in Agreeableness engage in more cooperative behavior with unrelated individuals and display low interpersonal hostility, both essential to social living. In addition, Sociability and Grooming Equity found in chimpanzees seem similar to Conscientiousness in the Big Five, especially with regard to friendship. Conscientiousness is associated with tracking reciprocity and delayed gratification. Chimpanzee and human friends must not only tolerate being physically close to each other, they also must be comfortable with unequal exchanges, such as attending to the immediate needs of the other individual and delaying gratification of one's own needs or finding satisfaction in helping a friend. Echoing findings regarding personality among chimpanzees, researchers have reported that Western European young adults entering university are most likely to form new friendships with people who share similar personality characteristics (Selfhout, Burk, Branje, Denissen, van Aken, & Meeus, 2010). Specifically, friends tend to match on Extraversion, Agreeableness, and Openness. What is more, men preferred male friends, and women preferred female friends. Similarly, adults on Facebook and their friends also tend to match in personality (Youyou, Stillwell, Schwartz,

& Kosinki, 2017). Using behavioral-based personality assessments that looked at similarity in language and social media "likes", researchers found that 5,674 Facebook friendship pairs were similar on measures of Openness to Experience and Extraversion.

In sum, there is good evidence of close preferential same-sex alliances with unrelated individuals among male and female chimpanzees and among female bonobos, with some alliances lasting for many years. Same-sex alliances among both male and female chimpanzees play an important survival role in defending against aggression and facilitating food acquisition. Same-sex alliances among male and female chimpanzees and among female bonobos also function to maintain and increase social rank within the same-sex group, which has reproductive benefits such as preferential mating. Thus, long-term preferential same-sex alliances appear to have ancient origins. Recent findings demonstrate that chimpanzees prefer the company of individuals who are socially similar (Massen & Koski, 2014). Humans also prefer friends who are similar in personality (Nettle, 2006; Selfhout, Burk, Branje, et al., 2010; Youyou, Stillwell, Schwartz, & Kosinki, 2017). Personality traits associated with close social contact with unrelated individuals among chimpanzees appear similar to personality traits associated with friendship among humans. Respectively, both chimpanzees and humans may find individuals with similar characteristics to be more predictable, familiar, and less threatening than individuals with dissimilar characteristics. That is, social similarity may foster a sense of comfort.

The Evolutionary Adaptiveness of Friendship Among Early Humans

Now that we have identified evidence of friendship-like behavior among chimpanzees and bonobos, is there evidence of friendship among early humans? As a reminder, about 4 million years ago, the Australopithecines were walking exclusively on two legs and living in mixed woodlands and grasslands in Africa (Taylor, 1996). They looked like tall bonobos and may have shared many of the same characteristics, like living in small multimale-multifemale fission-fusion groups. Small bands may have merged temporarily into larger communities to shelter or share access to water or food supplies (Grueter, Chapais, & Zinner, 2012). Like chimpanzees, male Australopithecines likely formed close alliances with other males within linear hierarchies. Temporary male coalitions defended the group's territory from predators and participated in cooperative hunting. Like chimpanzees, female Australopithecines likely grouped together to care for immature offspring and shield themselves from aggressive males. They may have formed close kin alliances like chimpanzees, as well as alliances with unrelated females in the group. By about 2.5 million years ago, a cooler, drier climate had further reduced forests and promoted the spread of grasslands across Africa and into Europe, promoting a greater diversity of species (Taylor, 1996). By then, our early ancestors lived mainly in open grasslands on a diverse diet. Like other species in these new ecologies, early hominins had begun to diversify, growing taller, less dimorphic, and less chimpanzee-like. By just two million years ago, several species of early hominins (*Homo*) were spreading throughout Africa, across Europe, and into Asia. Around 300,000–200,000 years ago, early *Homo sapiens* appeared. By roughly 70,000 years ago, early modern humans began moving out of Africa and spreading across the world (Dunbar, 2010).

Archaeologist Timothy Taylor (1996) has argued that late Australopithecines and early archaic humans, our direct ancestors, were hunters and gatherers. Sometime between two million and 500,000 years ago, our early hominin ancestors began to wear clothing, as they experienced a changing climate or encountered new ones. As nomadic and semi-nomadic archaic humans followed migrating herds, they encountered a wide range of climates compared to the African savannah. They adjusted to different ecologies by wearing clothes, varying their diets, building semi-permanent shelters, and developing innovations in weaponry, hunting, controlling fire, cooking, and medicine. Archaic humans had also begun to express themselves through vocal and gestural communication, art, and culture. Their social organization was becoming more complex. Living in small hunter-gatherer cultures became an enduring pattern of life (Gurven, 2012). For more than 90% of human history, humans have lived as hunter-gatherers.

Long-term mating pair-bonds, discussed in the previous chapter, fueled the complexity of hunter-gatherer cultures by creating multiple social levels. Distinct couples were embedded within larger families who lived cooperatively with other families in small groups of 35–80 individuals (Dunbar & Sosis, 2018; Grueter, Chapais, & Zinner, 2012). Multiple small groups joined occasionally to form larger communities or bands of 150–500 individuals, and then split off into small groups again. Families and communities may have been linked by kinship ties through marriage. Distant bands stayed connected through bride exchange and trade. Cooperation and coordination within and between families likely involved a hierarchical and authoritarian structure that stressed obedience and honoring the family (Goodwin, 1999). Men likely held authoritarian roles. While small hunter-gatherer camps may have been largely egalitarian, bigger communities were probably less so (Dyble, Salali, Chaudhary, Page, Smith, Thompson, Vinicius, Mace & Migliano, 2015). Group living likely afforded early humans, like chimpanzees, protection against predators and hostile groups (Watts, 2012). Cooperative living also ensured greater success in various activities of daily life—building shelters, hunting, defending against threats, foraging, and child-rearing. Early archaic human females likely engaged female relatives and unrelated women in the community (cooperative breeding) in raising their large-brained, slow-developing children (Burkart, Hrdy, & van Schaik, 2009). Complex cooperative relationships with non-relative community members for childcare, as well as hunting and foraging, required coordination, communication, and tracking of obligations. The need for specialized skills and cooperation to complete activities of living—tracking and hunting big animals, gathering edible foods, preparing foods daily, keeping fires burning, monitoring and caring for young children, making and repairing clothing, weaving baskets and mats, making tools/weapons, crafting pots/containers, tooling leather, building shelters, settling quarrels among group members, and negotiating contact between groups or bands—suggests an early division of labor (Taylor, 1996). Dividing and assigning time-consuming tasks by gender allowed for specialized skill development and better ensured survival of the group. The division and gendering of labor mostly followed reproductive roles, although these divisions may not have been absolute.

The archeological record provides limited evidence about how early hunter-gatherers lived. Fossil evidence is spotty and restricted to durable materials that survive time and weather. However, we can draw some inferences about ancestral human life by examining contemporary hunter-gatherer societies. These societies are not, of course, preserved relics of our distant past, so our inferences require caution. Contemporary hunter-gatherer societies have been touched, sometimes violently, and changed by modern cultures. Sometimes scholarly reports on contemporary hunter-gatherers refer to a past way of life that has long disappeared. For example, the Aché (Guajagui), an indigenous people of eastern Paraguay, first experienced Western contact by Jesuits in the seventeenth century (Hurtado, Hawkes, Hill & Kaplan, 1985). By the late eighteenth century, however, the Jesuits had left the region, and the Aché were left alone for 100 years. In the early twentieth century, the Paraguayan government violently moved the Northern Aché to two reserves, acquiring their land and reducing their territory from 20,000 square kilometers to just 50 square kilometers. One settlement, Chupa Pou, is only about 30 kilometers from a town (Curuguaty). In the recent past, Aché adults still made extended hunting trips in the forest and lived on wild foods but also grew some vegetables and traded hunted game for consumer goods (Hurtado, Hawkes, Hill & Kaplan, 1985). However, most Aché children and adolescents attend school in the mission. Another contemporary hunter-gatherer society, the Aka, spend approximately 17% of their time working for nearby agriculturalists (Konner, 2005). The Aka are a small-stature people living in the tropical forest of the southwestern Central African Republic and northern People's Republic of the Congo. They consume mainly farm-produced foods obtained by trading hunted game. Contemporary hunter-gatherer societies have had varying amounts of contact with modern cultures, which has undoubtedly changed their traditional way of life in many ways that we cannot know. Nevertheless, observations about these societies can provide suggestive insights about our ancient past.

Contemporary Hunter-Gatherer Societies
and Devoted Male Friendships

In general, contemporary hunter-gatherer societies are highly cooperative (Marlowe, 2010). Living in small groups, members depend on each other for survival and, therefore, need to work together. Social organization often does not extend beyond the camp level. Small camps are often non-hierarchical and largely egalitarian, although members have different and sometimes distinct roles (Marlowe, 2010). Bigger camps or bands of multiple groups tend to be more hierarchical and less egalitarian. Among the Hadza of northern Tanzania around Lake Eyasi, for example, multiple families live in small groups of about 30 (but up to 100) and move often. Moving camp is determined when women have exhausted local plant resources. In camp, men and women socialize together, and couples sleep together. During the day, men and women largely live separate lives; men are off hunting together, while women stay close to camp and forage, take care of children, sew, and process food (Marlowe, 2010). Disagreements among camp members are often public and managed publicly. Women have loud arguments with their husbands. In small groups or camps, everything is public. Among the Aché of eastern Paraguay, men and women have different roles (and perhaps status), but women are involved in discussions about camp matters (Hurtado, Hawkes, Hill & Kaplan, 1985). Men leave camp early in the morning and spend the day hunting in the forest. Hours later, women pack up the camp and follow them, sometimes foraging along the way, but primarily attending to young infants. Women provide most of the childcare and engage in activities that keep them in proximity to the children. Women also clean small game, process foods (e.g., palm starch), cook meals, gather wood, and collect water. When living in the forest, Aché men supply about 87% of the camp's subsistence with hunted game or prized foraged food, like honey. Big game is highly valued by camp members. Aché men are efficient hunters, but successful hunting requires 15–20 years of experience (Gurven & Hill, 2009). Consequently, Aché males spend most of their time hunting.

In these two examples of well documented but distinct contemporary hunter-gatherer societies, a general pattern emerges: Men hunt, and women forage and care for children, although there are several exceptions (Goodman, Griffin, Estioko-Griffin, & Grove, 1985). Among 179 contemporary hunter-gatherer societies, men alone hunt in 166 of them (Ember, 1978). Both men and women hunt in 13 societies. No society has women hunters alone. However, women are the primary foragers in two-thirds of the 179 examined societies. Exceptions to rigid divisions of labor are related to camp characteristics (e.g., size of the group, sex ratio), the availability and size of game, and the richness of the ecology. For example, among the Tiwi of Australia who live on Bathurst and Melville Islands, women regularly hunt small animals while men alone hunt big game (Goodale, 1971).

Among the Matsés (Mayoruna) of the Peruvian Amazon rain forest, women collaborate with their husbands in the hunt by driving game, calling dogs, and hitting prey with sticks or machetes (Goodman et al., 1985). Among the two Agta populations, the Palanan and the Maconacon, from the Northern Sierra Madre Natural Park in northeast Luzon in the Philippines, women, even nursing mothers, hunt. The rain forest environment of the Agta provides plentiful game and plant foods. However, the Agta are different from other hunter-gatherer societies in several ways. Agta men tend to hunt alone, while women almost always hunt in groups and with dogs. Agta women are hunters in their own right and not simply assistants in male-organized hunts. In one observational study, Agta women accounted for 30% of the big game captured by the camp (Goodman et al., 1985). Another study found that Agta women killed about half of hunted game (Konner, 2005). Even so, Agta women spend fewer hours hunting than men and hunt closer to camp (Goodman et al., 1985).

Successful hunts and foraging expeditions are highly variable. Big game does not keep people fed for long, and success today may be failure tomorrow. Many variables make hunting success unpredictable, such as season, climate, weather, plentifulness of game, and hunter illness or injury. Therefore, hunting and foraging are closely intertwined. Anthropologist Nicole Waguespack (2005) compared women's foraging activities across different groups of contemporary hunter-gatherers. The groups spanned diverse ecologies with a wide variety of available plant foods. In a study of 71 hunter-gatherer societies, groups that depended less on hunted game for food (< 50% of their diet) used a wider range of plant foods, including nuts and seeds which require more time and effort to process (Keeley, 1995). However, when groups depended more on hunted game (> 50% of their diet), they used a narrow range of plant foods, mostly fruits and roots. Waguespack (2005) then examined spent time in daily foraging, percent of meat in the diet, and time spent in non-subsistence activities by gender among eight hunter-gatherer societies. Except for the Agta (where women hunt), there was a trend among societies that as meat contributed less to the diet, women worked increasingly longer hours in subsistence activities. Among more meat-dependent societies, women spent more time in other valuable non-subsistence activities, such house building, leather working, and carrying materials usually associated with moving camp. While both men and women participated in many of these activities, they became female-dominated as the camp depended more on meat for their diet and men spent more time hunting. Waguespack (2005) concluded that women shifted activities and foraged more when hunters were less successful. Women foraged less and took on additional tasks when hunting was good.

Survival in small groups requires considerable cooperation and coordination. Close cooperation is important whether or not group members are relatives. If everyone in the group is related, then helping each other directly benefits the genetic line. Thus, one might think that small groups or camps are made up of relatives. However, most contemporary hunter-gatherer societies are composed of several unrelated dyads or families (Dyble et al., 2015). The presence of unrelated camp members requires that individuals work closely and reciprocally with each other to survive. Unsurprisingly, among small-group hunter-gatherer societies, men tend to form alliances with unrelated men, and women engage unrelated women in childcare. Researchers collected data on camp composition from 191 Agta adults across 11 camps and from 103 Mbendjele adults across 9 camps to examine associations among related and unrelated individuals (Dyble et al., 2015). As noted earlier, the Agta live in the Philippines. The Mbendjele (BaYaka) are small-stature hunter-gatherers who live in the northern region of the Republic of Congo. Investigators compared the two hunter-gatherer societies to 49 farmers in Parana, Brazil and their residential group. Despite comparable size between groups, the Brazilian farmers had significantly fewer unrelated individuals living with them than did the two hunters-gatherer societies. That is, farmers had mostly kin living together, while hunter-gatherers lived mainly with unrelated individuals. Clearly, different ecologies and ways of life favor or necessitate different cooperative associations.

In this section, I have provided a broad description of contemporary hunter-gatherer societies and alluded to the early division of labor, gendered tasks, and sex-segregated activities. As a consequence, early humans likely spent most of their time in same-sex environments. I have hypothesized that devoted same-sex friendships are an adaptation to living in such environments. The next section explores in more detail evidence for sex-segregated social environments among early human societies. I will then present evidence for devoted friendships in contemporary hunter-gatherer societies.

Sex-Segregated Social Environments among Hunters-Gatherers

Division of labor and gendered tasks may have fueled sex-segregation among early hunter-gatherers. In the brief description above of contemporary hunter-gatherer societies, we have seen that meat is highly valued among many groups, and hunting is primarily a male activity. Successful hunting, especially big game hunting, requires skill and many years of experience (Gurven & Hill, 2009). Beginning in adolescence, young boys in hunter-gather societies spend a considerable amount of time learning to hunt with other boys and men (Ember, 1978; Konner, 2005). Their learning often continues through late adulthood. Extended hunting trips are frequent and may stretch quite a distance from camp. Thus, from an early age, males in hunter-gatherer societies spend much of their time with other boys and men. Consequently, women also spend much of their time with girls and women in the camp. Among most contemporary hunter-gatherer societies, women are the primary foragers (Ember, 1978). Women and older children can forage for roots and vegetables and fruits, while remaining near camp and near smaller children who need attention. Women's daily experience with plants contributed to their greater knowledge about edible and toxic plants as well as the medicinal or spiritual benefits of certain plants. Women's breadth of knowledge about plant properties positioned them to function as healers and shamans. While contemporary hunter-gatherer men often collect non-meat foods, they usually focus on fruits, nuts, and palm starch that are more difficult-to-reach and riskier to obtain, like collecting honey from stinging bees (Konner, 2005). The specialized knowledge and skills required for efficient hunting and effective foraging largely group men together and women together for much of their time.

Childcare is a gendered task that hunter-gatherer women engage in apart from men. In no known contemporary hunter-gatherer society are men the primary caregivers of children (Konner, 2005). Childcare provided by men is highly variable across hunter-gatherer societies. Among the !Kung San of northwestern Botswana, mothers account for about 75–80% of physical contact with an infant in their first 20 months of life. !Kung fathers hold the infant for only short periods of time and generally provide no childcare (Konner, 2005). Additional childcare is provided by adult women in the group, either kin or non-kin (Lee, 1984). Similarly, among the Aché, mothers and other women provide nearly all childcare, although fathers interact with their young children. Aka fathers provide more infant caregiving than fathers of almost any other hunter-gatherer society (Konner, 2005). Even so, Aka mothers provide most childcare and engage various female camp members in childcare. On average, infant Aka have seven different female caregivers during the day. In addition to childcare, other mostly female tasks among contemporary hunter-gatherer societies include food preparation and cooking, fetching water, weaving baskets and mats, leather working, and making and repairing clothing, because these activities can be performed close to camp and without disrupting childcare demands. Some tasks like weaving, leather working, and manufacturing textiles require specialized skill and experience. While men sometimes engage in these specialized tasks, mostly they do not (Konner, 2005).

Thus, at a young age, boys and girls' lives in hunter-gatherer societies diverge. From about puberty to end-of-life, most days males are engaged in activities with other males, including their father, brothers, uncles, and unrelated boys and men in the group. Similarly, most days, females are engaged in activities with other females, including their mother, sisters, aunts, and unrelated girls and women in the group. Success in these same-sex environments means acquiring the skills and resources needed to survive by forming cooperative same-sex alliances and friendships. Among the !Kung, for example, young children usually play in mixed gender, mixed age groups because their camps are small in size (Konner, 2005). However, at puberty, !Kung boys undergo an initiation rite and subsequently begin spending large amounts of time with other boys and men, primarily learning to hunt. !Kung girls are often married before they reach menarche (around 16.5 years of age), usually to a man who is about 10 years older (Lee, 1984). After marriage, !Kung girls spend much of their time in the camp with other women. Young Aka children also play in mixed-gender, mixed age groups, although they sometimes form same-sex groups (Konner, 2005). By age 11–12, Aka children spend most of their time with same-sex peers. At puberty, boys are circumcised. Post-puberty, Aka boys spend their time hunting small game with other boys and eventually hunting bigger game with men in the camp. Aka boys also spend more time outside of camp, often traveling to visit relatives in neighboring camps. By puberty, Aka girls are collecting water, fruits, roots, and nuts with other girls and women. Like other hunter-gatherers, Aché children also spend their early years playing in mixed-gender, mixed age groups (Konner, 2005). By age 8, Aché children are learning about edible plants, dangers to avoid in the forest, and how to track adults as they travel through the forest. By age 10, Aché boys and girls are increasingly independent and engaged in sex-segregated activities: boys carry a bow and arrows and travel long distances to visit relatives, while girls stay close to camp and watch younger children, fetch water, and run errands for adults. By puberty, girls are usually married. Adolescent Aché boys spend their time hunting, visiting neighboring camps, and making friends with other boys and men. Aché boys touch, tickle, and joke with male friends, even adults. These friendships can turn into lasting alliances across camps. By adulthood, Aché men have formed close alliances with other men within the camp and across camps.

Close male alliances among hunter-gatherers likely facilitated hunting success and reduced friction within and between camps (Tiger, 1969/1984). Cross camp alliances promoted trade and expanded access to suitable mates for men and their children. Thus, boys directly benefited their survival by forming close alliances with age mates, and men to learn to hunt and defend against internal camp hostilities. Boys also benefited from alliances that reduced hostilities across camps and promoted trade. Equally important, boys indirectly benefited their reproductive success by expanding access to quality mates through personal connections with other camps. While intra-camp and inter-camp male alliances were critically important, the anthropology literature on male alliances in hunter-gatherer societies usually presents these relationships as unemotional and transactional activities based on reciprocity. While observers and theorists cannot know for certain what men in alliances feel toward each other, it is unimaginable that enduring interpersonal relationships between humans lack emotional significance. Human relationships are inherently emotional. Voluntary enduring affiliations are not simply reciprocal interactions; they are emotional relationships infused with feelings of trust, mutual respect, empathy, gratitude, satisfaction, affection, and even pleasure. While not all alliances or friendships are the same, strong alliances and friendships are beneficial, mutual, affectionate, and meaningful.

Although we have little information about women's alliances in contemporary hunter-gatherer societies, girls and women spend much of their time together engaged in shared activities. Girls likely receive support and protection from their mothers, grandmothers, and sisters. Mothers and grandmothers surely share their broad knowledge about plant properties and other domestic tasks with their children and grandchildren. Unrelated women in the camp care for each other's children and likely share their knowledge and resources at times. If the camp exchanges girls in marriage (exogamy) to promote cross-camp alliances, young girls around puberty face unfamiliar and potentially unwelcoming groups of women in their new husband's camp (Kauth, 2000). Thus, if early humans were like contemporary hunter-gatherers, girls directly benefited their own survival by forming close alliances with female relatives and with unrelated women in the camp. For new young brides migrating to an unfamiliar camp, forming close alliances would have been critical for survival and reproductive success. A young migrating bride may have formed close alliances with older, higher status resident women in the new camp, particularly her mother-in-law and friends of her mother-in-law. Without those alliances, the young bride and her future children would be vulnerable. Further, close female alliances within hunter-gatherer societies would have been emotional experiences. Close enduring alliances require trust, respect, empathy, affection, and pleasure.

With this brief background on the division of labor and sex-segregation among contemporary hunter-gatherer societies, we are now ready to review evidence for devoted male friendships.

Devoted Male Friendships Across Contemporary Hunter-Gatherer Societies and Recent Agricultural and Pastoral Societies

Strong evidence suggests that contemporary male hunter-gatherers value alliances and close friendships. Hunter-gatherers typically live in small camps comprised of several families (Apicella, Marlowe, Fowler, & Christakis, 2012). Thus, most camp members are unrelated to each other, requiring close cooperation and coordination with non-relatives to survive and raise their children. Although camp membership changes regularly as dyads or families leave and others join, cooperation, agreeableness, and reciprocity are likely unspoken requirements for staying in the camp. Close cooperation and alliances are the norm. Further, once formed, alliances or close friendships often continue when members leave, extending one's social network. In a study of preferential personal relationships, investigators asked 205 individuals from Hadza camps in Tanzania with whom in the next camp they would like to live and to whom they would like to give an actual gift of honey (Apicella et al., 2012). Honey is a prized food. Unsurprisingly, Hadza men and women wanted to live with people who had privately identified them as "friends", suggesting that participants also thought of these individuals as friends. Also, unsurprisingly, men and women more often chose to gift individuals who had exchanged resources with them in the past. Researchers noted that high cooperators within the camp tended to connect with other high cooperators. In other words, cooperation and friendliness breeds further alliance and friendship. Other field researchers have observed that cooperation, like food-sharing, while quite common, is not equitable across contemporary hunter-gatherer societies (Gurven, 2012; Gurven & Hill, 2009). That is, individuals favor relatives, neighbors, and cooperative partners when food, especially highly-prized meat, is shared. Close alliances have direct benefits.

A recent study examining cooperative behavior among the Agta in the Philippines reported that individuals preferentially gifted (with rice) needy, less cooperative individuals rather than friends who could or have benefited them (Smith, Dyble, Major et al., 2019). The implication is that the Agta are a generous people who give to the needy rather than to those who may benefit them later. However, the needy, less cooperative individuals tended to be older and often related to the giver. When age was controlled, the effect of need-based sharing was not significant. While the investigators interpreted need-based sharing with older relatives as charitable and counter to benefiting cooperative friends, that conclusion misses the point. This was not a study about friendship or cooperation. Clearly, the Agta have complex relationships and do not view all relationships as transactional. Agta givers appear to help older relatives who can no longer help themselves (or the giver) but who may well have benefited the giver in the past. The researchers' concepts of cooperation, friendship, and reciprocity seem oddly narrow.

In a clever study to identify who contemporary hunter-gatherers interact with, anthropologists had 200 individuals from six Agta and BaYaka camps wear a portable wireless device to track their movements over the course of a week (Migliano, Page, Gómez-Gardeñes, et al., 2017). The Agta live in the Philippines. The BaYaka are small-stature hunter-gatherers who live in the Republic of the Congo and Central African Republic forests. Researchers found that overall Agta and BaYaka men and women maintained very strong connections to between one and four close friends in unrelated families. In fact, men and women interacted with their close friends as frequently as they interacted with close relatives, reflecting the value of these friendships. The investigators hypothesized that friendships with non-relatives greatly expanded individuals' social networks and shared knowledge (Migliano, Page, Gómez-Gardeñes, et al., 2017). In fact, shared knowledge about plant properties was greater between friends than between kin dyads, such as spouses, siblings, or parent-child. Close friends readily exchanged information, which has enormous benefits. Although not measured in this study, Agta and BaYaka men and women likely spent so much time with friends because they experienced their friendships as important and meaningful.

In *A Talent for Friendship*, anthropologist John Terrell (2015) illustrates the extreme lengths, literally, that New Guinea hunter-gatherers go to in order to make and keep friendships. Terrell notes that scholars once thought that hunter-gatherer bands in New Guinea were isolated from each other, given the rugged, treacherous terrain on the island. Their geographic isolation was thought to explain the approximately 1,000 different languages that developed across these groups. Yet through his field work, Terrell documented that many individuals in New Guinea societies have long had distant personal connections with other groups that have been maintained for years and even passed down to their children. One man on Tumleo Island off the Aitape coast of New Guinea reported maintaining friendships with individuals in 15 different communities spanning an area of 250 kilometers (155 miles). A man on Tarawai Island also off the coast of Aitape reported friendships in 33 communities covering a distance of 270 kilometers (168 miles). Another man from Kep near the mouth of the Sepik river had friendships in 28 communities over a distance of 140 kilometers (86 miles). A large effort and significant amount of time are necessary to maintain even a few friendships when one lives on an island or in a difficult-to-access area. To invest such effort, these distant friendships must be very important and meaningful. The benefits of close friendships with people in other New Guinea communities include hospitality, safe passage through the region, provision of food or building materials (especially for those on islands) when needed, and allies for defense when one's family or community are attacked. Terrell asserts that an emotional connection between individuals or families ensures a warm reception in the community and future support. He describes these distant friendships, even inherited ones, as warm, friendly, and personally meaningful. While visits routinely involve gift exchange and trade, Terrell refutes the notion that these are transactional relationships. In recounting expeditions with informants to visit friends in other communities, Terrell describes these visits as mostly social events, even formal festivals, that involve sharing food, hunting and fishing together, sharing news since last contact, joking, dancing, presentations of gifts, and sometimes engaging in sexual activities with friends' wives. For children accompanying their parent(s), this is an opportunity to get to know their parents' friends, as well as form their own friendships with age-mates in the community.

The Bangwa of Cameroon, a diverse group of isolated farmers, traders, and hunters, so highly value close friendships that Bangwa parents strongly encourage their male children to find a best friend, as well as a spouse (Brain,

1976). In some ways, the Bangwa view male friendships as more valuable than marriage because close friendships often last longer than marriages. What is more, when a Bangwa man dies, his devoted male friend, not the family, pays for the funeral. The friend's loss is treated more seriously by the community than the family's loss, suggesting that in this culture close male friends share a particularly deep emotional bond. There are numerous examples of devoted male friendships across hunter-gatherer societies. Among the Azande of the upper Nile in Central Africa, men formalize their devoted friendships with an elaborate "blood-brother" ceremony before the entire community (Spain, 1992). The concept of male friends becoming "blood brothers" or "sworn brothers" appears across a variety of cultures throughout history. (See Chapter Four for historical examples). Similarly, Akan men of Nzema in southwestern Ghana "marry" their best friend in a public ceremony (Spain, 1992). The marriage between Akan devoted male friends includes payment of a bride price to the parents of the younger friend (Brain, 1976). In the Azande and Akan communities, blood brothers are called *bakurëmi* or "my cut-blood", referring to the bonding ritual of mixing their blood (Miller & Donovan, 2009/2013). Azande and Akan blood brothers vow to assist each other against enemies, share hunted game, and not sleep with each other's wife. If a blood brother is accused of witchcraft, upon their death, the brother / friend is responsible for cutting open the corpse to demonstrate that the entrails are normal and the deceased was human.

Many other African cultures have blood brotherhood traditions, and it is worth citing some of these to illustrate the staggering prevalence of devoted male friendships. Several cultures with blood brother traditions are contemporary hunter-gatherers, while others are now pastoralists or agriculturalists. Some members of pastoral or agricultural societies now spend large amounts of time living among urbanized people in industrialized towns or cities as paid labor. Nevertheless, these various groups originated as hunter-gatherer societies and remained so until relatively recently. The continued existence of blood brotherhood traditions speaks to its deep significance in these cultures. Many, but not all, blood brotherhood traditions presented here are documented in *Blood Brotherhood and Other Rites of Male Alliance* (2009/2013) by independent scholars Nathan Miller and Jack Donovan.

The small-stature Twa people who live as foragers around Lake Kivu in central Africa in Congo and Rwanda and the Gua-Tumbwe subgroup of Sanga people of the southeastern Congo have blood brotherhood traditions (Miller & Donovan, 2009/2013). The Babwa, Bangala, Havu, and Ngata people of the Democratic Republic of Congo, as well as the Lunda people along the Kalanyi River of the Democratic Republic of Congo, Angola, and Zambia, all have blood brotherhood traditions. The agricultural Mbunda of Angola, who have lost most of their traditional ways, still maintain blood brotherhoods. The matrilineal clans of the Lungu people on the west coast of Lake Tanganyika in the Democratic Republic of Congo and southwestern Tanzania, and northeastern Zambia also recognize the special friendship bond between blood brothers.

In Tanzania, blood brother traditions can be found among the mostly agricultural Zaramo (or Dzalamo, Saramo) who represent 200–300 matrilineal clans (Miller & Donovan, 2009/2013). Blood brotherhoods are also found among the Shambala (or Kishambala) and Gogo people. Among the Kaguru (or Kagulu) of central Tanzania, two male friends close in age participate in a formal ceremony where they exchange vows and mix their blood. The devoted friends call each other *wandugu* or "kin", and are viewed by the community as closer than relatives. The Chaga (or Chagga, Wachaga, Jagga, Dschagga) of Mount Kilimanjaro, Mount Meru, and the Moshi area of Tanzania are terrace farmers composed of 400 patrilineal clans who immigrated to the area around the eleventh century. Chaga blood brothers, or *mma*, are formally bonded by a chieftain, although unofficial *mma* are common in the community. Among the agricultural Pare people of the Pare Mountains of northern Tanzania and part of the Kilimanjaro region, blood brothers directly suck blood from each other via cuts enacted during a formal ceremony. The Pare people are mainly patrilineal clans and are closely connected to the Chaga. The Haya people of northwestern Tanzania maintain blood brotherhoods as part of their ancient tradition. Among the Sagara (or Sagala) and Sumbwa people of central Tanzania, blood brothers are quite common. The Kerewe (or Wakerewe) people on the Ukerewe Island of Lake Victoria in the Tanzania section also practice blood brotherhoods, as do the Nyamwezi (or Wanyamwezi) of west central Tanzania. The Kerewe are a polygamous, patrilineal people who farm and own cattle.

In Kenya, blood brotherhood traditions have been documented among the Maasai people of northern, central and southern Kenya and northern Tanzania (Miller & Donovan, 2009/2013). The Maasai are mainly pastoralists and raise cattle but were once known as fierce fighters. They are a polygamous group whose ancestors migrated to the region in the fifteenth century. The Kikuyu (or Agīkuyu, Gikuyu), the largest ethnic group in Kenya, also practice blood brotherhoods. The Kikuyu are a matrilineal people who arrived in the Mount Kenya area around the third century. Among the Kamba (or Akamba) people who live in the lowlands of southeast Kenya from Mount Kenya to the coast, blood brotherhood traditions are common. The Kamba are agriculturalists, traders, and sometimes paid laborers in the city. Blood brotherhoods are also found among the Duruma, subsistence farmers, and the Giriama (or Giryama) ethnic group of the Mijikenda people. The Giriama now largely work as service workers in cities along the coast, like Mombasa.

In south central Uganda, the Ganda (or Baganda, Waganda) people refer to blood brotherhood as *mukago* (Miller & Donovan, 2009/2013). In the distant past, traditional Ganda men could have two or as many as six blood brothers who had the status of kin. A Ganda boy's father chooses his first *mukago* brother. After that, men can choose additional blood brothers. Today, the Ganda are mainly farmers and pastoralists. The Lango people of central and northern Uganda also have a longstanding blood brother tradition, as do the Nkole (also Nkore, Ankori, Ankole, Banyankole, Banyankore) and the Nyoro (also Nyoros, Banyoro, Bunyoro) people.

In Nigeria, ancient blood brotherhood traditions can be found among the Bassa in Kogi state, the Ibibio in the south, and the Ekoi (or Ejagham) people of southeast Nigeria and southwest Cameroon (Miller & Donovan, 2009/2013). The Ibibio are thought to have arrived in the area around the fourteenth or fifteenth century. They are now predominantly Christian. The Ewe people of Ghana and Togo, along coastal West Africa, also have blood brotherhoods, as do the Tallensi (or Talensi) of northern Ghana. The Ewe, who have a patrilineal society, are now mainly traders, while the Tallensi are small scale agriculturalists. The mostly Islamic Bambara (or Bamana, Banmana) of Mali, Guinea, and Senegal trace their origins back to about 2500 BCE and have long maintained blood brotherhoods. The Bambara were once mighty warriors who ruled several empires over the past 4,000 years. The Bozo along the Niger river in Mali and the Dogon people of central Mali maintain blood brotherhood traditions. The Dogon are now primarily agriculturalists, although they also hunt game and gather fruits.

On Madagascar, off the eastern coast of Africa, the Tanala and Malagasy people have long held blood brotherhood traditions. The Tanala were once great warriors but are now agriculturalists. The Malagasy people represent a variety of Austronesian and South African ethnic groups who have lived on the island for centuries.

Moving on to Indonesia, among the Asmat of Western New Guinea, boys frequently form enduring devoted friendships with age-mates (Neill, 2009). An Asmat boy's devoted friend is called *mbai,* or bond-friend. The relationship is voluntary, mutual, trusting, loyal, intimate, sexual, and lifelong. The devoted friendship is formally recognized by the community and continues after marriage. Anthropologist Tobias Schneebaum, who lived among the Asmat for an extended time, described *mbai* relationships in *Where the Spirits Dwell* (1988). According to Schneebaum, families promote *mbai* relationships between boys at an early age to strengthen ties between clans or as part of a marriage arrangement. Nevertheless, in many villages, boys freely choose their *mbai*. One Asmat man described *mbai* relationships like this: "*Mbai* are always friends and always help one another when there is trouble. They remain *mbai* all their lives, until one of them dies" (Schneebaum, 1988, p. 195). Regarding their intimacy and loyalty to each other, the informant stated, "Sometimes one is jealous because his *mbai* has been with another man. He is not jealous when he goes with a woman who is not his wife, only when he is with another man" (p. 195). When asked about a *mbai*'s sexual behavior with other men, the Asmat informant declared, "It is all right [*sic*] to play with another man. He may suck his penis or even enter his ass; that is all right [*sic*]. But he may not have an orgasm. Then, his *mbai* is very angry" (p. 195). Jealousy suggests that *mbai* friends are emotionally committed to each other and expect sexual fidelity. Sex with women, however, raises no such concerns. *Mbai* friends share their wives with each other, as part of a tradition called *papisj*. The Asmat place a strong emphasis on balance in their *mbai* relationships. Attention to balance, or equity, may be a way to avoid putting their friend in a subordinate role. As an Asmat man explained, "There must be balance. There must always be balance between *mbai*. There is no other way" (p. 195). The Asmat informant then gave an example about sexual equity that also illustrates the ordinariness of sex between *mbai* friends,

> When one *mbai* sucks the penis of his friend, the two may not part until the friend turns around and sucks his penis. If one enters the ass of another, the other must turn around and enter his ass. *Mbai* must always give back what they take. When I bring fish to the house of Kayet, my *mbai*, he will bring me sago the next time he goes into the jungle (...). We must share what we have. Everything must remain in balance. (Schneebaum, 1988, pp. 195–196)

Among the Tiwi hunter-gatherers of the Australian Torres Straits, young boys live in a "bachelor's camp" away from women and the main camp (Greenberg, 1988). Eventually, boys form a devoted friendship with an age-mate—often someone who may become their brother-in-law. The friends become regular sexual partners. Among the Barasana of Columbia, relatively isolated agriculturalists, young boys form devoted friendships with their brother-in-law, who is often older (Greenberg, 1988). Brother-in-law friendships among the Barasana are characterized as affectionate, intimate, trusting, and sometimes sexual. The close friendship between the two continues after the boy marries.

Among the Akwe-Shavante (Xavante) of Brazil, young boys form lifelong devoted friendships while living in the bachelor hut during their initiation period (Spain, 1992). The Akwe-Shavante are an indigenous people of eastern Mato Grosso state in Brazil who are genetically related to the Australasian people of New Guinea, unlike Native American tribes. The Akwe-Shavante were enslaved in the eighteenth century. Later emancipated, they withdrew from outside contact, but were "rediscovered" in the 1930s. Today, the Akwe-Shavante are a polygamous society and largely agriculturalists, supplementing their diet with hunting and fishing. Around age seven and for about five years, young boys live in the bachelor hut, isolated from females, where they are taught vital skills of manhood, such as making weapons, fighting, performing ceremonial songs and dances, and taking leadership roles in the community (Maybury-Lewis, 1967). Each boy is encouraged to develop one or two close age-mate friendships, who become their constant companion(s) and partner(s) for life. The friend is called *i-amo* ("my other" or "my partner") and formally recognized by the community. *I-amo* friends work together, sleep together, and dance together in ceremonies holding hands. *I-amo* friendships are critical for acquiring positions of authority in the Akwe-Shavante community.

Devoted male friendships in the form of blood brotherhoods appear to have been common among aboriginal North American Indians. About 25,000 years ago, Native Americans' ancestors split off from people living in Siberia (Greshko, 2018). Groups of hunter-gatherers made their way across a land bridge to Alaska and the Pacific Northwest, arriving in North America at least 13,000 years ago (Saey, 2018). People among the first wave split, with one group slowly moving east across Canada and the other rapidly moving south along the coastline. Multiple waves of people migrated south, eventually reaching the Andean highlands. Around 9,000 years ago, groups in Mexico or Central America moved north into the US Plains (Greshko, 2018). Evidence suggests that these Paleo-Indians had a largely meat-based diet. Early Native American people hunted a wide range of prey but specialized in hunting large-bodied animals, such as mammoth and bison (Waguespack, 2005).

In *The Spirit and the Flesh: Sexual Diversity in American Indian Culture* (1992a), anthropologist Walter Williams summarizes a wide-range of reports on first contact with Native American societies and offers observations about contemporary Native Americans. According to Williams, most Native American societies have long maintained a gendered division of labor, with men and women spending most of their time with same-sex others in the community. Elsewhere, Williams (1992b) provides examples of devoted male friendship traditions among early Native Americans. For instance, among Cherokees in southeastern North America and the Yupik Eskimos of Alaska, males age ten or older moved into the men's house where they stayed and slept, while women and small children stayed in their own homes. Nearly everyone among the Cherokee and Yupik married. In these societies, marriage was viewed largely as an economic arrangement between a man and a woman to produce offspring, gather and supply food, manage the household, and provide protection. Williams (1992b) argued that in most first contact and contemporary Native American cultures, marriage was not a central part of an individual's life, and remains so. Among most early North American Indians, male friendships or blood brotherhoods were likely the primary social and emotional relationship in a man's life. These friendships were intimate and recognized as special. According to Williams (1992b), if devoted male friends or blood brothers engaged in sexual activity, early Native American cultures would have viewed this as a private matter and no one else's business. There would have been no public discussion about sex between blood brothers and no stigma.

When making first contact, early Westerner explorers, soldiers, trappers, and missionaries often commented on the unusual closeness of male friends, or blood brothers, among North American Indian cultures. A nineteenth-century United States Army officer describes the "brothers by adoption" that he observed during his tours of duty on the western frontier (cited in Williams, 1992b). The officer notes that Arapaho men "really seem to 'fall in love' with men; and I have known this affectionate interest to live for years" (p. 191). In many North American Indian cultures, the bonding of two men is publicly celebrated by a Friendship Dance that the two partners dance together. American historian Francis Parkman traveled to the far west in 1846 and lived with Native American Indian societies for several weeks (cited in Williams, 1992b). He later wrote about his experiences in a popular book titled, *The Oregon Trail*, presenting a sympathetic portrayal of Native American Indians. Parkman describes two "blood brothers" among the Lakotas who were "inseparable; they ate, slept, and hunted together, and shared with one another almost all that they possessed" (Williams, 1992b, p. 191). Parkman goes on to state, "If there be anything that deserves to be called romantic in the Indian character, it is to be sought for in friendships such as this, which are common among many of the prairie tribes" (Williams, 1992b, p. 191).

In early eighteenth-century Canada, French Jesuit missionary, Joseph Francois Lafitau, commented on the intense socially recognized "special friendships" that were common among young men in many tribes "from one end of America to the other" (Katz, 1992). Lafitau viewed these devoted male friendships as very close, strong, and "highly ancient in origin". He stated that "the union cannot be dissolved, unless one of the two makes himself unworthy of the union by acts of cowardice that would dishonor his friend and is compelled to renounce his alliance" (Katz, 1992, p. 289). Lafitau observed that male "special friendships" are revered among Native American societies, and parents in these communities actively encouraged their sons to develop devoted friendships with other boys.

In short, overwhelming evidence, across a wide range of cultures, demonstrate that men in hunter-gatherer societies and in relatively recent agricultural and pastoral societies have formed devoted friendships with other men, often referring to the relationship with a special term, such as *bakurëmi*, *mma*, *mbai*, *i-amo*, blood brothers, bond brothers, or adoptive brothers. Devoted male friendships were frequently formalized in a public ceremony. In many cultures, devoted male friends were age-mates, and friendships were egalitarian and lifelong. Sometimes the friendships involved sexual intimacy. Devoted male friendships functioned in parallel to marriage. Although we have little evidence, age-disparate devoted friendships may have existed in these cultures but went unnoticed by observers. Brother-in-law friendships, for example, were likely age discrepant. In the next chapter, I describe devoted male friendships from early literate cultures up until fairly recent times. Many of these friendships were age-disparate and dominance-role based but also loving, loyal, lifelong, and sometimes sexual.

I have not included male initiation rites in this discussion of devoted male friendships. Although some male initiation rituals have elements of friendship, most initiation rites that I am familiar with do not involve an intimate lifelong bond between two individuals. Male-male sexual behavior during initiation is also not necessarily reflective of emotional intimacy or friendship. For example, anthropologist Gil Herdt thoroughly documented Sambian male initiation traditions in *Guardians of the Flutes: Idioms of Masculinity* (1981), *The Sambia: Ritual and Gender in New Guinea* (1987), and an edited volume titled, *Ritualized Homosexuality in Melanesia* (1984/1993). Among the Sambia (a pseudonym created by Herdt to protect the identities of these New Guinea societies), young boys, around ages seven to ten, move into the bachelor lodge, avoiding contact with females. Boys spend the next 10–15 years engaged in rituals to become men. Later when masculinized, these individuals led rituals to grow other boys into men. Nearly every night, young boys fellate older males to orgasm to receive their male-growing semen (Herdt, 1981, 1987). After puberty, male adolescents switch roles and are themselves fellated by young boys. Sambia men continue to be fellated until the birth of their second child (long after marriage), when males reach full manhood. Among the Marind-Anim people of New Guinea, boys are also separated from females at a young age and receive semen from an older adult, frequently a maternal uncle, through anal intercourse (Herdt, 1984/1993). However, Marind-Anim initiations have a mentoring component, and the close relationship continues after marriage, blurring the distinction between initiation and devoted friendship. Certainly, male-male relationships that initially appear largely sexual can evolve over time into something different. From outside the culture, it is difficult to discern any individual's motivations and feelings or know for certain how people perceive their relationship changing over time.

I also have not included here discussion regarding relationships with androgynous or third-gender individuals. I have found no mention of devoted male friendships in the literature that include androgynous or third-gender individuals. It is possible that such friendships were undetected by observers. From what we know of early Native American cultures, for example, many *two-spirit* individuals were born with male genitalia and later adopted the androgynous two-spirit role. There is some evidence of two-spirit individuals who were born with female genitalia. Many early Native American societies—the Cherokee, Chippewas, Comanche, Dakota, Eskimo, Florida, Iroquois, Navaho, Sioux, Zuni—recognized two-spirit people as neither man nor woman, but something else (Greenberg, 1988; Williams, 1992a). These individuals represented a third gender with mixed-sex characteristics. Early observers referred to two-spirit individuals pejoratively as *berdache*, a French word that loosely translates as "sodomite" (Greenberg, 1988). In several

Native American societies, two-spirit people acquired privileged tribal roles as shaman. In those cultures, adult men engaged in sexual activity with two-spirit people (as the receptive partner) to gain good luck through sexual magic, but these encounters were not generally personal, loyal, lifelong friendships (Neill, 2009; Williams, 1992a). Many other cultures have recognized a third-gender, including the Dongo, Kwayama, and Ovimbundu of Angola; Nandi and Meru of Kenya; Dinka and Nuer of Sudan; Konso and Amhara of Ethiopia; Sarawak in northwestern Borneo; Ngadju Dyak of southern Borneo; Fanti of Ghana; Lango, Iteso, Gisu, and Sebei of Uganda; Wolof of Senegal; Tanala and Bara of Madagascar; Bugis of South Sulawesi (Celebes); the Pelew Islands; and Tahiti in French Polynesia, to name a few (Bleys, 1995; Greenberg, 1988). However, this text is not focused on the history of same-sex sexuality specifically. For comprehensive histories of same-sex sexuality in its many forms, see Louis Crompton, *Homosexuality & Civilization* (2003); David Greenberg, *The Construction of Homosexuality* (1988), and James Neill, *The Origins and Role of Same-Sex Relations in Human Societies* (2009).

In closing this survey of devoted male friendships among contemporary hunter-gatherer, agricultural, pastoral, and early Native American societies, it is unfortunate that documented evidence has almost exclusively focused on male friendships. On rare occasions, observers have mentioned female-female friendships off-handedly, often adding that female friendships are like male blood brotherhoods, with no additional details. At other times, observers and informants appear to have given little or no thought to women's relationships. For many (male) observers and informants, what women did together was of little concern. For others, their phallic-centric view of sexuality could not imagine women engaging in sexual affection with a woman, because neither have a penis. Schneebaum's Asmat informant illustrates this point perfectly. Schneebaum asked,

> "What about women having sex together?" I asked one day.
> "What do you mean?"
> "You know. I mean women playing with one another sexually".
> Akatpitsjin burst into laughter. He explained to the others and everyone laughed. The man and boys grabbed at one another's crotches. They hugged one another and pressed their bodies together. They rolled on the floor; they jumped up and down. They held their bellies, sat up, lay down, rolled back and forth.
> "But why would they want to play with each other?"
> "For the same reason they play with men, to have pleasure".
> "But that's impossible with another woman!"
> Everyone laughed again, trying to visualize two women having sexual intercourse. They denied any such possibility. I never got a proper answer to this since I was never able to question the women themselves on the subject. (1988, pp. 198–199)

Of course, the absence of evidence for devoted female friendship is not evidence of its absence. Asmat women (and women in other cultures) could well have had long traditions of devoted friendships similar to men's, and it seems likely that Asmat men and others would not know or even recognize female friendships as such. The long history of sex-segregation across cultures has ensured that boys and men, as well as outside observers, do not know what women do together. Further, for much of human history, women have not been in positions of power that would have spotlighted their activities and relationships, and pre-literate women had no ability to document their way of lives.

In this section, I have presented clear evidence that men in many contemporary hunter-gatherer societies and in relatively recent agricultural and pastoral societies have long traditions of devoted male friendships. Their communities have supported these friendships. If contemporary hunter-gatherer societies are at all like ancient hunter-gatherer societies, then devoted male friendships are quite old traditions. Are devoted male friendships simply a trivial coincidence? Why would such emotionally intense and sometimes sexual relationships between men persist across different human cultures for tens of thousands, if not hundreds of thousands, of years? What function might these friendships have? In the next section, I explore in more detail a possible adaptive function of devoted male friendships. Unfortunately, little direct evidence demonstrates the adaptive function of devoted male friendships because this research has not been done. In anticipation of this research, I offer several hypotheses regarding adaptive devoted male friendships that can be tested.

Devoted Male Friendship as an Adaptation

Research on the history of friendship across cultures is slim. Research on friendship among hunter-gatherers is also very limited. Even when writers mention friendship, they often fail to differentiate between alliances and intimate friends. When friendships are mentioned at all, writers typically emphasize the transactional, reciprocal nature of friendship, rather than its adaptive function or personal meaning to individuals. Associations or alliances are not necessarily friendships, and friendships vary in depth of intimacy. The focus in this text is on voluntary, loving, mutual, committed friendships between unrelated individuals.

Several writers have presented male alliances as adaptive cooperative associations to aide hunting and warfare. In particular, Lionel Tiger (1969/1984) described "male bonding", a term he coined, as an evolved trait that benefited men when hunting big game and fighting hostile groups. Bonds with other males ensured cooperative partners and allies when facing conflicts. As an adaptive trait, male bonding should be heritable and should enhance survival and reproductive success. In their review of contemporary hunter-gatherer societies, anthropologists Michael Gurven and Kim Hill (2009) found support for this idea. They noted that among hunter-gatherer societies, successful hunters usually form cooperative male alliances and share more resources with allies. They also observed that successful hunters generally have better mate choices than men who are poor hunters or who do not hunt. What is more, women highly value successful hunters as mates, in part because hunting skill increases the likelihood of meat in the diet. Further, among hunter-gatherer societies, women's total average fertility is positively correlated with the amount of meat that men contribute to their diet. In short, the most skilled hunters have male allies and better reproductive options than less skilled hunters or non-hunters, with or without allies. Gurven and Hill (2009) found hunting skill and male alliances associated with greater reproductive success in every hunter-gatherer society examined.

Tiger (1969/1984) argued that the adaptive benefit of male bonding resulted in men's desire to spend time with other males, although he did not distinguish between kinds of associations. Preferences for male association are evidenced by male-dominated activities, such as hunting, military and paramilitary occupations, team-based competitive sports, fraternities and secret societies, youth gangs, business and work life, and social drinking. In other words, Tiger sees men's preferences for male company as resulting in sex-segregated social environments. In contrast, I have argued that early division of labor and gendering and specialization of tasks produced sex-segregated environments and same-sex friendships are an adaptation to managing life in such environments.

Tiger further argued that male associations are largely hierarchical dominance-based relationships. He described dominance-based relationships as emotional, satisfying, and erotic, contrary to our contemporary cultural beliefs about unequal relationships. Dominance characteristics include various factors, such as physical size, strength, social status, age, skill, knowledge, and wealth. To illustrate, Tiger described early Cree Indian boys of the American Plains who formed close bonds with young adult men who were good hunters and brave warriors and, thus, had high social status in the community. The older mentor-friend teaches the young boy how to be an accomplished hunter and fighter. The bonded pair are constant companions and refer to each other as *niwitch ewahaken*, which means "he with whom I go about" (p. 108). As devoted friends, the Cree novice and mentor share their resources with each other, including their wives, which suggests that this friendship continues past marriage. Consistent with other cultures, Tiger noted that Cree boys choose their mentor-friend, while their parents choose their sons' spouse.

If male friendships are adaptive, it is reasonable to suppose that men highly value traits in their same-sex friends that would have assisted in solving ancient adaptive problems: for example, traits related to hunting and fighting. However, people in Western cultures no longer live in environments

Table 3.2 Evidence Supporting Devoted Male Friendships

- Blood brother, adoptive brother, and sworn brother (and other special terms) ceremonies across many pre-literate and literate cultures; sometimes an exchange of vows or mixing blood; public recognition of the lifelong bond
- In some traditional cultures, parents/community encourage young boys to develop a lifelong devoted friendship with a mentor or peer
- Among contemporary hunter-gatherer cultures—
  - communities are mainly composed of unrelated dyads/families, requiring alliances and close friendships to survive
  - men (and women) prefer to live with and spend time with close same-sex friends
  - men give preferences in food sharing to male allies/friends

where their survival depends on good hunting and warfare skills. So when asked to rate traits among their same-sex friends, heterosexual male college students most valued male friends who liked athletic activities and team sports, activities that exemplify cooperative alliances (Lewis, Al-Shawaf, Raja, DeKay, & Buss, 2011). Interestingly, college men were likely to maintain male friendships based on their friend's social status, social connections, and economic resources, suggesting that male friendships provide important social benefits such as increasing one's social status and access to resources. However, in the same study, heterosexual female college students did not favor female friends with skill in childcare or nurturing or anything close. Researchers did not assess for traits like emotional closeness, empathy, or dependability. I suspect that men and women's preferences for same-sex friendship are directed toward an emotional bond with an equal or higher status person and not a specific skill possessed by someone.

If devoted same-sex friendships are adaptive, we would expect to see evidence of devoted same-sex friendships across cultures and throughout history. Considerable evidence for devoted male friendships across cultures has been presented above and is summarized in Table 3.2 Additional evidence for devoted male friendships throughout history is presented in the next chapter. Further, if devoted same-sex friendships are adaptive, at least six predictions follow and can be tested.

Predications about Same-Sex Friendships

1. Aside from contact with relatives, *men and women should prefer to affiliate with same-sex individuals because same-sex associations and friendships aided survival in sex-segregated environments.* Same-sex alliances and friendships facilitated navigation of sex-segregated environments in order to survive and acquire resources to support a mate and family.

   Although most human cultures have some degree of sex segregation, it is very unlikely that inherent preferences for same-sex affiliation *caused* sex-segregation. Rather, sexual competition, division of labor, and gendered tasks collectively promoted sex-segregation among early humans. With limited contact, fairly quickly early human males and females began to view the other as foreign, emphasizing their differences and ignoring similarities. Once set in motion, social beliefs about gendered tasks, gender role, and sex-segregation contributed to men and women perceiving the other as dissimilar, strange, and unequal.

It may be worth stating explicitly that men and women are different. From an evolutionist perspective, humans are biological organisms living in a physical world that has shaped them through natural selection. Differential reproductive investment and sexual competition have promoted biological and psychological differences between men and women. Our large brains, mentalizing abilities, language skills, and complex social relationships have in turn created social and cultural forces that have shaped how men and women, living in sex-segregated environments, experience each other and the world. Social and cultural forces sometimes falsely attribute meaning to biological differences between men and women or create fictional differences because those narratives fit the current social power dynamic. From an evolutionist schema, biological differences between men and women are not inherently problematic and do not denote innate superiority or inferiority. They are just differences.

2. *Men should more strongly prefer same-sex alliances and close friendships than women.* The word "strong" is relative. However, given that male reproduction is more variable than female reproduction, since not all males reproduce, selection should strongly favor men who make alliances and form devoted friendships. This may explain in part why male alliances and devoted male friendships are so clearly evident across traditional cultures. By contrast, in traditional cultures, most women reproduce, so there is less variability. Thus, selection for friendship among women should be weaker than among men, but not absent. Childcare is resource intensive. Reproducing women still need support from allies in same-sex social environments, because support from relatives may be insufficient.

3. *Men with male alliances and one or more devoted male friends will experience greater reproductive success than men with no or few alliances and no devoted friends.* Cooperative male alliances indirectly benefit reproductive success. Men with alliances are better able to navigate their social environment, defend themselves, and gather resources for survival, find a mate, and raise a family than men without allies. What is more, men with devoted male friendships should be quite effective at navigating their social environment and acquiring resources, including a quality reproductive mate. Men with devoted male friendships should attain particularly high social status and influence in the community.

What is more, women should prefer male reproductive mates who have strong alliances and particularly desire men who have devoted male friendships because such relationships strongly signal a man's social status and means for acquiring resources in the future. Further, the wives and children of men who have devoted male friendships should be much better off than wives and children of men without devoted friends.

However, reproductive success is a long game and not simply the number of children fathered. Reproductive success is an outcome spanning generations. Thus, tracking reproductive success is difficult.

4. Given that male social environments are hierarchical, *age-different male alliances should be prevalent and dominance-structured because of differences in social status.* Aligning with an older male has several advantages: An older male likely has higher status within the social environment and many friends in the group and across other groups who can provide protection, support, and access to resources. Same-age peer alliances are more likely to be egalitarian because of similarity in social status. Peer allies are advantageous and offer protection, support, and companionship.

5. *Women who form alliances with non-relative females and have one or more devoted female friends will experience greater reproductive success than women with no alliances or close friends.* In traditional cultures, most women have children and receive support and assistance with childcare from both female relatives and non-relatives. Women with devoted female friends should be quite effective at navigating the female social environment, protecting themselves, acquiring necessary resources for survival, and caring for their children. Yet women with devoted female friends only *somewhat* enhance their reproductive success because women generally demonstrate a steady reproductive rate. Again, measuring reproductive success over generations is quite difficult.

Unlike male alliances, female alliances are more likely to be egalitarian and equitable and structured around sharing and empathy. While female groups are less hierarchical than male social environments, female social groups are not devoid of a hierarchy. For a young bride entering a new community in a traditional culture, aligning with an older, higher status female, like a mother-in-law or her friends, offers several social advantages.

6. Lastly, *men and women in traditional cultures will view their devoted same-sex friendships with the same importance as they do their marriages.* This should be evident in the social value placed on close friends and the amount of time men and women spend with their close friends compared to their spouses. Sexual expression is not a requirement of devoted friendships, although it may occur. Sexual intimacy between devoted friends may function to express affection or pleasure or to symbolize their special bond.

Summary

Friendship is a universal human phenomenon. Same-sex friendships are prevalent and valued across diverse cultures. I have argued that devoted same-sex friendships have persisted across cultures because they are an adaptive trait. That is, same-sex alliances and devoted friendships evolved within sex-segregated environments to directly benefit survival and indirectly support reproductive success. Most traditional human cultures throughout history have been sex-segregated. If same-sex friendships are an adaptive trait, people should long for and frequently form close intimate same-sex friendships, which is what we find across cultures.

An evolutionary analysis finds supportive evidence for preferential long-term same-sex bonds among chimpanzees and bonobos, suggesting that same-sex alliances/friendships are old, conserved traits. There is also strong evidence for male alliances and devoted male friendships among contemporary hunter-gatherer societies and among native people upon first encounter with Western observers. Across diverse cultures, devoted male friendships have been recognized with special terms such as blood brothers. There are only a few oblique references to devoted female friendships among contemporary hunter-gatherer societies, mainly because this work has not been a focus of research. There is little reason to believe that women in hunter-gatherer societies did not or could not form female alliances and devoted friendships with non-relatives.

Blood brotherhoods, or devoted male friendships, are common among contemporary hunter-gatherer societies and native people. In many cultures, same-age boys formed lifelong blood brotherhoods. These relationships were actively encouraged or orchestrated by their families. In some cultures, lifelong brotherhood bonds formed between young boys around puberty and young men, such as future brothers-in-law. In general, devoted male friendships have been passionate, intimate, long-term relationships. These friendships sometimes included sexual activity to express affection, pleasure, or the specialness of the bond. Male alliances and devoted friendships were often structured around differences in social status or role. Forming a close friendship with a higher status male would have had many advantages for a young male, but peer alliances with age-mates would also have had advantages. Hunter-gatherer societies formally recognized devoted male friendships with public rituals, such as vows and mixing blood, that paralleled marriage. In traditional cultures, marriage was about establishing a family, while friendship was about finding a mentor or equal, as well as an ally and companion.

Sex-segregation in early human cultures was likely fueled by sexual competition, the division of labor, and specialization of tasks. Later, social customs and distrust helped maintain sex-segregation. Once men and women began spending large amounts of time apart in same-sex social environments, survival and reproductive success depended on effectively maneuvering through those environments, overcoming conflicts, organizing support, and gathering the resources needed (such as a mate) to produce and raise children to reproductive age. Within same-sex social environments, characteristic of most human cultures until recently, devoted male friendships benefited survival and reproductive success by helping friends gain status and resources needed to acquire a mate and support a family. Although there has been little research on the reproductive benefits of same-sex friendship, this idea generates several predictions about male and female alliances and friendships that can be tested in traditional cultures.

Most people long for a close friend. The desire for a devoted companion—a second self—is part of our human nature because close friendships provided adaptive benefits for our early ancestors. Quite possibly, devoted male friendships (and probably female friendships) have been part of our ancestral history for more than a million years. In the next chapter, I further explore the history and function of devoted friendships from early recorded history up to the modern era.

Take Home Points:

- Preferential same-sex alliances are common among chimpanzees and bonobos, our closest living primate relatives.
- Sexual competition and the division of labor resulted in early humans spending most of their time in same-sex environments.
- Same-sex alliances and devoted friendships facilitated navigation of same-sex social environments, cooperation in complex tasks, care for children (for females), defending against aggression, and acquiring status and resources, such as a mate (for males).
- Among diverse hunter-gather societies and native people, devoted male friendships or blood brotherhoods formed early and were lifelong. Devoted friendships were formalized with public rituals and vows. Some friendships included sexual activity.

References

Angers, L. (2020). Symbols of friendship around the world. *Betterhelp.com*. https://www.betterhelp.com/advice/friendship/symbols-of-friendship-around-the-world/

Apicella, C. L., Marlowe, F. W., Fowler, J. H., & Christakis, N. A. (2012). Social networks and cooperation in hunter-gatherers. *Nature, 481*(7382), 497–501.

Bleys, R. C. (1995). *The geography of perversion: Male-to-male sexual behavior outside of the West and the ethnographic imagination, 1750–1918*. New York: New York University.

Brain, R. (1976). *Friends and lovers*. New York: Basic Books.

Burkart, J. M., Hrdy, S. B., & van Schaik, C. P. (2009). Cooperative breeding and human cognitive evolution. *Evolutionary Anthropology, 18*(5), 175–186.

Crompton, L. (2003). *Homosexuality & civilization*. Cambridge: Belknap Press.

DeScioli, P., & Kurzban, R. (2009). The alliance hypothesis for human friendship. *PLOS ONE, 4*(6), e5802.

Dunbar, R. (2010). *How many friends does one person need? Dunbar's number and other evolutionary quirks*. Cambridge, MA: Harvard University Press.

Dunbar, R. I. M., & Sosis, R. (2018). Optimising human community sizes. *Evolution and Human Behavior, 39*(1), 106–111.

Dyble, M., Salali, G. D., Chaudhary, N., Page, A., Smith, D., Thompson, J., ... Migliano, A. B. (2015). Sex equality can explain the unique social structure of hunter-gatherer bands. *Science, 348*(6263), 796–798.

Ember, C. R. (1978). Myths about hunter-gatherers. *Ethnology, 17*(4), 439–448.

Friendship bracelets. (2020). *Wikipedia*. https://en.wikipedia.org/wiki/Friendship _bracelet

Friendship day. (2020, February 14). *Wikipedia*. https://en.wikipedia.org/wiki/Frien dship_Day

Goodale, J. C. (1971). *Tiwi wives: A study of the women of Melville Island, North Australia*. Seattle, WA: University of Washington Press.

Goodman, M. J., Griffin, B. P., Estioko-Griffin, A. A., & Grove, J. S. (1985). The compatibility of hunting and mothering among the Agta hunter-gatherers in the Philippines. *Sex Roles, 12*(11/12), 1199–1209.

Goodwin, R. (1999). *Personal relationships across cultures*. London: Routledge.

Greenberg, D. F. (1988). *The construction of homosexuality*. Chicago: University of Chicago Press.

Greshko, M. (2018). Ancient DNA reveals complex migrations of the first Americans. *National Geographic.com*. https://www.nationalgeographic.com/science/2018/11 /ancient-dna-reveals-complex-migrations-first-americans/

Grueter, C. C., Chapais, B., & Zinner, D. (2012). Evolution of multilevel social systems in nonhuman primates and humans. *International Journal of Primatology, 33*(5), 1002–1037.

Gurven, M. (2012). Human survival and life history in evolutionary perspective. In J. C. Mitani, J. Call, P. M. Kappeler, R. A. Palombit & J. B. Silk (Eds.), *The evolution of primate societies* (pp. 293–314). Chicago, IL: University of Chicago Press.

Gurven, M., & Hill, K. (2009). Why do men hunt? A reevaluation of "Man the Hunter" and the sexual division of labor. *Current Anthropology, 50*(1), 51–62.

Herdt, G. H. (1981). *Guardians of the flutes: Idioms of masculinity*. New York: McGraw-Hill.

Herdt, G. H. (1984/1993). *Ritualized homosexuality in Melanesia*. Berkeley, CA: University of California Press.

Herdt, G. H. (1987). *The Sambia: Ritual and gender in New Guinea*. New York: Holt, Rinehart & Winston.

How to say friendship in different languages. (2019). *Indifferentlanguages.com*. https://www.indifferentlanguages.com/words/friendship

Hurtado, A. M., Hawkes, K., Hill, K., & Kaplan, H. (1985). Female subsistence strategies among Ache hunter-gatherers of Eastern Paraguay. *Human Ecology, 13*(1), 1–28.

Idani, G. (1991). Social relationships between immigrant and resident bonobo (*Pan paniscus*) females at Wamba. *Folia Primatologica; International Journal of Primatology, 57*(2), 83–95.

Katz, J. N. (1992). *Gay American history: Lesbians & gay men in the U.S.A. revised edition*. New York: Meridian.

Kauth, M. R. (2000). *True nature: A theory of sexual attraction*. New York: Kluwer.

Keeley, L. E. (1995). Protoagricultural practices among hunter-gatherers: A cross-cultural survey. In T. D. Price & A. B. Gerbauer (Eds.), *Last hunters, first farmers: New perspectives on the prehistoric transition to agriculture* (pp. 243–272). Sant Fe, NM: School of American Research.

Konner, M. (2005). Hunter-gatherer infancy and childhood: The !Kung and others. In B. S. Hewlett & M. E. Lamb (Eds.), *Hunter-gatherer childhoods: Evolutionary, developmental, and culture perspectives* (pp. 19–64). Piscataway, NJ: Transaction Publishers.

Konstan, D. (1997). *Friendship in the classical world*. Cambridge, United Kingdom: Cambridge University Press.

Lee, R. B. (1984). *The Dobe ![Kung]*. New York: Holt, Rinehart & Winston.

Lewis, C. S. (1960). *The four loves*. London: Geoffrey Bles.

Lewis, D. M. G., Al-Shawaf, L., Raja, A., DeKay, T., & Buss, D. M. (2011). Friends with benefits: The evolved psychology of same- and opposite-sex friendship. *Evolutionary Psychology, 9*(4), 543–563.

Marlowe, F. W. (2010). *The Hadza: Hunters-gatherers of Tanzania*. Berkeley, CA: University of California Press.

Massen, J. J. M., & Koski, S. E. (2014). Chimps of a feather sit together: Chimpanzee friendships are based on homophily in personality. *Evolution and Human Behavior, 35*(1), 1–8.

Maybury-Lewis, D. (1967). *Akwe-Shavante society*. Oxford: Clarendon.

Migliano, A. B., Page, A. E., Gómez-Gardeñes, J., Salali, G. D., Viguier, S., Dyble, M., … Vinicius, L. (2017). Characterization of hunter-gatherer networks and implications for cumulative culture. *Nature Human Behavior, 1*(0043), 1–6.

Miller, N. F., & Donovan, J. (2009/2013). *Blood brotherhood and other rites of male alliance* (2nd rev. ed.). Milwaukie, OR: Dissonant Hum.

Neill, J. (2009). *The origins and role of same-sex relations in human societies*. Jefferson, NC: McFarland & Company.

Nettle, D. (2006). The evolution of personality variation in humans and other animals. *American Psychologist, 61*(6), 622–631.

Number of social media users worldwide from 2010 to 2021 (in Billions). (2019). *Statista*. https://www.statista.com/statistics/278414/number-of-worldwide-social-network-users/

Saey, T. H. (2018). Ancient DNA suggests that people settled in South America in at least 3 waves. *Science News*. https://www.sciencenews.org/article/ancient-dna-fossils-south-america-populated

Schneebaum, T. (1988). *Where the spirits dwell: An odyssey in the jungle of New Guinea*. New York: Grove.

Selfhout, M., Burk, W., Branje, S., Denissen, J., van Aken, M., & Meeus, W. (2010). Emerging late adolescent friendship networks and Big Five personality traits: A social network approach. *Journal of Personality, 78*(2), 509–538.

Seyfarth, R. M., & Cheney, D. L. (2012). The evolutionary origins of friendship. *Annual Review of Psychology, 64*, 153–177.

Smith, D., Dyble, M., Major, K., Page, A. E., Chaudhary, N., Salali, G. D., ... Mace, R. (2019). A friend in need is a friend indeed: Need-based sharing, rather than cooperative assortment, predicts experimental resource transfers among Agta hunter-gatherers. *Evolution and Human Behavior, 40*(1), 82–89.

Spain, D. (1992). The spatial foundations of men's friendships and men's power. In P. M. Nardi (Ed.), *Men's friendships* (pp. 59–73). Newbury Park, CA: SAGE.

Taylor, T. (1996). *The prehistory of sex: Four million years of human sexual culture.* New York: Bantam Books.

Terrell, J. E. (2015). *A talent for friendship: Rediscovery of a remarkable trait.* Oxford: University of Oxford Press.

Tiger, L. (1969/1984). *Men in groups.* New York: Marion Boyers.

Waguespack, N. M. (2005). The organization of male and female labor in foraging societies: Implications for early Paleoindian archeology. *American Anthropologist, 107*(4), 666–678.

Watts, D. P. (2005). Sexual segregation in non-human primates. In K. E. Ruckstuhl & P. Neuhaus (Eds.), *Sexual segregation in vertebrates: Ecology of the two sexes* (pp. 327–347). Cambridge: Cambridge University Press.

Watts, D. P. (2012). The apes: Taxonomy, biogeography, life histories, and behavioral ecology. In J. C. Mitani, J. Call, P. M. Kappeler, R. A. Palombit & J. B. Silk (Eds.), *The evolution of primate societies* (pp. 113–142). Chicago, IL: University of Chicago Press.

Williams, W. L. (1992a). *The spirit and the flesh: Sexual diversity in American Indian culture.* Boston, MA: Beacon.

Williams, W. L. (1992b). The relationship between male-male friendship and male-female marriage: American Indian and Asian comparisons. In P. M. Nardi (Ed.), *Research on men and masculinities, vol. 2: Men's friendships* (pp. 186–200). Newbury Park, CA: SAGE.

Youyou, W., Stillwell, D., Schwartz, H. A., & Kosinki, M. (2017). Birds of a feather do flock together: Behavior-based personality-assessment method reveals personality similarity among couples and friends. *Psychological Science, 28*(3), 276–284.

Chapter 4

Life Partners

A Brief History of Devoted Friendships

Friendships appear to be universal. The persistence of devoted male friendships throughout history would suggest that this trait was engineered to benefit men across diverse cultures. In the first century, Roman lyric poet Horace proclaimed that a friend is valued above all else (Alessi, 2003). If this is so—if devoted male friendships are critically important—why do we not value friendships as much in contemporary Western culture? If devoted male friendships are adaptive traits, why are there not such friendships today? Why did they disappear? Answers to these questions demonstrate the persistence of devoted friendships as well as the transformative power of culture and language. Answers to these questions, as we will see, also illustrate how different contemporary Western culture is from past cultures and what we lose by not knowing our past.

Most evolutionary analyses of an evolved human trait explore its existence among non-human animals, especially primates and particularly chimpanzees, as I did in the previous chapter. Evolutionists then show evidence of the trait among contemporary hunter-gatherer societies, using these groups as a proxy for early human hunter-gatherers. That evidence was also presented in the previous chapter. Then, investigators typically leap ahead tens or hundreds of thousands of years to show evidence of the trait among contemporary humans—usually populations of mostly white men and women living in the urbanized West. What happened to that trait during the skipped span of time is generally viewed by evolutionists as peripheral to the story because relatively large, persistent evolved features can require a million years or more to stabilize and spread through the population (Uyeda, Hansen, Arnold, & Pienaar, 2011). Well, I want to know what happened during that unexamined period. Did the trait change? If so, how and when? Have cultures altered the trait's expression? Are those modifications evident in the present? I want to know what happened to devoted male (and female) friendships since this trait stabilized among early human nomadic hunter-gatherers.

While large evolutionary changes may take a million years to spread through the population, smaller evolutionary changes are possible in shorter spans of time. Humans have experienced significant changes in our bodies and minds in just the past 10,000 years—a blink of an eye in evolutionary time (Cochran & Harpending, 2009). Largely because of the introduction of agriculture and the domestication of animals, humans have undergone significant genetic, physiological, cognitive, and personality changes rather quickly. So, skipping large chunks of human history may lead us to miss important changes in the expression of a trait like friendship.

Over a relatively short period of time, sedentary farmers replaced most nomadic hunter-gatherers and dramatically influenced selection pressures. In *The 10,000 Year Explosion: How Civilization Accelerated Human Evolution* (2009), anthropologists Gregory Cochran and Henry Harpending provide a fascinating account of how farming and its consequences have fueled genetic variation in humans, including changes in personality traits that made living in denser, socially stratified communities more tolerable. With farming, food became more plentiful, but the human diet became less diverse. Humans experienced vitamin deficiencies that contributed to beriberi, rickets, and scurvy. People shrank by almost five inches in height. Infant mortality increased, likely due to changes in diet. Yet the time between births shortened, and birth rates increased, probably because humans were not regularly moving location. Major nutritional, environmental, and social changes tied to sedentary agriculturalism promoted a host of effects that changed human life, including greater task specialization, urbanization and the spread of disease, formation of governments, property ownership and the accumulation of wealth, social stratification and poverty, large scale warfare and mass killing, and the development of new technologies. Cochran and Harpending (2009) noted that just 7,500 years ago, a genetic mutation arose that permitted lactose digestion in adulthood. By this time, sheep, goats and cows had been domesticated as a source of meat and skins. Milk and milk products, such as yogurt and cheese, began to be exploited as food. Since dairying is a far more efficient calorie source than raising cattle for slaughter, lactose tolerance provided a survival advantage. By about 5,000 years ago, the mutation for lactose tolerance had spread across populations in Europe. Today, more than 90% of people on the planet have some degree of lactose tolerance. That is a remarkable spread in less than 8,000 years.

Obviously, the emergence of agriculture and new technologies associated with it has altered human experience and development and continues to do so. What effect have these major lifestyle and cultural changes had on devoted friendships? This chapter explores evidence of devoted friendships from agricultural societies to early civilizations in Mesopotamia up through the late Roman Empire in the fifth century and through pre-modern imperial China and Japan, only 200 years ago. Widespread evidence of devoted male (and some female) friendships across cultures illustrates the strength of this trait. The factors behind the devaluation of devoted male friendships demonstrate the transformative power of culture in shaping how we think about and experience ourselves and friendship today. The evidence presented here comes from a variety of literary and historical sources, including poetry, songs, plays, novels, essays, diaries, treatises, histories, laws, religious tracts, the Hebrew and Christian Bibles, and travel logs. Much of the information reported represents observations and thoughts from contemporaneous figures.

Devoted Friendships from Agricultural Societies to the Late Roman Republic and Imperial China and Japan

Around 12,000 years ago, the last ice age was coming to an end. The climate became warmer and more stable. Large mammals, like mammoths and mastodons, were disappearing, and so was the hunter-gatherer way of life. About this time, in several different parts of the world, humans began settling in one place and farming (Taylor, 1996). Because of climate change and possible population pressures around 11,000 years ago, farming people began migrating out of Anatolia (modern Turkey) in southwest Asia and into the Balkans (Curry, 2013). About 8,500 years ago, in Palestine, a farming village called Jericho became one of the world's first permanent settlements. Additional migrations of farming people occurred about 8,000 years ago. Two waves of migrants slowly spread out of the Balkans into Europe (Olalde, Schroeder, Sandoval-Velasco, Vinner, Lobón, Ramirez, et al., 2015). One wave closely followed the northern Mediterranean coastline, eventually spilling across southern Europe. The other wave followed the Danube River into Europe, then moved west, eventually encompassing all of central and northern Europe. These farming people began clearing forests in their path to create huge tracts of open land. Farming people finally reached Britain between 4,000 and 3,500 years ago (Taylor, 1996). As agriculture took hold, the human population grew and continued to spread. Migrating farming people occupied and settled lands already occupied by ancient nomadic hunter-gatherers. Historians once believed that hunter-gatherers in these lands decided to stop their nomadic way of life and take up farming, perhaps after intermarrying with encroaching farmers. However, analyses of mitochondrial DNA from early people across diverse geographic locations show little admixture of genetic profiles between migrating early farmers and local hunter-gatherers. In other words, intruding sedentary farmers did not marry local hunter-gatherers; they drove them out and replaced them (Bramanti, Thomas, Haak, Unterländer, Jores, Tambets, et al., 2009; Hofmanová, Kreutzer, Hellenthal, Sell, Diekmann, Díez-del-Molino, et al., 2016).

Without a written record, only archeological evidence can provide clues about the beliefs and social organization of early farmers. Looking at this evidence, archeologist Timothy Taylor (1996) described early farming societies as patriarchal with "a fundamentally exploitive attitude toward everything" (p. 149). Taylor asserts that early male farmers began viewing their settlement and everything on it, including livestock, resources, wives, and children, as their (private) property—as things they owned. Farming was also difficult and required everyone in the family to do a job. Tasks became further specialized, and men's and women's work became more separated. Arduous, repetitive tasks necessary to manage livestock, raise crops, and manage the household further reinforced gendered divisions of labor and strengthened the view that wives and children were labor resources governed by the male heads of the family. Further, early farming societies had several families living close together in permanent settlements, which required considerable cooperation within and between groups, including providing aid when needed and respecting each other's property and boundaries.

With the domestication of grains, food production increased, leading to surpluses, trade, and the accumulation of wealth. Communities emerged around the exchange of goods, and civil governments formed to keep the peace. With increased productivity and wealth, individuals could specialize in non-farming and pastoral tasks, such as leather tooling and pottery making, textile production, shop keeping, healing, civil administration, and soldiering. Roles for women were more restricted and hidden from the view of unrelated men. Even so, women (and some men) began holding two newly specialized roles: prostitutes and cult priestesses/attendants (Neill, 2009; Taylor, 1996). Taylor (1996) has speculated that farmers' close attention to seasons and recurrent life-death cycles, inherent in animal husbandry and agriculture, promoted a general belief in "Mother Earth" and goddess worship. Even so, Mother Earth was only a vessel for men's fertile seed. Consistent with a focus on fertility, early farmers erected stone phalluses as symbols of fertility and good luck (Taylor, 1996). Unfortunately, without written records, it is unclear how early farmers related to each other and formed friendships.

Commerce and the exchange of wealth, labor specialization, and civil authorities promoted social stratification in early civilizations (Neill, 2009; Taylor, 1996). One of the first cities, Uruk, in central Sumer, sits between the Tigris and Euphrates rivers in Mesopotamia. Established around 7,000 years ago (5,000 BCE), Uruk became a center for trade because early Sumerian farmers were highly productive (Sumer, 2020). Uruk, Ur, Kish, Adab, and other cities, collectively formed Sumer, one of the world's first civilizations. The Sumerian civilization (c. 2900–2350 BCE and 2112–2004 BCE) was absorbed by the expanding Akkadian Empire in the third millennium BCE (c. 2334–2154 BCE), which then became the Babylonian Empire (c. 1900–539 BCE). The northern Assyrian Empire (c. 1900–612 BCE) is also part of ancient Mesopotamia. The Assyrian Empire encompassed modern Iraq and parts of modern Turkey, Syria, and Iran (Nemet-Nejat, 1999). The Sumerian, Akkadian, Babylonian, and Assyrian cultures largely blended into each other, representing a greater Mesopotamian civilization that lasted for a few thousand years. These civilizations were surrounded by Neolithic tribal warrior bands who envied their wealth and resources. After repeated raids by Indo-European Hittites from Anatolia, the Babylonian Empire fell into decline (Babylonia, 2020).

Writing first emerged in ancient Mesopotamia, perhaps initially for record-keeping. The earliest written texts date to around 5,000 years ago (approximately 3300 BCE) and come from Uruk (Sumer, 2020). One of the earliest pieces of written literature is the epic poem *Gilgamesh*, which dates to the middle of the third millennium BCE but has origins in earlier stories. *Gilgamesh* is loosely based on a historical king of Uruk who reigned about 2750 BCE. The poem *Gilgamesh* is at least 1,000 years older than Homer's *Iliad* or the collection of texts that became the Bible (Mitchell, 2004). Like the *Iliad*, *Gilgamesh* originated in an earlier oral tradition of spoken poems. Epic poems like the *Iliad* and *Gilgamesh* were not solely entertainment. These poems conveyed artfully crafted moral lessons that reflected the larger culture's history, customs, values, and beliefs (Neill, 2009). These stories were meant to educate and inspire their audiences, as well as entertain. *Gilgamesh*, for example, depicts an important existential life lesson for its listeners—the meaning of life. The poem also provides the earliest evidence for how the ancient world viewed devoted male friendships, so it is worth a long look.

Ancient Mesopotamia: Gilgamesh and Enkidu

In the poem, Gilgamesh is king of the Sumerian city of Uruk. He is the son of a king who became a god and the goddess Ninsun, making Gilgamesh "two-thirds divine and one-third human" (Mitchell, 2004). Because of his divine nature, Gilgamesh possesses exceptional strength and great beauty, and a large penis (Neill, 2009). His divinity gives him insatiable appetites, including sexual desire. As the poem opens, Gilgamesh is terrorizing the citizens of Uruk by taking their sons (into forced labor or sexual submission) and having sex with their daughters on their wedding day. King Gilgamesh is incredibly powerful. No one can stop him. The citizens of Uruk pray to Anu, father of gods, for help. Anu asks Aruru, the creator of humans, to make a companion for Gilgamesh: "Now go and create a double for Gilgamesh, his *second self* (italics added), a man who equals his strength and courage, a man who equals his stormy heart. Create a new hero, let them balance each other perfectly, so that Uruk has peace" (Mitchell, 2004, p. 74). Note that Anu does not ask Aruru to make Gilgamesh a wife. He requests a male companion. As king, Gilgamesh likely has multiple wives. Anu also asks Aruru to create an equal, a soulmate, a "second self" for Gilgamesh. The idea of a devoted friend as another self is a persistent theme across diverse cultures.

Aruru creates Enkidu, a fierce, powerful, hairy wild man, who roams the wilderness naked. When Gilgamesh hears about this wild man, he sends the priestess Shamhat to the wilderness to bring him to the city. Shamhat casts a spell on Enkidu causing them to have sex for seven days, without Enkidu losing his erection. After seven days of sex with the priestess, Enkidu is changed! He now understands language. He has consciousness. Enkidu also feels a desire he has never felt before: "Deep in his heart he felt something stir, a longing he had never known before, the longing for a true friend" (Mitchell, 2004, p. 80). It is worth noting that after seven days and nights of sex with a woman, Enkidu wants a male friend! He goes to Uruk to meet Gilgamesh.

Meanwhile, Gilgamesh is having strange dreams that foretell his meeting Enkidu. He asks his goddess mother to interpret his dreams. In one dream, a star falls to earth and lands at Gilgamesh's feet. The star is too heavy for him to lift. He embraces and caresses the star like a man caresses his wife. Ninsun tells Gilgamesh that the star is his "second self" (Enkidu). She says Gilgamesh will hold and touch this man like a wife and he will be the "companion of your heart" (Mitchell, 2004). A different translation has Ninsun telling Gilgamesh, "I myself put him on a par with you, over whom you did bend as over a woman. He is a strong companion, one who helps a friend in need ... . That you did bend over him as a woman means that he will never forsake you" (Neill, 2009, p. 88). In another version of the story, Gilgamesh dreams about a great ax, which he loves and caresses and sleeps with (Neill, 2009). The ax is always at his side. Ninsun tells Gilgamesh that the ax is a man and he will love and embrace this man like a wife. What is impossible to experience from the English translations of the Akkadian text are the multiple sexual puns in the two dreams (Neill, 2009). The obvious erotic and sexual references in the dreams illustrate the sexual nature of Gilgamesh and Enkidu's relationship in a humorous, winking way. The early third millennium BCE audience would have understood the puns and been unfazed by the sexual part of Gilgamesh and Enkidu's relationship. Even so, the sexuality between Gilgamesh and Enkidu is treated obliquely and metaphorically, almost reverently, compared to the explicit, crude references to obligatory sexual activities with women in the story. In general, the poem exalts male-male relationships and portrays male-female relationships as somewhat negative.

When Enkidu arrives in Uruk, people recognize him as Gilgamesh's equal and are relieved. Enkidu learns that Gilgamesh is on his way to a wedding with plans to bed the virgin bride. Objecting to this behavior, Enkidu arrives first and blocks Gilgamesh's entry to the wedding. The two men fight violently, nearly destroying the house. Finally, Gilgamesh overpowers Enkidu. Rather than treat each other as enemies, they acknowledge each other's greatness: "They embraced and kissed. They held hands like brothers. They walked side by side. They became true friends" (Mitchell, 2004, p. 90). Later, Gilgamesh's mother accepts Enkidu as her son "not born from my womb" and recognizes him as "a brother for Gilgamesh". Ritual bonding and kinship references are also common across cultures with devoted male friendships.

Gilgamesh and Enkidu are inseparable. Further, Gilgamesh is changed. He no longer terrorizes Uruk's citizens or violates virgin brides. He is a good king. Later, the two men go on a long journey together to kill an evil being, Humbaba, in a faraway forest. While successful, they also kill the goddess Ishtar's sacred Bull of Heaven. Enkidu then insults Ishtar, and she kills him. Gilgamesh is inconsolable in his grief: "He began to rage like a lion ... . This way and that he paced round the bed, he tore out his hair and strewed it around" (Sandars, 1972, p. 95). Gilgamesh places a veil over Enkidu's face, like a wife. For six days and seven nights, he mourns over his companion's body until maggots appear. Enkidu's death shakes Gilgamesh to the core. Grieving and fearful for his own mortality, Gilgamesh begins a journey in search of the meaning of life. He meets a tavern keeper who tries to comfort him. The man philosophies, "Humans are born, they live, then they die, this is the order that the gods have decreed. But until the end comes, enjoy your life, spend it in happiness, not despair" (Mitchell, 2004, p. 168). Gilgamesh replies, "What can your words mean when my heart is sick for Enkidu who died" (p. 169). As Gilgamesh continues on, he meets an immortal man, Utnapishtim, who tells him, "Gilgamesh, why prolong your grief? Have you ever paused to compare your own blessed lot with a fool's? ... . Can't you see how fortunate you are?" (pp. 176–177). Finally, Gilgamesh accepts that life goes on without his beloved Enkidu. He returns to Uruk and his kingdom.

There are many remarkable elements of *Gilgamesh* that are beyond the scope of this book. As a popular story about two masculine heroic men, it is a glimpse into how the ancient world viewed devoted male friendships. While this story cannot tell us how ordinary people lived their lives or how prevalent devoted male friendships were in ancient Mesopotamia, we learn that devoted male friendships were admired. We can assume that the Mesopotamian people who listened in rapt attention to the story of Gilgamesh and Enkidu were comfortable with close male friendships that included sexual affection. While men were expected to marry and have children—real companionship—like a second self, like one soul in two bodies—was not found in marriage. Real companionship was found in male friendships. For Gilgamesh, his relationship with Enkidu was the most important one in his life. It was literally life-transforming. Contemporary readers may fixate on the sexuality between Gilgamesh and Enkidu, but ancient Babylonians would have understood that sexuality is present in many non-kin relationships, including close male friendships. Sex is not the defining characteristic of the relationship; love, respect, loyalty, and adherence to customary social roles are more important. Sex expressed affection, produced pleasure, and symbolized the roles of partners in the relationship. Even so, many scholars have insisted that Gilgamesh and Enkidu's relationship was not sexual. Historian George Held, for example, strongly argued that the sexual imagery in *Gilgamesh* is merely symbolic or allegorical and without sexual intent, much like the sexual imagery in the later *Song of Solomon* from the Hebrew Bible (Neill, 2009). Historian James Neill (2009) has refuted that claim by pointing out that the *Song of Solomon* is not allegorical at all. The *Song of Solomon* is most likely a product of love songs that preceded ritual consummation of a sacred marriage by a king and a temple prostitute representing a goddess. Neill (2009) also rebutted Martti Nissinen's (1998) argument that Gilgamesh and Enkidu's relationship was primarily spiritual. The anti-same-sex asceticism that Nissinen attributes to *Gilgamesh* did not emerge until 2,000 years after the poem was written.

Unfortunately, *Gilgamesh* tells us little about female friendships in ancient Mesopotamia. Contemporaneous sources suggest that women's roles were fairly limited. In the ancient world, a woman's primary role was to bear children, preferably a boy who could inherit his father's property and provide for his parents when they grew old (Nemet-Nejat, 1999). Motherhood garnered respect. A song attributed to the goddess Eula describes the stages of a woman's life in the ancient world: "I am a daughter, I am a bride, I am a spouse, I am a housekeeper" (Nemet-Nejat, 1999, pp. 97–88). In ancient Mesopotamia, girls in their teens married young men who were at least ten years older. Usually, the marriage was arranged and brokered to join two families for their mutual benefit. In the ancient world, marriage had at least four stages: 1) an engagement, usually orchestrated by the fathers or parents of the two families; 2) payments to both families in the form of the bride's dowry and the bridegroom's price; 3) transitioning the bride into her father-in-law's house to live with her husband; and 4) sex with her husband (Nemet-Nejat, 1999). Women in the ancient world were overseen by men. If a woman's husband died, his father or the senior male in the household decided the woman's fate. Wives had to be faithful, and isolation made access to potential male partners very difficult. Married men could have other sexual partners, such as a concubine (slave) who might also bear children. Nevertheless, married couples in the ancient world were expected to love each other and, hopefully, fall in love. Married men and women wanted to feel sexual passion and romantic love for their spouse. Love songs, love poetry, love potions, and love magic were quite popular in ancient Mesopotamia, although the popularity of love magic could mean that love was frequently absent in marriages (Nemet-Nejat, 1999). At least for men, love was not limited to marriage. Married men in ancient Mesopotamia sometimes fell in love with their concubines.

In summary, the earliest example of written literature, the Akkadian poem *Gilgamesh*, features a devoted male friendship between heroic men. The audience would have understood and been amused by the many punning references to sexuality between the two men. While in the ancient world heroic men were depicted as having profound relationships and adventures, real life for men may have been less heroic but centered around men. Women's real-life roles were to marry, be available for sex, care for her children, and run the household. It is inconceivable that women in ancient Mesopotamia did not form intimate, devoted friendships with non-kin women in their social circles. Women's primary emotional relationships were with other women.

The Early Israelites: David and Jonathan, Ruth and Naomi, and the Book of Leviticus

Given the later influence of the Hebrew Bible on Christianity and the popularity of the David and Jonathan story, it is worth examining the culture of the early Israelites to understand the context of these stories. Neill (2009) has provided a concise but informative description of this history. During the second millennium BCE, a collection of Semitic warrior tribes led by priests emerged from the southern deserts in the Levant. These tribes violently attacked and conquered the indigenous people of Canaan, which encompassed lands just east of the Mediterranean Sea. These Bronze Age early Israelites worshipped Yahweh, a male warrior god credited with leading the Hebrew tribes to the "promised land". Like most invaders, as the early Israelites settled into Canaan, they began to blend their worship of Yahweh with the native Canaanite worship of fertility deities, goddess Asherah, and her son and companion, Baal (Neill, 2009). Yahweh, a god of war, unlike Asherah and Baal, had little to do with the daily activities and worries associated with farming and raising livestock, like: Will it rain at the right time for plants to grow, and will the newborn lambs survive? Worship of Asherah and Baal filled this gap. Canaanite fertility rituals included phallic totems, food gifts and animal sacrifices to Asherah or Baal, and ritual sex with female temple priestesses and/or male temple priests or attendants. Pleas for rain for crops involved ritual masturbation before an idol of Baal. Like many early cultures without a contemporary understanding of biology, fertility was attributed to men, not women. At this time, the early Israelites had no general prohibition against same-sex sexual activity, and many participated in Asherah and Baal fertility rituals, including ritual sex in temples. From about 1400 BCE to the sixth century BCE, the early Israelites worshipped Yahweh, Asherah, and Baal (Neill, 2009). As noted in 1 Kings, during King Ahab's reign (c. ninth century BCE), about 900 Israelites were priests of Asherah and Baal. While Israelite priests of Yahweh condemned goddess worship and polytheism, many Israelites, especially women, combined fertility rituals with their worship of Yahweh. After the capture of

Jerusalem in 587 BCE, early Israelites from the Kingdom of Judah became further exposed to polytheistic religious practice while exiled in Babylonia.

The Persian king, Artaxerxes, defeated Babylon in 539 BCE. Artaxerxes appointed Ezra, a Hebrew Aaronite priest, as the religious leader of the Israelites and sent the captives back to Canaan (Neill, 2009). To unite the Hebrew tribes into one Jewish people, the priests orchestrated a national- ist campaign to distinguish the new Jewish people from their idolatrous neighbors. The priests compiled and re-edited early religious texts, taking a strong position against polytheism, especially the worship of Asherah and Baal. These updated texts became Exodus, Numbers, Deuteronomy, Joshua, Judges, 1 and 2 Samuel, and 1 and 2 Kings of the Hebrew Bible, in the form we know them (Neill, 2009). The priests and new texts blamed women for worshipping Asherah and for leading Israelite men away from Yahweh, the one true god. Priests railed against the evils of goddess worship and its associated rituals, including the sacrifice of pigs and eating pork, as well as sex with temple priestesses/priests. The Book of Leviticus, the Holiness Code, compiled and edited around 500 BCE, focused on religious, dietary, and behavioral standards for the Jewish people, including distinct gender roles (Nissinen, 1998). Leviticus contained strict rules for the Hebrew reli- gion and Jewish identity (Neill, 2009). One passage, Leviticus 18:22, has been read by many as generally condemning same-sex behavior between men (Boswell, 1980). The King James Version (KJV) of the Bible, familiar to most people, reads: "Thou shalt not lie with mankind, as with womankind: it is an abomination". Leviticus 20:13 repeats the same prohibition and adds the death penalty as punishment. No prohibition against same-sex behavior between women is mentioned anywhere. Christian writers have interpreted Leviticus 18:22 as a condemnation of same-sex acts between men (but not women), particularly anal sex (Boswell, 1980; Neill, 2009). Later Christian writers broadened this interpretation to mean a general condemnation of *all* same-sex sexual behavior and same-sex-attracted people. The radical twenty-first-century Westboro Baptist Church (2020) famously condensed Leviticus 18:22 to the slogan "God Hates Fags". However, these anti-same- sex sexuality interpretations of ancient Hebrew texts are not so clear-cut and must be viewed in context.

Modern scholars and historians, John Boswell (1980) and Rictor Norton (1993), have pointed to unusual words and phrasing in Leviticus 18:22 that direct this prohibition toward ritual sex with men during goddess worship. The Hebrew text uses an uncommon word, *zakar*, to refer to the man with whom the sexual act is performed, rather than the common term, *ish*, for "male" or "man" (Boswell, 1980). Boswell and Norton have argued that *zakar* refers to men with religious roles, like priests. If the Israelite priests had intended to generally condemn male-male sexual acts, they could have used common terms without religious associations (Neill, 2009). But that is not what they did. In addition, the Hebrew word *to-ebah*, translated as "abomination", means "unclean" and "ritually impure" in reference again to idolatrous practices (Boswell, 1980; Neill, 2009; Norton, 1993). "Abomination" has a very different meaning in English, suggesting strong disgust, abhorrence, or something detestable, consistent with later Christian writers' attitudes about sodomy and sexual pleasure in general. Leviticus 18 opens and closes with admonitions about not following the sinful, impure, idolatrous ways of the Canaanites. Thus, it is difficult to miss the direct connection to idolatry, rather than sexual immorality, in verse 22. However, many writers, including David Greenberg (1988) in his excellent book, *The Construction of Homosexuality*, have overlooked this association.

It is also worth noting that early Christians gave no special attention to Leviticus 18:22, largely because they understood the Holiness Code to apply to Jews, not Christians. Finnish Old Testament scholar Martti Nissinen (1998) understood that the prohibitions in the Holiness Code were not civil or criminal law, but more akin to principles of life for the Jewish people. Consistent with this view, no evidence exists for the enactment of the death penalty by the Israelites for receptive male sexual acts or for participation in ritual sex with male priests as part of goddess worship (Nissinen, 1998). Even so, the focus on strict gender roles made passive male sexual acts (viewed as woman-like) more problematic for the Jewish people.

In short, after conquering Canaan and for centuries after, the early Israelites incorporated goddess worship into their religious practices. These practices included totems, gifts to the gods, and ritual sex with the high priestess/priest to ensure fertile crops and livestock. After the early Israelites returned from exile in Babylonia, the priests began a nationalist campaign to unite and set apart the Jewish people from their ritually unclean, idolatrous, polytheist neighbors. The Holiness Code established strict principles for devout Jews. Leviticus 18:22 from the Holiness Code has been interpreted as a prohibition against male-male sexual acts, but recent scholars have demonstrated that this verse more likely condemns idolatry in the form of ritual sex, which was common at the time. The distinction between religious sexual rituals and consensual sexual intimacy between adults is very important. Although female-female sexuality is never mentioned in the Hebrew Bible, there is no reason to believe that it did not exist. With this background, the stage is set for the exploration of two highly popular Old Testament stories about devoted same-sex friendships: David and Jonathan and Ruth and Naomi.

David and Jonathan

The story of David and Jonathan is presented in 1 and 2 Samuel. The Books of Samuel were composed in the late seventh century BCE, while the Israelites were in exile in Babylon (Neill, 2009). Although little is known about David outside of the Books of Samuel, David became an important figure for both Jews and Christians. David (c. 1035–c. 970 BCE) is the young son of a shepherd, Jesse, and Jonathan is the son of King Saul (c. 1076–c. 1004 BCE). As the story goes, the early Israelites, who were frequently battling their neighbors, crowned Saul the first king of Israel in the eleventh century BCE. Soon after, Saul defied Yahweh's command to exterminate the Amalekites and destroy all that they possess. Yahweh punishes Saul with fits of melancholy. Saul searches for a musician to play for him and soothe his troubled mind. Eventually, David, a shepherd and skilled harp player, is sent to the palace in hopes that he can calm the king. Saul immediately likes David and appoints him as musician and armor bearer, which keeps him nearby. Although no mention is made of meeting Jonathan while in the palace, it seems likely that the two met about this time.

Soon the Israelites are again in conflict with the Philistines. Goliath, the Philistine hero, a large, ferocious warrior, calls for an Israelite champion to face him. When no regular solider steps forward, David, the armor bearer does. David approaches Goliath with only a sling and several small stones. He hits Goliath in the forehead with a stone, killing him. The Philistines retreat, and David is a hero. David later presents himself before King Saul carrying Goliath's head. According to scripture, Jonathan, also a successful soldier but crippled from a young age, meets David and instantly loves him. They become fast friends and swear a solemn oath of brotherhood. Historian John Boswell (1994) notes that the Hebrew word translated here as "covenant" refers elsewhere to marriage vows between a man and a woman. Jonathan gives David very personal gifts, including his own fine clothes and weapons. Saul invites David to live in the palace:

> And it came to pass, when he (David) had made an end of speaking unto Saul, that the soul of Jonathan was knit with the soul of David; and Jonathan loved him as his own soul. And Saul took him (David) that day, and would let him go no more home to his father's house. Then Jonathan and David made a covenant, because he (Jonathan) loved him as his own soul. (I Samuel 18:1–3, KJV)

Later, Saul gives his daughter Michal to David in marriage (one of eventually eight wives). Saul says to David that now he is a son-in-law "through two" of his children (Neill, 2009). The verse in the New Jerusalem Bible (NJB) reads: "On two occasions, Saul told David, 'Today, you shall be my son-in-law'". Saul seems to view David and Jonathan's relationship as a marriage or like a marriage.

Over time, Saul grows envious of David's military successes and popularity. He tries to kill David on several occasions, but Yahweh intervenes each time. Jonathan overhears Saul's plan to kill David and warns him. He then lies to his father about David's whereabouts. When Saul realizes that Jonathan has warned David, he is furious. In a rage, Saul exclaims, "Son of a rebellious slut! Don't I know that you side with the son of Jesse to your own shame and to your mother's dishonor?" (I Samuel 20:30, NJB). Biblical scholar and Episcopalian priest, Tom Horner (1978a), noted that Saul's accusation follows the form of early Semitic people and indirectly references the person being criticized: "son of a rebellious slut" (Jonathan) and "son of Jesse" (David). Insulting one's mother is another common convention among early Semitic people and even today. Horner (1978a) has suggested that Saul's slur on his wife and Jonathan's mother is another way of saying, "You're no son of mine if you don't put your own family first" (p. 31). The reference to "nakedness" may be an indirect reference to sex. But sex with whom? Horner explained that the Greek word *métochos* translated as "chosen" in the KJV Bible refers to an intimate partner or companion. In other words, Saul is acknowledging that Jonathan and David have an intimate sexual relationship, which he may or may not find displeasing. Saul is telling Jonathan to choose his family over David (Horner, 1978a; Neill, 2009).

Jonathan meets David in a secret place and tells him to flee the land. When David and Jonathan meet, "they kissed one another, and wept one with another, until David exceeded" (I Samuel 20:41, KJV). There is no mention of David saying goodbye to his wife Michal (Horner, 1978a). Sometime later, both King Saul and Jonathan are killed in battle. Upon learning of Jonathan's death, David cries, "Jonathan, by your dying, I too am stricken, I am desolate for you, Jonathan, my brother. Very dear you were to me, your love more wonderful to me than the love of a woman" (2 Samuel 1:25–26, NJB). David describes himself as a blood relative of Jonathan, reminiscent of blood brotherhoods (Horner, 1938). What is more, David proclaims that their love is stronger and closer than love between a man and woman (in marriage), implying that their relationship is more than a marriage and just as intimate (Horner, 1978a; Neill, 2009). David's lament also echoes Gilgamesh's cries of sorrow over the death of Enkidu.

Christian and Jewish writers have acknowledged that David and Jonathan's relationship was special, but many have insisted it was platonic (cf., Horner, 1978a; Nissinen, 1998). Often, these denials have echoed a modern anti-sexual Judeo-Christian perspective and implied that homosexuality is rare and against God. Writers proposing a non-sexual interpretation of David and Jonathan's relationship have argued that scripture never explicitly says that the pair slept together: That is, since the Bible did not *explicitly* mention sex—since David and Jonathan were not caught in the act—there was no sexual relationship. This insistence on witnessed same-sex sexual activity as proof reflects a modern bias towards defining relationships and people as inherently heterosexual and believing that same-sex sexuality is unusual and not normal. This way of thinking is quite different from how most ancient cultures have viewed devoted friendships and sexuality. David and Jonathan had a loving, intimate relationship. They made a sworn commitment to each other. In the ancient world, sexual intimacy within a loving, devoted adult friendship would have been private and certainly not the defining characteristic of the relationship. David and Jonathan's friendship was also not at odds with their marriages to women. Marriage was common, but friendship was special. David even described his love for Jonathan as stronger than his love for Michal, his wife. John Boswell (1980; 1994) noted that the Jewish Mishnah, the first written compilation of Jewish oral law tradition, which was published in the second century BCE, cited David and Jonathan as examples of lasting love and again contrasted the pair to male-female married couples. Boswell (1980; 1994) claimed that by this comparison, ancient Jewish writers acknowledged the physical and sexual intimacy between David and Jonathan.

Some may argue that the account of David and Jonathan is simply an allegorical story about heroic figures and not meant to reflect reality. Yet at the time that David and Jonathan lived, many early Israelite men had sex with men, at least in the context of fertility rituals (Neill, 2009). Many early Israelites had adopted the practices of neighboring peoples that included devoted male friendships. The story of David and Jonathan is consistent with the value placed on friendship by neighboring Canaanite cultures. Lastly, at the time exiled priests compiled the story of David and Jonathan, they had not yet initiated a nationalist campaign to distinguish the Jewish people from their pagan neighbors (Boswell, 1994; Neill, 2009).

Ruth and Naomi

The biblical story of Ruth and Naomi is one of the first written narratives about a woman's relationship with another woman. The Book of Ruth dates to around the fifth century BCE and has generally been used to demonstrate an accepting attitude toward those who convert to Judaism (Horner, 1978a). The story of Ruth and Naomi also includes one of the most passionate vows of friendship in ancient literature. As the story goes, there is a famine in Judah. Subsequently, Naomi, a Hebrew, moves with her husband, Elimelech, and their two sons to Moab, a kingdom east of the Dead Sea in what is now Jordan (Neill, 2009). Sometime after their arrival, Elimelech dies. Naomi's two sons, Mahlon and Chilion, marry Moabite women, Orpah and Ruth, respectively. About ten years later, Mahlon and Chilion are also dead, leaving the three women alone. With no male to oversee the family, Naomi must return to Judah to live with her natal family, as is the custom. She instructs her daughters-in-law to return to their natal families and find new husbands because they are still young. Orpah says her goodbyes and leaves. Ruth, however, refuses to leave and clings to Naomi. Ruth makes a passionate solemn vow to never leave Naomi. Ruth not only rejects her kin, but also her gods. She vows to follow the Hebrew god Yahweh, like Naomi.

> And she (Ruth) said, Entreat me not to leave thee, or to return from following after thee; for whither thou goest, I will go; and where thou lodgest, I will lodge: thy people shall be my people, and thy God my God: Where thou diest will I die, and there will I be buried: the Lord do so to me, and more also, if ought but death part thee and me. (Ruth 1:16–17, KJV)

In the New Jerusalem Bible, the last verse reads: "Let Yahweh bring unnameable ills on me and worse ills, too, if anything but death should part me from you!" Ruth says that only death will keep them apart but then, when they are both dead, they will be reunited. It is easy to imagine that Ruth became quite close to Naomi during the previous ten years. She likely married in her teens, and her survival, reproductive success, and emotional life would have depended on her close relationship with her mother-in-law, Naomi, and sister-in-law, Orpah (Neill, 2009). The women may not have lived together, but they likely spent much of their time together.

According to Boswell (1994), the Hebrew word in the text translated as "cleave unto" or "cling" appears elsewhere in Hebrew scripture to describe the attachment between a husband and wife. Does this kind of love attachment include sexual activity? There is no indication in the text that Ruth and Naomi slept together, which does not mean their relationship was non-sexual. Few writers have claimed that Ruth and Naomi had a sexual relationship. However, sex between women was not prohibited by Hebrew scripture. Neighboring matriarchal goddess-worshipping cultures, like early Dorian Sparta, would have viewed a sexual aspect of women's relationships with other women as unremarkable (Horner, 1978a; Neill, 2009). The male scribes who compiled the Book of Ruth in the fifth century BCE would have had little knowledge of or interest in what Ruth and Naomi did together behind closed doors, as long as they fulfilled their roles as women (Horner, 1978a). Like David and Jonathan and Gilgamesh and Enkidu, devoted love is the defining characteristic of Ruth and Naomi's friendship, not sex. As an interesting aside, the stories of Ruth and Naomi and David and Jonathan have a direct connection: Ruth's son, Obed, is the father of Jesse, who is the father of David. Ruth is David's great grandmother.

Invasion of the Indo-European Warrior People and Male Initiation

As scribes recorded the oral poem *Gilgamesh* in the early third millennium BCE, warrior tribes from the steppes of Central Asia began a series of migrations extending over the next one thousand years (Neill, 2009).

These warrior invaders disrupted native farming societies and imposed their hierarchical ruling structure, gods, and language on conquered people. Early sources describe these warriors as tall, blond or light-haired, with blue or gray eyes, and fierce fighters. The invaders gradually spread east into Asia and then moved south into northern India (Indo-European migrations, 2020). They later advanced into Persia and Syria and continued west into Anatolia. Additional waves of warriors from the steppes spread north and west into the Balkans and down into the Mesopotamian valley. Other tribes moved further west, spreading across Europe and south to Greece. These fighters and their culture strongly influenced several powerful early civilizations, including the Hittites, Kassites, and the Mitanni and Persian kingdoms of the ancient Near East. Descendants of these warrior people became the Greeks, Celts, Hindus, Persians, Romans, Scythians, French, Spanish, Slavs, Germans, and Scandinavians (Neill, 2009). Indo-European warriors' spoken language contributed to 11 language families, including most modern languages spoken in Europe today and what eventually became English.

It is unclear what prompted the Indo-European people to leave the steppes in droves. Possibly climate change leads to chronic drought, famine, competition for resources, and the collapse of urban centers (Indo-European migrations, 2020). Whatever the reasons, the Indo-European people were mobile and not content to stay in one place. They did not just move into a neighboring land and stop. Some settled, but many continued moving until eventually they had spread throughout the Near and Middle East and all of Europe. While the invaders lacked superior technology, they were skilled fighters with horses and chariots, which gave them an advantage in battle (Cochran & Harpending, 2009). They also herded cattle, sheep, and goats and engaged in dairying, which made them more mobile and competitive than farmers, especially in Europe. Cochran and Harpending (2009) have speculated that lactose tolerance was the critical element that helped the Indo-European people to leave the steppes. Consistent with this claim, the appearance and similarity of milk-related words across cultures support the special role of dairying among Indo-European people and their strong influence (Garnier, Sagart, & Sagot, 2017). Cochran and Harpending (2009) described the Indo-European invaders as aggressive "mobile pastoralists" who encroached on farms and villages by raiding their dairy animals and goods.

The invasion and spread of Indo-European people across the Near and Middle East and Europe significantly contributed to the spread of devoted male friendships. Their military culture promoted male initiation and devoted male friendships (Neill, 2009). Ancient Greek historian and mythologist Bernard Sergent (1986) has asserted that adolescent male initiation-to-adult status was universal among Indo-European cultures. Sergent linked adolescent male initiation to ancient hunter-gatherer practices to grow boys into men, sometimes through semen exchange. While no evidence supports semen exchange to grow men among early Indo-European cultures, young males in these cultures lived in sex-segregated male communities where they formed a close bond with an adult man whom they served as an attendant (Sergent, 1986). The adult warrior "made" the youth a man through extensive training in hunting, fighting, riding horses, and driving chariots. Sexual services may have been part of these mentor-mentee relationships, because we find this in later Celtic and Greek cultures. After the youths achieved manhood and the training period ended, the mentor-mentees remained lifelong friends.

The Hittites, Celtic people, Scythians, and Germanic Tribes

The Hittites became the first Indo-European descendants to establish an empire. Located in Anatolia (modern Turkey), the Hittites first appeared as a powerful force around the late third millennium BCE (Hardman, 1993). By the early second millennium BCE, the Hittites had established their capital of Hatussa and controlled most of Anatolia. They later expanded into Syria. By early 1600 BCE, the Hittites had conquered Babylonia, but then turned over control of the region to their Kassite allies (Neill, 2009). In 1274 BCE, the Hittites stopped the powerful Egyptian armies of Ramses III from entering Syria. By this time, centuries of war had severely weakened the Hittite Empire, and it began a slow decline. The Hittite Empire was eventually absorbed by the rising Assyrian Empire in the eighth century BCE.

The early Israelites drafted their Holiness Code in reaction to the secular laws and idolatrous customs of neighboring cultures, like the Hittites (Hardman, 1993). Two Hittite laws provide suggestive clues regarding how the culture viewed devoted male friendships. Law I #36 gave male slaves the right to offer a "bride-price to a free youth" and allow him to live in the household "as husband" without a loss of status (Hardman, 1993). This law appears to give male slaves the right to form a same-sex union with free male youths, much like a marriage, without the free youths losing their civil status—that is, becoming slaves. Boswell (1980) claimed that this law refers to same-sex marriage. Consistent with this view that the law permits a same-sex union, evidence points to a later translator incorrectly and misleadingly inserting the phrase "of his daughter" in the text to give the impression that male-female marriage was the law's focus (Hardman, 1993). Boswell has been heavily criticized for reading too much into ancient texts (e.g., Shaw, 1994; Young, 1994). Critics have claimed he is biased, although Boswell's critics often come across as ideologically biased themselves. Boswell aimed to reveal a history of acceptance of same-sex attraction, unions, and sexuality that had been denied by Christianity and scholars. The notion that same-sex attracted people were ever accepted or ever formed unions is unimaginable for many people. In this case, Boswell was not alone in his interpretation (e.g., Goetze, 1950/1974; Zimmern, 1922, and Riemenschneider, 1955, both cited in Greenberg, 1988, p.125n although Greenberg disagrees). Historian Paul Hardman (1993) also argued that the adulterated textual insertion "of his daughter" does not add up. It would be quite odd to grant a right to a female slave, even if she was also the daughter of the master of the household. Hittite law was written by men and for men; women were overseen by men and did not function independently. Siding with Boswell, Hardman further claimed that Law I #36 clarified a right for male slaves that was already practiced by male Hittite citizens—that is, the right to form a legal union like a marriage with another man. Hardman asserted that no earlier law explicitly mentioned a right for male citizens to form a union with another man because it was unnecessary; they already did this. Hittite men commonly purchased male slaves for sexual services. Hardman (1993) has read Law I #36 to suggest that men formed devoted relationships with male slaves and with males who were not slaves. Law I #36 protected the younger free man in the relationship from the loss of civil status. Importantly, Hittite law did not prohibit consensual same-sex relations (Hardman, 1993). If such activities were a concern for the Hittites, it is not apparent in their laws.

The Celtic people first appeared around the end of the second millennium BCE and became the first Indo-European group to wield power in Western Europe (Neill, 2009). Their reign peaked about the end of the first millennium BCE. At one time, their homeland encompassed much of Western Europe, including the British Isles and parts of Asia Minor. The Celtic people only reached the British Isles around 200 BCE. The northern Celtic tribes remained fairly out of reach from the Romans, who were never able to conquer Ireland, thus allowing Celtic traditions to survive longer in the British Isles (Greenberg, 1988). The Romans believed that the Celtic people came from what is now France and so referred to them as Gauls. Although spread over a large geographic area, the Celtic people shared a common language, military culture, and religious beliefs. They became more loosely associated as tribes spread further apart, some eventually separating entirely from the larger group.

The Celtic people had a militaristic culture and a reputation as fierce warriors. They ruled the farmers they conquered. Farmers paid their Celtic overlords for protection, creating the beginnings of a feudal system (Greenberg, 1988). By all accounts, Celtic warriors were terrifying in battle, sometimes charging their enemies naked (Neill, 2009). Diodorus Siculus (c. 90–c. 30 BCE), a Sicilian-born Greek historian, described Celtic warriors this way:

> Their aspect is terrifying … . They are very tall in stature, with rippling muscles under clear white skin. Their hair is blond, but not naturally so: they bleach it … washing it in lime and combing it back from their foreheads. They look like wood-demons, their hair thick and shaggy like a horse's mane. Some of them are clean-shaven, but others, especially

those of high rank, shave their cheeks but leave a moustache that covers the whole mouth. (Herm, 1975, p. 3)

The Celts terrified their neighbors by decapitating and displaying the heads of their enemies. According to Diodorus, "They cut off the heads of enemies slain in battle and attach them to the necks of their horses ... . And they nail up these firstfruits upon their houses. They embalm in cedar oil the heads of the most distinguished enemies ... and display them with pride to strangers" (Neill, 2009, p. 118). The Celts not only displayed their enemies' heads, they also used them as drinking vessels (Herm, 1975; Neill, 2009). Like warrior societies in contemporary Melanesia, the Celts believed that a man's power resided in his head. By possessing an enemy's head, they completely conquered him. By consuming his brains, they absorbed their enemy's spirit and power. Other Indo-European people, including the Scythians and Germanic tribes, also decapitated their enemies and drank from their skulls (Neill, 2009). Evidence of this practice lingers in the language these warrior people left behind. Across many Indo-European languages, the words for "cup" and "skull" are closely related.

As a military culture, the Celtic people idealized masculinity, dominance, power, and the phallus. The phallus represented virility and strength and served as the vehicle for the other life force: semen, which was also believed to be present in the brain (Neill, 2009). For the Celts, horns or antlers growing out of one's head (or helmet) symbolized virility and fertility, like a phallus. Celtic men spent most of their time together, and women stayed in the background and apart from men who were not relatives. According to several sources, around age 14, Celtic boys began their initiation into manhood. Boys lived in an all-male social group called the *fianna* (Greenberg, 1988; Neill, 2009). If the Celts were like the Germanic tribes, male youths bonded with an adult male warrior-mentor whom they served in all things until the young men proved themselves, received their animal name, and became full men. The warrior-mentor taught his attendant-novice how to hunt, fight, and rule over others like a man. Among Germanic tribes, and most likely the Celts, marriage and access to fertile women were restricted (Greenberg, 1988). Men's friends, companions, comrades, brothers, and lovers were youths or other masculine men.

Observers commented on Celtic warriors' love of male companionship. Diodorus, for example, stated:

the [Celtic] men are much keener on their own sex; they lie around on animal skins and enjoy themselves, with a lover on each side. The extraordinary thing is they haven't the smallest regard for their personal dignity or self-respect; they offer themselves to other men without the least compunction. Furthermore, this isn't looked down on, or regarded as in any way disgraceful. (Herm, 1975, p. 58)

Diodorus described a general atmosphere of male bonding, affection, and sexuality. However, Diodorus, a Greek, also portrayed Celtic men as shameless in their masculine role and morally inferior to the Greeks. He objected to adult men having sexual relationships with adult men. From Diodorus' perspective, the Celts were shameful because they did not love males in the correct way—the Greek way—where an adult man courts an adolescent boy (*paiderastia*). Diodorus added that despite the beauty of Celtic women, "The men will have nothing to do with them. They long instead for the embrace of one of their own sex" (Herm, 1975, p. 57). That was not quite true. The Celts had children! Many children. Again, Diodorus is making a moral criticism. Even so, Aristotle (384–322 BCE), writing in the fourth century BCE during the Classical Greek period, also noted that Celtic warriors favored sexual relationships with other men and publicly celebrated these relationships, which may refer to formal brotherhoods (Greenberg, 1988). While critics have argued that Aristotle, like Diodorus, is trying to elicit disgust of Celtic behavior, Sergent (1986) has dismissed these claims, citing corroborating reports from other contemporaneous observers.

Descendants of early Indo-European warriors, the Scythians first appeared around the ninth century BCE and survived until the fourth century CE (Neill, 2009). The Scythians were several loosely associated semi-nomadic, Iranian-speaking warrior groups who lived north of the Black Sea in what is now the Ukraine and Crimea and throughout the western Eurasian Steppe. Witnesses described them as tall, blond, green or blue-eyed, and fair-skinned. The Scythians wore trousers and fought on horseback. Like the Celts and early Germanic tribes, the Scythians collected their enemies' heads, deified the phallus and semen, and formed brotherhoods (Boswell, 1994; Neill, 2009). Greek historian Herodotus (c. 484–c. 425 BCE) traveled through Scythian territory in the fifth century BCE and met them or learned about them from traders. Herodotus claimed that Scythian warriors made solemn oaths to each other, suggestive of blood brotherhoods (Boswell, 1994). Centuries later, Syrian-born satirist and rhetorician, Lucian of Samosata (c. 125 CE–after 180 CE) also described Scythian warriors as forming blood brotherhoods (Boswell, 1994; Konstan, 1997). In his dialogue, *Toxaris or On Philia*, Lucian has a Greek, Mnesippus, and a Scythian, Toxaris, debate which of their people are better at friendship—by which they mean devoted male friendships. Lucian's source of information on Scythians, or whether he relied on any source, is unclear. During the second century CE, Greeks and barbarians, including Scythians, lived under Roman rule. While Lucian idealizes the Greeks in his dialogue, he presents a sympathetic portrayal of the Scythians. In the story, Toxaris declares that Scythians make better friends because, unlike the Greeks, they do not just talk about friendship; they practice it (Kuin, 2017). Toxaris states,

We consider appropriate to [devoted friendship] what you do in regard to marriage—wooing for a long time and doing everything similar so that we might not fail to obtain the friend, or be rejected. And when a friend has been preferred to all others, there are contracts for this and the most solemn oath, both to live together and to die, if necessary, for each other, which we do … . It is allowed to enter into such contracts at most three times, since a man who had many such relations would seem to us like a promiscuous and adulterous woman, and we would not consider that his devotion was as strong if it was divided among many affections. (Boswell, 1994, p. 94)

How much historical information we can draw from a fictional account is debatable. Boswell (1994) noted that the Greek word translated here as "friendship" is the same word used to describe Achilles and Patroclus' relationship, which the ancient world viewed as erotic. In the ancient world, the idea of being "just friends" in a modern platonic, somewhat distant manner, would have made no sense. According to Boswell (1994), in the ancient world, "no relationship was more emotional, more intimate, more intense than friendship" (p. 76).

The various Germanic tribes (also known as Teutons, Suebian, and Gauts) also descended from Indo-European warriors. The Germanic tribes emerged from the Battle-Axe culture of Scandinavia around the beginning of the Nordic Bronze Age (1700–500 BCE) (Neill, 2009). The Battle-Axe culture arose from the Yamnaya people, very early Indo-European tribes who arrived in the plains of Denmark and Sweden from the eastern Caucasus at the beginning of the third millennium BCE. The Battle-Axe culture was significant for introducing new burial customs in which the dead were buried singly or in pairs: men and women, and men and men. The burial of two similar-age men together is suggestive of blood brotherhood customs.

Like the Celts, the Germanic tribes encompassed several related groups who shared a similar language and culture (Neill, 2009). These tribes became more diverse and distinct over time as they spread out and lived apart. Around 1000 BCE, the Germanic tribes in Scandinavia began expanding south, confronting and pushing out the Celts and eventually reaching the edge of the Roman frontier. Like the Celts, the Germanic tribes ruled over their conquered people, who mainly worked farms. Like the Celts, the Germanic tribes revered masculinity, virility, and domination. They despised passivity and cowardice. Given their hyper-masculine values, it is easy to imagine the Celtic and Germanic tribes viewing peasant farmers and townspeople as weaklings and cowards who deserved to be ruled by dominant men (Neill, 2009). Celtic and Germanic male warrior gods also dominated and began to supersede the feminine or transsexual fertility goddesses who were frequently worshipped by early farmers.

In the patriarchal Germanic tribal culture, only the eldest son married and inherited all his father's land and wealth (Greenberg, 1988). Younger sons received nothing, so they had to leave home to seek their livelihood and fortune within the warrior community. Young males lived in all-male groups (*fianna*) or clubs (*Männerbünd*) where they trained with other boys and men (Greenberg, 1988). They wore animal skins, hunted, fought, robbed, and engaged in drug-induced frenzies. Germanic warriors remained bachelors for life, unless they left the *fianna* society for some reason: e.g., their older brother dies and they inherit the family estate. In most cases, Germanic warrior men spent most of their time with youths or other men.

Evidence suggests that male youths served as attendants to warrior men until they reached adulthood and became warriors themselves. Some warriors formed a special bond with their attendant and swore brotherhood for life. In the late fourth century CE, Roman historian, Ammianus Marcellinus (c. 330–c. 391/400), wrote about the Taifali, a Germanic tribe related to the Gauts (Goths) (Greenberg, 1988). Marcellinus probably had direct experience with this tribe when stationed as a soldier on the frontier or while living along the northeastern frontier (Neill, 2009). Marcellinus described how Taifali male youths engaged in close sexual relationships with adult warriors as part of their training and initiation into manhood (Greenberg, 1988). The sexual relationship continued until the youth achieved adult status by killing a bear or boar. Late Byzantine Greek scholar Procopius (c. 500–after 565) described a similar custom of male initiation among the Heruli, another Germanic tribe (Greenberg, 1988). Procopius traveled widely and accompanied a general in Emperor Justinian's wars in the sixth century, so he may have had direct contact with the Heruli. Procopius wrote that male youths were called "slaves" and served adult warriors, until the youths proved themselves in battle. Services included meeting the warrior's sexual needs.

Observations regarding the Hittites, Celtic people, Scythians, and Germanic tribes make clear that these military cultures idolized masculinity, strength, fighting skills, and male friendship and brotherhood. As conquerors, these tribes set themselves apart from farmers, merchants, and traders. As masculine men, they ruled others. Within these cultures, inheritance and marriage were restricted. Most men's opportunities for survival, fortune, and love lay with forming devoted relationships with other men, first as initiates and then as warriors. Among the Celtic people, Scythians, and Germanic tribes that spanned Europe and the Ukraine, young males joined a society of warriors where they learned to hunt and fight (Greenberg, 1988; Neill, 2009). They formed alliances and grew their reputations within the community. Male alliances were essential for survival. Successful men bonded with other men. Male initiates lived and trained with and served adult warrior-mentors, including providing menial and sexual services. In these cultures, sexually submitting to men with higher status presented no stigma for male youths. Some warrior-mentors and attendant-novices formed devoted friendships or brotherhoods that continued for life, while the young man, as a warrior himself, took on his own attendant. Adult warriors formalized their close bond with a sworn oath that observers described as like marriage, suggesting love, intimacy, and sexual expression. Witnesses reported that adult male warriors had sexual relationships with male youths and other warriors. While we do not know how prevalent sex was among devoted friends (most? some?) or other men, it really does not matter. Love, respect, devotion and performance of established roles defined the pair's relationship, not sex. For warrior-mentors and attendant-novices, adherence to dominant-subordinate roles was necessary in the eyes of the community. If social roles and respect were maintained, there was no stigma in mutual, reciprocal sexual affection between devoted adult male friends.

Ancient Greece

From Archaic Greece through the Classical and Hellenistic periods, we find many examples of devoted male friendships. We also find rare documentation of devoted female friendships. In *Friendship in the Classical World*, David Konstan (1997) describes the practice of friendship among the Greeks. Counter to traditionalists, Konstan argues that devoted male friendships in the Classical world were affectionate and emotional and not simply exchanges based on obligation. The words, *philos* and *philia*, for "friend" and "friendship", respectively, are used in complex ways in Greek texts to refer at times to devotion to someone, being loved, affection and intimate familiarity with someone, and friendship. *Philos* and *philia* are not devoid of sexuality. For the Greeks, intimacy and affection were erotic and important components of friendship.

The Greek word *xenos*, commonly translated as "foreigner" or "stranger", can also mean "guest-friend" (Konstan, 1997). The concept of guest-friend is common throughout the ancient world. A guest-friend from another land is treated with hospitality and respect as part of an understood reciprocal obligation that the host-friend will receive the same hospitality when visiting the guest-friend's land. Homer's *The Odyssey* provides several examples of guest-friends and their treatment in the ancient world. One celebrated reference to guest-friend *and* male friendship in *The Odyssey* is the story of Telemachus and Pisistratus. Telemachus is the son of Odysseus who has not come home from the Trojan War. Telemachus is now a young man, and suitors of his mother are on the verge of destroying the family estate; the suitors are treated as guests and are eating and drinking the family into poverty. While searching for his father, Telemachus visits Nestor, king of the Pylians and a senior commander during the war. Nestor welcomes Telemachus as a guest-friend and introduces him to his youngest son, Pisistratus. They are roughly the same age. Pisistratus is also unmarried but old enough to captain a boat. After a banquet, Nestor sends Telemachus to bed with Pisistratus. While two people sharing a bed is not unusual in ancient times, this pairing parallels Nestor going to bed with his wife. Telemachus and Pisistratus become good friends during his stay. Pisistratus even accompanies Telemachus to Sparta and during the trip the pair continue to share a bed.

In his survey of friendship in the Classical world, Konstan (1997) identified common characteristics of male friendships: They are voluntary, mutually beneficial, devoted, loyal, and affectionate. Gift-exchange is common but not the basis of male friendship. Affection and loyalty are critical; friends like each other and come to each other's aid. In *Memorabilia*, Greek philosopher Xenophon (c. 431–354 BCE) has Socrates, the good citizen, reproach a group for not appreciating and valuing their friends. Socrates advises his audience to be the friend they expect in others, adding that those who do not help their friends when needed deserve to lose them. Importantly, Konstan (1997) noted that Classical world friendships were not structured around social equality and self-disclosure, unlike friendships today. Disclosing one's personal feelings or secrets to create a sense of shared intimacy was not a value in the Classical world.

In this section, I explore the friendship between mythic heroes Achilles and Patroclus, devoted female friendships, male initiation rituals in military cultures, and educational *paiderastia* in Classical Athens.

Achilles and Patroclus in Archaic Greece

There is no better example of male friendship in the Classical Greek world than Achilles and Patroclus. Ancient writers frequently presented Achilles and Patroclus as having a friendship that was erotic, passionate, and likely sexual (Sergent, 1986). The poet Theocritus (c. third century BCE), the poet Bion of Smyrna (early second/late first century BCE), orator and historian Dio Chrysostom (c. 40–c. 115 CE), and biographer and essayist Plutarch (c. 46–c. 120 CE) all celebrated Achilles and Patroclus as ideal friends (Konstan, 1997). In the *Symposium*, Plato (c. 428/427 or 424/423–c. 348/347 BCE) describes Achilles and Patroclus's friendship as noble (Neill, 2009). However, writers could never quite agree on whether Achilles, a semi-divine masculine warrior, was the older penetrating lover (*erastēs*) of Patroclus or the younger receptive beloved (*erōmenos*). The pair were cousins and close in age. Some ancient texts made Patroclus slightly older and, thus, the active penetrating partner, while others portrayed Patroclus as Achilles' squire, a subservient role that is incongruent with being older (Konstan, 1997). These issues mattered to the Greeks because friendship typically involved symmetrical roles, whereas love relationships (*erōs*) involved complementary roles and adhering to social convention was important. Achilles and Patroclus' relationship had elements of both. Despite uncertainty about their roles, the Classical world viewed Achilles and Patroclus as exemplars of masculine male friendship.

The story of Achilles and Patroclus is recounted in Homer's *The Iliad*, which is subtitled *The Story of Achilles* in W. H. D. Rouse's translation.

Before taking its current written form in the eighth century BCE, *The Iliad* had a long oral history as a sung poem. *The Iliad* tells the epic story of the Trojan War set in the Mycenaean Age, between the thirteenth and twelfth centuries BCE. Achilles is central to the battle and the story, and Patroclus' death marks the major turning point in the war. Achilles is the son of Peleus, king of the Myrmidons, a Thessalonian tribe in northeastern Greece. His mother, Thetis, is a sea nymph and immortal, making Achilles semi-divine. Achilles is described as tall, strong, fast, and handsome. He is raised in Phthia with his cousin Patroclus, and the two become close friends. Meanwhile, the beautiful Helen, wife of King Menelaus of Sparta, is kidnapped by Paris, a prince of Troy, and taken to Troy. Menelaus and his brother, Agamemnon, king of Mycenae, lead an army of Greek tribes to punish Troy and rescue Helen. The Greek armies' war with Troy in Anatolia lasts ten years. Well into the war, Agamemnon receives a prophecy that the battle at Troy can only be won with Achilles fighting on their side. Odysseus visits Achilles and convinces him to join the war. At 15, Achilles leads the Myrmidons to Troy in 50 ships with Patroclus at his side. The two friends share a tent in the camp. Achilles quickly proves himself a great warrior by helping the Greeks kill countless Trojans and capture 12 cities.

In the tenth year of the war, Agamemnon and Achilles quarrel over the spoils of war. The king demands that Achilles give him his captured slave girl, Briseis. Achilles is furious and humiliated by the confiscation of his property commemorating his success in battle and refuses to fight any longer. The Greeks begin losing battles. Later, as the Trojans come dangerously close to the Greek camps, Patroclus pleads with Achilles to let him wear his armor and lead the Myrmidons into battle. Patroclus believes the ruse will terrify the Trojans who will think that Achilles has rejoined the fight. The trick may also inspire the Greeks to fight harder. Reluctantly, Achilles agrees. He prays to the gods that only he and Patroclus will survive the war and capture Troy—everyone else should die: "If only not one single Trojan could be left alive, and not one Achaean, but you and I might be left, that we alone might tear off the sacred diadem of Troy!" (Homer, *Iliad*, XVI, 189).

At first, Patroclus is successful. Eventually, Hector, the Trojan champion, engages and fatally wounds Patroclus, thinking he is Achilles. Patroclus dies on the battlefield wearing Achilles' armor, like a second skin. The Trojans abuse Patroclus' body to demoralize the Greeks. When Achilles learns of Patroclus' death, he is devastated: "Sorrow fell on Achilles like a cloud. He swept up the dust with both hands, and poured it over his head and smirched his handsome face, till the black dirt stained his fragrant tunic. He tore his hair and fell flat in the dust" (Homer, *Iliad*, XVIII, 216). A friend holds Achilles hands fearing that in his grief he might take his own life. Thetis appears and tells Achilles not to grieve because he will be victorious and legendary. Achilles responds, "But what good do I get of all that now, if my dear friend Patroclus is dead? I cared more for him than all my companions, as much as for my own life. He is lost!" (Homer, *Iliad*, XVIII, 217). Achilles wishes aloud that he had never been born. He lies with and embraces Patroclus' dead body for several days.

When Achilles finally returns to battle, he kills Hector and desecrates his body. Without their champion, Troy's destruction is certain. Yet Achilles pauses to hold a funeral for Patroclus. That night the spirit of Patroclus visits Achilles and asks him to bury their bones together so they will never be apart: "Do not lay my bones apart from yours, Achilles, but with them ... . Then let one urn cover my bones and yours" (Homer, *Iliad*, XXIII, p. 267). Achilles designs a grave for both himself and Patroclus, knowing he will not survive the final battle. Thetis again visits Achilles and finds him still mourning Patroclus. She suggests that being with a woman might provide some comfort, but Achilles rejects that idea. He cannot be comforted. *The Iliad* ends before we learn Achilles' fate. Other texts describe Achilles being killed by Paris with an arrow to his heel, his only vulnerable spot (Konstan, 1997; Neill, 2009). In the *Odyssey*, which takes place after the Trojan war, the ghost of Agamemnon tells the ghost of Achilles that the Greeks built a memorial to him after his death on the battlefield and their ashes were placed together in a single urn.

Achilles and Patroclus' friendship is legendary. Homer structured *The Iliad* around their relationship. Their passion and intimacy to the exclusion of others is unmistakable. Achilles and Patroclus are a couple, and ancient audiences would have viewed them that way (Konstan, 1997; Neill, 2009). The pair's passionate devotion to each other also inspired ancient audiences. Classical Greek writers pointed to Achilles and Patroclus as a model for others. Although the legend of Achilles and Patroclus tells us little about how ordinary men structured friendships in Ancient and Classical Greece, the popularity of the pair suggests that devoted male friendships were admired. The celebration of Achilles and Patroclus' friendship in the Classical world does not mean that men's friendships were necessarily sexual. However, if they were sexual, there is little indication that this would have been viewed with disgust or disapproval. Indeed, Classical writers enjoyed musing over whether Achilles was the top or bottom in his relationship with Patroclus.

Konstan (1997) argued that the passionate story of Achilles and Patroclus's friendship mattered so much to Classical world audiences because their bond reflected an older tradition of devoted friendship between pairs of warriors. Achilles and Patroclus were not the only warrior friends in the Classical world. Seventh century BCE Thessalonian hero, Cleomachus, brought his soldier-lover to fight with him at his side against the Eretrians in the Lelantine War (Neill, 2009). Cleomachus led the Chalcidian army to victory but died in the battle, inspiring the Chalcidians to honor him and his companion. Third- century BCE poet, Theocritus, in the *Idylls* tells the story of Diocles of Athens who died in a fifth-century BCE battle near Megara protecting his beloved, a fellow warrior (Neill, 2009). Theocritus used this story to explain the traditional Festival of Diocleia, in which young men kiss each other for a prize.

Sappho and Women Who Love Women

Sappho's poetry represents the first documentation of romantic love between women in the world (Greenberg, 1988). During her lifetime, there is no evidence of disapproval or concern about the virtue of love between women. Since the sixth century BCE, Sappho's work was enormously popular and revered. At least seven biographies about her existed in late antiquity (Brooten, 1996). Plato called her the "Tenth Muse" (Neill, 2009). Socrates (c. 470–399 BCE) described her soul and verse as beautiful. Greek philosopher and historian Strabo (c. 64 BCE–24 CE) called her poems "miraculous". Seven hundred years after her death, Greek physician and philosopher Galen (129–c. 200/216) compared Sappho to Homer. Sappho produced over 12,000 verses in her lifetime, yet only about 600 fragments exist today, thanks to systematic efforts by zealous Christians to completely destroy her work, including a Vatican-led purge by Pope Gregory VII in 1073 (Brooten, 1996).

Sappho was born around 630 BCE (died c. 570 BCE) to an aristocratic family on the Aeolian island of Lesbos near Anatolia (Neill, 2009). She married an older man named Cercylas and had a daughter named Cleis (Brooton, 1996). At the time, Greek women were taught to read and write (Horner, 1938). Sappho openly voiced her anti-government political views and was briefly exiled twice as a result. After her second exile, now a widow and still a young mother, Sappho returned to her hometown of Mytilene and founded a school for girls (*thiasoi*). Sappho served as headmistress of the school. Similar schools soon spread across other Greek islands. The *thiasoi* functioned as a school and temple where girls learned to dance, sing, and play music, as well as worship their deities. Young girls in the *thiasoi* had crushes on and possibly sexual relationships with same-age girls and with the adult headmistress. The *thiasoi* held formal sisterhood ceremonies, representing a union between two girls, like marriage. However, a sisterhood bond would not have prevented later marriage to a man. During Sappho's lifetime, Spartan lyric poet Alcman (dates unknown) wrote a poem-song for a sisterhood ceremony between Agido and Hagesichora, two girls in the *thiasoi* who were in love (Neill, 2009). The chorus, representing the pair, sings that no other girl will tempt them to love another. The song proclaims that not even the headmistress of the *thiasoi* can break up Agido and Hagesichora's sisterhood: "Nor will you go to Aenesimbrota and say, if only Astaphis were mine, if only Philylla were to look my way and Damareta and lovely Ianthemis; no, Hagesichora guards me" (Neill, 2009, p. 162).

Sappho herself writes cheekily of her love of a girl in *Prayer to Aphrodite*:
Who is it this time, Sappho? (...)
if she flees from you now, she'll return;
and if she refuses gifts, later she'll bring them;
and if she doesn't want love, eventually she will—
even if she isn't completely convinced. (Horner, 1978b, pp. 67–68)

In the poem, *Watching You with a Man*, Sappho comments on her feelings for a young girl sitting next to the man she will marry:

I envy him as if he's one of the gods,
that man who is close beside you
and listens to the sweet sound
of your voice (...).
My tongue sticks to my throat;
a hot fire runs under my skin;
my vision is blurred and I can hear
nothing
But a rushing sound in my ears.
My whole body trembles and I blanch,
like dead grass. I myself am but one step
from death.
But life goes on. (Horner, 1978b, pp. 70–71).

In the first stanza of a poem to Anactoria, who has married and left Lesbos with her soldier husband, Sappho contrasts her love of Anactoria with her husband's: "Some think that the most beautiful thing in the world is cavalry, others think it to be infantry, while still others say it is a fleet of fast ships. But I say it's the one you love" (Horner, 1978b, p. 71). Sappho suggests that her love of Anactoria is more profound and personal than her husband's.

Despite similarities, there is no evidence that Greek women's devoted friendships in the seventh and sixth centuries BCE were modeled after male relationships. While there is evidence of both same-age and age-disparate friendships, female friendships did not mimic male initiation rituals or Athenian *paiderastia* ("the love of boys") (Canatrella, 1992; Neill, 2009). Too little evidence exists to discern the roles of women in devoted female friendships.

The *thiasoi* were short-lived. The codification of laws in Athens that began in the seventh century BCE spread throughout Greece and brought with it a resurgence of conservative values. Greek women became increasingly confined to the home and secluded from men. In Sparta and other Dorian islands, women retained greater freedoms for longer but, by the fourth century BCE, the *thiasoi* had disappeared. Most women no longer received an education (Cantarella, 1992). Upper-class women were an exception. Consequently, women lost their voice to describe their relationships. Women were viewed largely as vehicles that made babies.

Religious scholar, Bernadette Brooten (1996) claimed that the Classical world of Greece and the Roman Empire knew about women who loved women and even had a concept of erotic/sexual orientation. However, counter to Boswell, Brooten (1996) concluded that Greek and Roman writers viewed love between women with disapproval. As seen through the male model of sexuality based on masculinity and the phallus, ancient writers engaged in bizarre contortions to explain love between women. Classical scholar Kenneth Dover (1989) and ancient legal scholar Eva Cantarella (1992) also concluded that Greek and Roman writers perceived women who love women as peculiar, disgusting, and somewhat threatening, yet titillating. In the Classical world, women who loved women may have lived with some fear of discovery, disapproval, and reprisal by family members (Cantarella, 1992). Even so, Brooten (1996) cited post–Classical age sources from geographically widespread urban areas that refer to sisterhood unions or marriages, suggesting some level of recognition and tolerance. Both Greek astrologer Ptolemy in Egypt (c. 100–c. 170 CE) and Greek Christian Clement of Alexandria (c. 150–c. 215 CE), who were widely traveled, referred to a custom of women unions or marriages in surrounding cultures.

Whether for titillation, comedy, or ridicule, novelists also depicted women loving women. In the fifth of his *Dialogues of Courtesans*, Lucian, writing in the second century CE, tells the story of two courtesans, Clonarium and Leaena, who share secrets with each other at a banquet (Cantarella, 1992). Clonarium has heard that Leaena is involved in a loving sexual relationship with Megilla, a rich woman from Lesbos, who loves Leaena "like a man". Leaena admits this and expresses shame over her behavior. Clonarium wants to know more about Megilla, whom Leaena describes as masculine. She says Megilla hired her as a musician for a party held at her home. Leaena stayed late after the event and agreed to spend the night at Megilla's house. Megilla and a party guest, Demonassa of Corinth, began kissing each other. They then tried to seduce Leaena. Megilla removed her wig to reveal a shaved head similar to a male athlete. Megilla described herself as like a man, but not physically. She does not have a penis, but she has something better—a dildo! Megilla said her mind and sexual desires are like those of men. Then Megilla demonstrated her sexual skills with Leaena. The story is clearly a man's version of women's relationships with forced stereotypes. While the story is fiction and Lucian has designed it to excite and slightly shock its readers, the subject matter suggests that second-century Roman and Greek readers were aware that some women love women.

Well-known Syrian novelist, Iamblichus (c. 245–c. 325), wrote a racy romance story, *Babyloniaka*, that included a woman-loving-woman subplot (Brooten, 1996). The novel, now lost, remained popular well into the

Byzantine period. A tenth-century patriarch, Photios, described the plot in a separate text. In the story, Berenice, the daughter of the king of Egypt, is in love with "the beautiful Mesopotamia", who was kidnapped by the cruel Babylonian king, Garmos (Boswell, 1980). The king plans to kill her. Berenice's female servant, Zobaras, "having drunk from the spring of love and seized with passion for Mesopotamia", through a series of improbable events, manages to rescue her (Boswell, 1980, p. 84). Mesopotamia returns to Berenice, who is now the queen of Egypt following her father's death. Berenice and Mesopotamia marry, which ignites a war with Garmos.

Despite evidence for devoted female friendships, particularly in the North Aegean Islands and Dorian Sparta on the mainland, the prevalence of such friendships is unknown. Few women could write, and few wrote about their relationships. There are references to women-loving-women as plot devices in novels, but these works, written by men, were intended to entertain, not document women's relationships. Nevertheless, for at least several centuries in ancient Greece, particularly in the North Aegean and Doric Sparta, same-age girls, as well as women and girls, formed devoted friendships. These friendships were loving, often compared to marriage, and likely sexual. We do not know to what extent these friendships provided social benefits to women because this information is missing. Sisterhood friendships did not circumvent marriage to a man, and such friendships may have continued after marriage, like male friendships (Brooten, 1996). Given the increasing seclusion of Greek women in the Classical world, devoted female friendships could have continued unabated. From the Classical period on, references to women's loving friendships by men conveyed modest disapproval, mild disgust, and sexual excitement. The depiction of women-loving-women in novels and satire suggests that Greek and Roman readers understood that such relationships existed and were not so shocked or disgusted that they stopped reading.

Early Dorian Greeks and Military Culture

By 1600 BCE, Indo-European tribes had reached mainland Greece and begun to spread across the islands, mixing with the indigenous people. These warrior invaders brought with them chariot warfare, new gods and religious beliefs, and a language that became the foundation for modern Greek. The Minoan Crete culture soon became a superpower and dominated the Aegean and early Greek people for over a thousand years. In 1450 BCE, the volcano on Thera (or Thira, now called Santorini) erupted, burying the Minoan colony of Akrotiri and devastating coastal Crete miles away. The Minoan civilization did not recover. The mainland Mycenaean Greeks emerged as the major power in the region for the next 400 years. The Mycenaeans revived Minoan trade routes, especially with the Hittites, and reestablished a palace at Knossos on Crete. However, repeated invasions by the mysterious "Sea Peoples" eventually left Aegean cities in ruins, disrupted trading routes, and ultimately led to the collapse of Mycenaea. Around the twelfth and eleventh centuries BCE, Dorian Greeks from the northern edge of the Mycenaean Empire began moving into depopulated Peloponnesian lands, including Crete in the far south. One main Dorian city was Sparta in Laconia. Militaristic Dorian culture flourished alongside and initially held in check the growing urbane Ionian culture of Athens. However, by the time Greek writers described Dorian culture, it was already in decline, and many customs had changed.

Most of what we know about Dorian culture comes from Greek historian Ephorus (c. 400–330 BCE), writing in the fourth century BCE (Neill, 2009). Much of Ephorus' work has been lost, though heavily referenced by other ancient historians. Citing Ephorus, Strabo in the first century CE described an older Cretan custom in which an armed warrior mock-abducts a youth from his home (with the complicity of friends), and the two live in the wild alone for two months. The warrior teaches the youth to hunt and fight. The youth serves the warrior and attends to his needs, including sexually submitting to him. Strabo stated,

> [The Cretans] have a peculiar custom in regard to love affairs, for they win the objects of their love, not by persuasion, but by capture. The lover tells the friends of the boy three or four days beforehand that he is going to make the capture … . And when they meet, if the abductor is the boy's equal or superior in rank or other respects, the friends pursue him and lay hold of him, though only in a very gentle way, thus satisfying the custom. And after that they cheerfully turn the boy over to him to lead away. If, however, the abductor is unworthy, they take the boy away from him. (Neill, 2009, pp. 153–154)

At the end of the initiation period, the Doric Cretan warrior presents the youth with gifts, including armor and a drinking cup (Neill, 2009). The drinking cup symbolized his entry into adult male society, since women and children were not allowed to drink wine. After a sacrifice is made by the youth, he publicly declares that his abduction and relationship with the adult warrior were consensual (and not forced). The young male moves into the men's house. The youth's relationship with his warrior-mentor and his training continues until he marries around the age of 30. All men were expected to marry and produce children. Neill (2009) noted the striking resemblance between Cretan warrior-attendant male initiation customs and male initiation ("boy wives") among Azande warriors of North Central Africa.

Male youth abduction was not universal on Crete. Some Cretan cities banned the practice, and it is not difficult to imagine how this custom could go wrong. Doric Sparta also did not practice male youth abduction, although they had a highly militaristic culture that included adult warrior-mentors pairing with youth attendant-novices until marriage at 30 (Neill, 2009). Some sources have referred to the Spartan warrior's relationship with a young attendant as a "breathing-in" or "inspiring", which referred to the transfer of virtue and manhood to the youth (Neill, 2009). The intake of adult male breath or spirit to grow Spartan boys into men is reminiscent of semen exchange customs among some Melanesian hunter-gatherer societies.

In ancient Sparta, men lived apart from women and children. Around age seven, boys moved into the men's house and began training as warriors. Initially, boys lived in troops with other same-age boys, supervised by an older youth who was supervised by an adult warrior. Dover (1989) has suggested that Spartan boys developed strong, lifelong peer friendships in these same-age troops. Spartan boys also bonded with an adult warrior. According to Plutarch, at age 12, a Spartan boy was entrusted to an adult warrior with whom he lived and served until he married (Neill, 2009). How this pairing occurred is unclear. The youth's training included learning to hunt and fight, tending to the warrior's armor and weapons, and maintaining the warrior's comfort and household. The warrior's comfort included his sexual needs. Attendant-novice boys also served as cupbearers to warrior-mentors during their meals, where men discussed military strategy, politics, history, and ethics, and boys listened. During this period, the warrior and attendant developed a close emotional bond. While Spartan males became adults at 20, they continued their role as attendants to their warrior-mentor for another decade. Spartan warrior-friends shared quarters for nearly 20 years, even though most warriors were married and had children of their own. According to Roman historian Aelianus (c. 175–c. 235 CE), Spartan warriors who refused to take an attendant-novice faced punishment (Neill, 2009). As well, boys who did not accept a warrior-mentor, or chose a mentor of less noble status, were punished. It is unclear who decided that these customs had been violated or the nature of the punishments.

Plutarch wrote that "this type of love" (adult warrior-mentor and youth attendant-novice) was so admired by the Doric Spartans that even "the young girls had love relations with beautiful and good women" and "the most respectable women became infatuated with girls" (Plutarch, *Life of Lycurgus*, 18.4, in Neill, 2009, p. 160). Young Spartan girls also lived with troops of same-age girls supervised by a headmistress. Girls trained in singing and dancing, as well as fighting. Special sanctuaries for girls and women existed at Sparta, Limnai between Laconia and Messenia, and at Brauron near Athens. No evidence exists that young girls participated in coming-of-age initiations at these sanctuaries. Little is known about mentor-mentee friendships between adult women and youths, largely because women's activities were of no interest to learned men in the ancient world. While women in ancient Dorian cultures had greater freedom than in other

Greek cultures, men and women had very different statuses and privileges. Training for boys and girls served different purposes. Male youth initiation and mentoring in Dorian cultures aimed to develop virtuous men who led and defended the community, while female youth training aimed to cultivate virtuous wives and mothers (Neill, 2009).

Spartan military efficiency and success were admired throughout the ancient world. Observers credited Spartan warriors' fierceness in battle to their desire to protect their devoted friends and their own honor. Plutarch told the story of a Spartan who, when fatally wounded in battle, pleads for his adversary to spear him through the chest so his friend will not find him with a spear in the back—as if running away (Vanggaard, 1972). Aelianus related a similar story about a warrior in Crete (Vanggaard, 1972). To emphasize the point, Aelianus reported that before going to battle, Spartans offered sacrifices to Eros, the god of love, rather than to Ares, the god of war. Without mentioning the Spartans by name, Plato praised the idea of warrior-friends-lovers in battle in the *Symposium*:

> Let me then say that a man in love, should he be detected in some shameful act or in a cowardly submission to shameful treatment at another's hands, would not feel half so much distress at anyone observing it, whether father or comrade or anyone in the world, as when his beloved did … . And such men as these, when fighting side by side, one might almost consider able to make even a little band victorious over all the world. For a man in love would surely choose to have all the rest of the host rather than his favorite see him forsaking his station or flinging away his arms. Sooner than this, he would prefer to die many deaths. (Plato, *Symposium*, 178c, 178d)

Over three centuries (669–371 BCE), the Spartans were defeated only once—by another army of warrior-friends/lovers, the Sacred Band of Thebes. Along with Sparta and Athens, Thebes in Boeotia on the Greek mainland was a major military power in the region. The Sacred Band, composed of 150 pairs of warriors, were so successful in battle that they were thought to be invincible. However, in 338 BCE, Philip of Macedonia (382–336 BCE) famously defeated the Sacred Band, to the last man, near Chaeronea. Philip was so deeply moved by the men's valor that he built a monument to them.

In sum, the custom of male youth initiation and warrior bonding among Dorian Greeks persisted for several centuries. From an early age, male youths lived exclusively with other boys and men until they reached the age of marriage at 30. Male youths received an education and military training and learned civil and sexual servitude. Participation in male initiation/training was mandatory, as was marriage and producing children. Yet for most of men's lives, their primary relationships were with boys and men. Male youths formed strong peer friendships and lifelong devoted friendships with their warrior-mentor. The social advantages of bonding with an older, higher status man in this culture are obvious. Allies are needed, not just on the battlefield, but also within the male social community in order to gain status, develop and expand social networks, gain leadership roles, and acquire access to valued resources, including a high quality female reproductive partner and resources for one's family.

Not all men in Dorian cultures were warriors. Some men were merchants, tradesmen, craftsmen, farmers, and slaves. Non-noble men and slaves would not have participated in male initiation rituals or military training. We do not know how the values and customs of elite men in Dorian culture influenced the lower classes. Lower-class men may not have been prohibited from forming devoted male friendships, but their social environment was not structured around devoted male friendships. Even so, merchants, tradesmen, craftsmen, and farmers also lived and functioned in a sex-segregated society. Dorian men and women's primary social contacts and emotional relationships were mainly with same-sex others.

Young Dorian girls of noble birth participated in training with other girls and developed close emotional and sexual relationships with other girls or with the headmistress, an adult woman, within all-female schools. Devoted female friendships may have continued after marriage, like men's friendships. Close devoted friendships with peers and older women were likely important sources of social support and help with childcare. Strong female alliances and devoted friendships may have eased the burden of boring domestic tasks and offered some protection against male aggression.

Adult-Youth Love (Pederasty) and Friendship in Classical Athens

The rise of the Athenian merchant class in the seventh century BCE created class tensions and eventually led to 50 years of tyrannical rule by Peisistratus and his family in the sixth century BCE. During the Peisistradid, the upper classes lost much of their political power and so turned their attention to cultural pursuits, such as poetry, plays, and symposia, laying the foundation for the Classical Age (Konstan, 1997). With the fall of the tyrants, urbane Athens adopted a democratic system of government in the fifth century BCE that continued even after Philip of Macedon conquered Athens. Athenian democracy required all male citizens to participate in government. All (male) citizens had the opportunity to vote on new laws. From the fifth century BCE on, Athens dominated Greece culturally and politically.

As Athenian democracy emerged, writers began to refer to a complicated form of age-structured adult male relationships with youth among the upper classes called *paiderastia* or pederasty: literally, "the love of boys" (Dover, 1989). Athenian pederasty involved a tutoring relationship between a noble adult man (30 and older) and an adolescent boy of good birth no younger than 14. If the pair bonded, the relationship continued until the youth had a full beard, around the age of 22 (Greenberg, 1988; Hardman, 1993). The adult mentor provided a formal education to the young boy and conveyed to him his knowledge and experience. This period of tutelage aimed to prepare the youth for introduction into elite Athenian male society and his role as a citizen. Male youth received tutoring in reading, writing, politics, philosophy, civil values, the pleasures of life, and the values of self-control and moderation. Like Dorian warrior-attendant relationships, Athenian adult-youth relationships also involved sexual activity, mostly intercrural sex (between the thighs), rather than anal sex. Athenian pederasty may be a variation of an older military warrior-attendant custom that evolved with Athenian urbane culture and the establishment of a paid military. Unlike warrior relationships, Athenian pederasty involved a period of intense romantic courting of the youth by the adult man. The adult *erastēs* ("lover") expressed a romantic obsessive love for the beautiful young boy that included giving gifts, writing love poems, and stalking. The younger *erōmenos* ("loved one" or "beloved") supposedly received this attention impassively. The *erōmenos* youth selected an *erastēs*, accepted his gifts, received an education and social introductions, and submitted sexually to his lover. Some texts have described the *erōmenos* youth as not in love with the *erastēs* and not experiencing sexual pleasure during their encounters, although that seems implausible. The age and status differences in the relationship mirrored the pair's sexual roles: The adult male took the active penetrating (masculine) role (between the thighs), and the male youth had the passive receptive (non-masculine) role.

The complicated rules of etiquette around Athenian pederasty helped to protect the noble youth's virtue and honor (Neill, 2009). For adult Greek men, acceptable sexual objects included male youths, girls, and women. However, for a youth of good birth, sexual submission to an adult man ran several risks for the soon-to-be adult citizen. Even as an adolescent, sexual submission to a man of lesser social status diminished the youth's status and brought dishonor. Sexual submission also risked looking like prostitution by the youth accepting gifts. Lastly, the youth risked appearing unmanly, and even womanly, if he enjoyed or preferred the sexually submissive role, especially anal penetration. The relationship had to be carefully orchestrated for the youth not to lose status in the eyes of the community. Despite these potential problems, Plato presented Athenian pederasty as the highest form of love (Neill, 2009). In Plato's *Symposium*, from the fifth century BCE, Pausanias describes two kinds of love: heavenly love and common or earthly love. Heavenly love is spiritual, moral, profound, and only possible between men and male youths. Sexual pleasure, while obviously present, is not the objective. For earthly love, sexual pleasure is the goal, whether with a boy, girl, or woman. Only earthly love was possible in marriage. Plato also saw refined Athenian pederasty as superior to the coarser custom of indiscriminate adult man-adolescent youth devoted friendships common in Elis and

Boeotia (Neill, 2009). Writing a few years later, Xenophon made the same point, complaining that in Boeotia, men and boys "were living together like married couples" (Vanggaard, 1972, p. 27). In his own *Symposium*, Xenophon commented that male youths in pederastic relationships do not enjoy sex, unlike girls and women. While misrepresenting the experience of sexual pleasure, Xenophon argued against Plato's ideal of the love of male youths and advocated for the love of women (in marriage).

Neither Plato nor Xenophon were journalists. They did not attempt to describe real life in Athens. As philosophers, Plato and Xenophon offered their ideal ways of life for the benefit of the less informed and uninitiated. They aimed to persuade their audiences. While Plato presented Athenian pederasty as a superior love that followed strict rules of honor, his argument implies that this was not how same-sex friendships were practiced. If his ideal for adult-youth love was the norm in Athens, there would have been nothing to say. Plato is likely responding to a cultural climate in which adult-youth loving relationships (and perhaps adult male friendships) were not following the "rules", which raised ethical and moral concerns and necessitated a defense. Plato argued that the love of male youths is superior, when it conforms to certain rules. In contrast, Xenophon objected to the celebration of love of male youths to the exclusion of female love. He voiced a minority opinion about male love, while making the point that the practice of male youth love is not as noble as Plato presents. Xenophon also acknowledged the reality that some men love women and their wives.

Evidence suggests that Athenian pederasty, while common, differed from both Plato and Xenophon's models. In the sixth century BCE, chief magistrate of Athens, Solon (c. 630–c. 560 BCE) enacted a law forbidding classes of men from seducing free male youths at the *gymnasia* (Cantarella, 1992; Neill, 2009). The *gymnasia* were popular places for men to exercise, socialize, and admire beautiful youths. Some scholars have interpreted Solon's law to mean that Athenians banned or at least disapproved of adult-youth love. Not so. Solon himself had several young male lovers (Neill, 2009). The law prevented lower class, less noble men (for example, slaves) from seducing and exploiting free youths, which would damage their reputation and status as a citizen (Cantarella, 1992). Noble male citizens remained unencumbered in their ability to seduce free male youths at the *gymnasia*. Solon's law suggests that the Athenian model of upper-class men courting male youths was being mimicked by lower-class men and had become a problem. Elite men may have had to compete with lower-class men for a youth's affection, or young men may have been misled by disingenuous suitors. Solon's law implies that male youths were frequently pursued for less noble ends, like sexual gratification, rather than mentoring.

Evidence also suggests that Athenian male youths formed close friendships with same-age peers, counter to the age-disparate pederastic model. Xenophon made several references to same-age devoted male friendships (Neill, 2009). Harmodius and Aristogeiton, who aided the end of the Peisistradid tyranny in late sixth century BCE, were close in age and celebrated as a couple. The pair assassinated Hipparchus but were unsuccessful in killing his brother, Hippias, the real tyrant of Athens (Neill, 2009). Hippias immediately executed Harmodius but tortured Aristogeiton to death in hopes he would reveal his co-conspirators. Hippias' extreme reaction to the assassination attempt led to greater public discontent and his eventual removal.

Numerous images on vases of same-age male youths in erotic activity also suggest that male sexual partners could be similar in age. In addition, contrary to Athenian pederasty, some devoted friendships continued long after the youth reached manhood around age 22. In the *Symposium* where Plato makes his case for the love of male youths, an adult Alcibiades voices his continued love for Socrates, his older mentor (Neill, 2009). While Plato may be mocking Alcibiades and idealizing Socrates (executed for "corrupting" youth), other evidence suggests this was not the case. In the *Protagoras*, Plato, describing a banquet that occurred several years before events in the *Symposium*, begins with Socrates being questioned about his pursuit of the handsome Alcibiades, who, while young, already has facial hair (Plato, *Protagoras*, 309a). Further, in the *Protagoras*, Pausanias and Agathon appear as long-time companions. They share a couch to signify their closeness (Plato, *Protagoras*, 315e). In the *Symposium*, set years later, Agathon, now roughly 30 years old, is still very intimate with Pausanias, who is in his fifties. In real life, their relationship continued until Agathon's death in his late forties. Plato implies that Pausanias and Agathon are among the few who have found their ideal love match (Plato, *Symposium*, 193b). Plato also mentions two other devoted friends who remained together long after the beloved had reached manhood. In the *Parmenides*, Greek philosopher Zeno of Elea (c. 495–c. 430 BCE) visits Athens with fellow philosopher and long-time companion, Parmenides (late 6th or early 5th century BCE). Parmenides, the *erastēs*, is around 65 years old, while Zeno is almost 40 (Neill, 2009). In the *Politics*, Aristotle noted two devoted friends who lived together most of their lives and were buried together: Philolaus, a Theban legislator, and Diocles, an Olympic athlete (Neill, 2009). Clearly, Athenian Greek male friendships did not always follow the pederastic model.

Classical Greek philosophers may have been the first to opine on the nature, structure, and value of friendship. Although they often spoke in general terms, philosophers described friendship as a relationship between noble men. Philosophers were uninterested in friendships among women or among lower-class men or slaves. Pythagoras of Samos (c. 570–c. 495 BCE), an Ionian Greek mathematician and mystic, was one of the first philosophers to comment on friendship (Konstan, 1997). In the sixth century BCE, Pythagoras founded a monastic school where initiates lived an ascetic communal life, swore themselves to secrecy about mystic knowledge, and referred to each as friends. Several oral sayings about friendship attributed to Pythagoras have survived: for example, "The possessions of friends are common", "The good will of friends is the worthiest good", and "They above all are friends who help you toward wisdom" (Konstan, 1997, pp. 114–115). Within the community, Pythagorean friends were expected to share what they had and help each other become wiser. The legend of Damon and Pythias (or Phintias) illustrates the Pythagorean view of friendship. These devoted friends were so well known in the Classical and pre-Modern world that their names "Damon and Pythias" signified "true friendship". According to the story, Pythias is condemned to death by the tyrant Dionysius of Syracuse in the early fourth century BCE for plotting against him. Pythias pleads with Dionysius to let him return to his homeland and settle his affairs. His friend Damon agrees to take Pythias' place in prison and, if Pythias fails to return, receive his sentence and be executed. Pythias returns at the last moment. Dionysius is so amazed by their commitment that he frees them both. In one version of the story, Dionysius asks Damon and Pythias to allow him to be their friend. They refuse.

The most famous explanation for friendship and love in Classical Greek literature is Plato's description of original humans in the *Symposium* (189e–192b). Aristophanes explains that humans originally had two heads, four arms, four legs, and two sets of genitals. They were a proud and arrogant people, eliciting Zeus' punishment by slicing each in half. The new humans longed to be reunited with their other half. Thus, according to the myth, friends and lovers (because Greek does not make a distinction) seek their other half as a companion to feel whole again. For this reason, some men seek a union with male youths or men, other men bond with girls and women, and some women prefer girls and women.

Hellenism

In 431 BCE, Athens instigated the Peloponnesian War with Sparta which spanned 30 years, devastating trade routes and the Athenian economy. By the end of the Classical Age (360 BCE), the Greek city-states were severely weakened by two centuries of wars with the Persians and with each other (Neill, 2009). Philip, king of Macedon, a Greek-speaking backwater country, had already begun to expand his territory with the ambitious goal of conquering Persia. In the process, Philip took advantage of the weakened Greek city-states, eventually uniting all of Greece under Macedonian rule. After his assassination in 336 BCE, Philip's son, Alexander (356–323 BCE), took the throne, marking the beginning of the Hellenistic Age. Hellenism refers to the spread of Greek culture and identification with the Greeks throughout the civilized world. Alexander brought all the lands of the ancient civilizations in the Middle East from Egypt to India, including Persia, under Macedonian rule (Neill, 2009). Greek was the common language across the empire.

With Macedonian rule, warrior-mentor/attendant-novice friendships and Athenian male youth love gained new recognition and acceptance throughout the empire. Philip himself had many male friends-lovers, some of whom were soldiers (Neill, 2009). A former lover assassinated Philip after feeling rejected by him. Alexander and members of his army also had devoted male friends-lovers. While later historians stressed Alexander's relationship with women and his three marriages, his emotional and sexual relationships with men were more important to him. Alexander's closest friend, Hephaestion, had been his companion since childhood. They were similar in age. Hephaestion was a former bodyguard and a general in Alexander's army. Their relationship drew comparisons to Achilles and Patroclus. Roman historian Valerius Maximus (early first century CE) illustrated their closeness with an anecdote about mistaken identity. When Alexander first met with the conquered Persians, King Darius' mother threw herself at the feet of Hephaestion, thinking he was Alexander. Reportedly, Hephaestion was taller and more handsome than Alexander. Upon realizing her mistake, Darius' mother was greatly embarrassed. Alexander tells her there is no need for embarrassment because "Hephaestion is Alexander too" (Williams, 2012, p. 11). When Hephaestion died while on campaign in Babylonia, Alexander refused food and contact for two days.

Alexander's friendships may have been strongly influenced by his tutor, Aristotle. Like Plato, Aristotle's views on friendship have been highly influential. Aristotle described three kinds of *philia* (friendships) in the *Nicomachean Ethics* and *Eudemian Ethics*: friendships based on utility, on pleasure, and on virtue (Konstan, 1997). Friendships based on utility are relationships built on exchange, like business partners or coworkers. Friendships based on pleasure are, of course, enjoyable. These are drinking buddies, teammates, and casual acquaintances. Utility- and pleasure-based friendships are common but may be relatively short-lived, according to Aristotle. By contrast, friendships based on virtue are grounded in respect, good will, and reciprocity. Aristotle believed that true friends are attracted to each other's good character (Konstan, 1997). True friends are naturally few in number. True friends are like a second self, implying equivalent social status. To illustrate this point, Aristotle listed relationships between individuals of unequal status that are *not* friendships. These included a father and son, an older and younger man (as in Athenian pederasty), a ruler and his subject, and husband and wife. Aristotle granted that under certain circumstances husbands and wives can be friends, especially if they have children (Ward, 2008). While Aristotle never mentions a sexual element of devoted friendships, two cited "imperfect" friendships—Athenian pederasty and marriage—have a sexual component. Again, sexuality was simply not an important defining characteristic of intimate relationships. Aristotle stressed that affection and pleasure in each other's company were key elements of true friendships.

In this lengthy section on ancient Greece, spanning several centuries, we find devoted male friendships among men and youths in Dorian military cultures, like other warrior cultures. Adult warriors benefited from the service of a devoted attendant, which could include lifelong allegiance and a wider social network of allies, if the pair bonded. Male attendant-novices gained a mentor-protector with friends in leadership roles, life skills, entry into male society, and greater access to resources that could benefit their families. Devoted friendships continued after the youth reached adulthood. Both parties likely experienced pleasure from the emotional and sexual component of the relationship. During the Classical period, Athenian age-disparate male pederastic relationships were common in Attic and Ionian cultures. Sometimes these relationships continued after the youth reached adulthood. At some point, the mentoring aspect of the relationship shifted to friendship. Plato's argument for heavenly love suggests that Athenian men often pursued male youths for sexual pleasure rather than the young man's education. Athenian youths and men also formed same-age devoted friendships. Same-age friends likely provided each other an ally and extended social networks that helped in navigating the urbane Athenian male society. There is little evidence regarding adult-youth or peer friendships among the non-noble classes. Merchants, traders, and craftsmen left few records about their friendships. However, Solon's law implies that lower-class men courted male adolescents, perhaps in imitation of the Athenian elite. During the Hellenistic Age, same-age devoted friendships among military men are frequently mentioned.

From the sixth century BCE in the North Aeolian Islands and Dorian cultures, devoted female friendships thrived between same-age girls and sometimes with the adult schoolmistress. Little information has survived about the nature and longevity of these friendships. Devoted female friendships likely continued after marriage, and friends assisted with childcare and household tasks.

Lastly, during this period, philosophers expounded upon the nature of (male) friendship, emphasizing the importance of true friends. Aristotle said that true friendship was a function of good character. True friendship included good will, respect, reciprocity, and pleasure in each other's company. Plato and Aristotle's views on friendship greatly influenced later writers, including Christians, well into the late Middle Ages.

The Roman Republic and Empire to the Late Fifth Century

Friendly, intimate relationships among men appear quite varied in ancient Rome. Roman men were quite class conscious but had close relationships with men from different social classes (Williams, 2012). Young men formed devoted friendships with older, more powerful men. Within the military and government, a bond with a powerful man could facilitate a young man's rise to power. Julius Caesar and Mark Antony are two examples discussed later. While not friendships, Roman men had sexual relationships with male slaves and concubines, and some masters expressed deep affection and romantic love for their male slave/concubine. While not the life preferred by slaves and concubines, some male slaves remained devoted to their master after being freed. Cicero's slave Tiro and Manlius Torquatus' male concubine are two examples discussed later. Particularly during the Empire, Roman men valued devoted friendships among social equals. There are many examples of similar age and status (or uncertain social status) devoted male friend-ships in real life and in literature, where it is unclear whether the men also had wives and children. Roman poet Martial (38/41–102/104) commented disapprovingly about a "marriage" between two men and made no mention of them having wives. In one popular novel, a man partners with a similar age young man who later dies; he then marries an older rich woman for her money. After his wife dies, he partners with another man, which seems to be his preference. Discerning social status among friends, benefits of a friend-ship, or conformity to convention from our distant perspective is difficult. However, individuals likely benefited from love and companionship. It is possible that the common Roman practice of same-sex adult adoption was as much a public declaration of friendship as it was a legal arrangement to ensure the lower status friend's future financial support.

Before digging into this rich source material, a brief overview of Roman history may provide helpful context. By the mid-eighth century BCE, Italic tribes of Indo-European settlers occupied the region that is now Rome. According to legend, Romulus and Remus, twins nursed as infants by a she-wolf, founded Rome. In another legend, Trojan War hero and refugee Aeneas founded the city. Later Roman writers recounted these origin sto-ries to emphasize early Roman hardscrabble agrarian roots and strict moral values, which was as much a fable as twins raised by a wolf (Neill, 2009). Beginning in the sixth century BCE, early Rome was dominated by a north-ern culture of Etruscan people, themselves descendants of Indo-Europeans. The Etruscans had grown rich and powerful trading with Celtic people in the north. They admired Greek culture and brought those influences to Rome. The Etruscans ruled early Rome, built the first city walls, and introduced the alphabet, although remarkably, the Romans retained their Latin language. By the early fifth century BCE, the Romans succeeded in overthrowing their Etruscan rulers and established a Republic that lasted almost 500 years. Political conflict and civil wars eventually destabilized the Republic (Neill, 2009). In 45 BCE, Julius Caesar (100–44 BCE) became the perpetual dic-tator (magistrate) of the late Republic but was assassinated the next year. Caesar had named his nephew, Gaius Octavius Thurinus (Octavian) (63 BCE–4 CE), as his son and heir. Octavian, Mark Antony (83–30 BCE), and Marcus Lepidus (c. 89/88–13/12 BCE) co-ruled for a time as the Second

Triumvirate. Quarreling between the three led to Octavian overthrowing Lepidus and Antony. Octavian became the first emperor of Rome in 27 BCE and received the title of Augustus. He stabilized and dramatically enlarged the Roman Empire and, for 200 years, the empire experienced peace.

By the third century, a series of crises led Emperor Diocletian (244–311) to divide the empire into four regions, with four co-rulers. This structure quickly collapsed into an east-west division. Constantine I (c. 272–337) became the emperor in the East in 306. Constantine converted to Christianity in 312 and actively promoted the religion, linking church hierarchy to the government. He briefly reunited the Empire. In 380, Emperor Theodosius (347–395) made Christianity the state religion and banned all other religious practices. Political, military, and environmental crises continued to destabilize the western empire. Warrior people from the north badly stretched the Western empire's military resources. In 476, the Goths dethroned Romulus Augustus (c. 460–after 476), formally ending the Western Roman Empire. The better defended Byzantine Empire in the east lasted for another 1,000 years.

Roman Religious Values, Gender Roles, and Devoted Friendships

To understand Roman friendships, some knowledge of Roman religious values, gender and sexual roles, and the function of marriage is needed. As noted above, early Rome was heavily influenced by Etruscan and Greek cultures. All three cultures shared roots in fertility cults in which the phallus symbolized fertility and good luck. Erect phalluses adorned Roman and Greek shops, chariots, gardens, and roads, and phalluses were worn as jewelry (Hardman, 1993). The cult of Bacchus, prominent in early Rome, was closely associated with fertility worship and ritual sexual activities. Bacchanalias were famous for their sexual licentiousness and violation of social norms. Roman historian Titus Livius (Livy) (64/59 BCE–12/17 CE) wrote that early Bacchanalia celebrations in Rome involved young men engaging in receptive anal sex as part of their initiation into the mysteries of the cult (Neill, 2009). While Rome generally accommodated a wide range of religious practices and gods, including later Christian sects, the sexual deviance of Bacchanalias was too much. By the second century BCE, Rome had banned Bacchanalias as dangerous (Hardman, 1993). Other religious practices, even those involving ritual sex, were fine. Rome encouraged the populace to make temple offerings and sacrifices to their gods and participate in cult festivals up to the Christian era.

From the early Republic on, marriage was largely a private matter in Roman culture (Hardman, 1993). Marriage functioned to establish the legitimacy of a man's children and, thus, rights of inheritance. Marriage was not about love, although one should love one's spouse. Romans were expected to marry and produce children as a duty to the state. As an obligation, Roman men did not find marriage particularly pleasurable (Cantarella, 1992). Throughout the Republic and Empire, men tried to avoid or delay marriage, and government officials demanded that men marry for the good of the state. In 131 BCE, censor Metellus Numidicus (c. 160–91 BCE), responsible for supervising public morality, stated: "If we could get on without a wife, Romans, we would all avoid that annoyance; but since nature has ordained that we can neither live very comfortably with them nor at all without them, we must take thought for our lasting well-being rather than for the pleasure of the moment" (Cantarella, 1992, p.136). More than 100 years later, Emperor Augustus made the same point, enacting a law that punished Roman men who did not marry or who remained childless (Hardman, 1993). Two hundred years after that, rhetorician Titus Castricius (second century CE) felt compelled to agree with Metellus' argument that the needs of the state are the best argument for marriage (Cantarella, 1992). By contrast, for women, the role of matron—a married woman—was an honored one. Married women were respected in Roman society. In general, wives had the right to divorce their husbands and inherit property (Hardman, 1993). During the Empire, some women became quite wealthy and influential through inheritances. However, husbands could also easily divorce their wives and even kill them with impunity under certain circumstances, like catching one's wife in the act of adultery. Wives had to be faithful to their husbands, but husbands could seek sexual satisfaction wherever they wished. The poet Horace (65–8 BCE) remarked that if a man has a sudden irrepressible sexual desire the easiest solution is a nearby (male or female) household slave (Cantarella, 1992). For a woman, non-marital options for sexual pleasure were few and risky. Some married women found sexual gratification in self-pleasure or through the services of a female household slave.

Romans viewed themselves as a superior race destined to conquer the world; they felt born to dominate others (Neill, 2009). Men's masculine role included sexual domination. Roman men took the dominant, penetrative sexual role, while everyone else had the subordinate, receptive role. The penetrator sexual role was powerful and respected; the receptive role was womanly and weak. Real men were penetrators, never penetrated. This focus on the active, penetrator role made the sexual object less important. For Roman men, appropriate sexual objects included girls, women, male and female slaves and prostitutes, and foreign-born boys. Adult Roman men and freeborn boys were off-limits. Contemporaneous Greeks viewed sex with free male youths by honorable men as ennobling, but Romans believed that free youths were degraded and humiliated by sex with men, especially men of lesser social status (Neill, 2009). Roman preoccupation with domination may have even enhanced men's sexual pleasure with males, since a male partner, even a slave, had more (status) to lose by the experience than a female partner. Sex with male youths and men also eliminated the risk of unintended progeny of mixed birth. During the Republic, freeborn bachelors often kept a handsome male slave (*concubinus*) as a sexual companion until marriage (Neill, 2009). Alternatively, some bachelors preferred a "kept boy" (*scorti*) or high-class prostitute, even though street prostitutes (both male and female) were plentiful and legal. While visiting Rome in the early second century BCE, historian Polybius (c. 208–c. 125 BCE), a Greek, observed that young men in Rome showed little restraint in sexual matters since most had male concubines (Neill, 2009). First-century CE satiric poet and epigrammatist Martial found it amusing to advise a bridegroom to try to enjoy a new kind of sexual pleasure—sex with a woman: "Enjoy feminine embraces, Victor; enjoy them, and let your poker learn an activity unknown to it" (Neill, 2009, p. 199).

Romans portrayed the concubinage relationship as pleasurable and meaningful for both parties, although we only have the Romans' word for it. Supposedly, men no longer needed a concubine or sexual slave after marriage, but many men kept them anyway. The playwright Plautus (c. 254–184 BCE) makes numerous references to master-slave sexual activity in his scripts, suggesting that this practice continued after men married (Neill, 2009). In the play *Casina*, from the second half of the third century BCE, male slave characters are teased about being sexually used by their masters. The practice is never ridiculed or treated as bizarre. In the play *Truculentus*, Plautus makes joking references to sex between a courtesan and her female slave, suggesting that at least some women were known to satisfy themselves with a female slave (Neill, 2009).

However, expressing romantic love for one's male slave or concubine was not proper. Historian Valerius Maximus tells the story of a man charged with killing a farmer's ox while on an outing in the country with his male concubine (Neill, 2009). Killing a work animal was a punishable offense. The man confessed that his concubine had wished to eat tripe and the ox was the closest source. What else could he do? In another example, respected Roman statesman and orator, Marcus Tullius Cicero (106–43 BCE) is chastised by his brother Quintus in a letter for the inappropriateness of his relationship with a former slave. Cicero, who had penned love poems to his male slave, Tiro, had freed him. While freeing a slave after years of service was not unusual, Cicero now treated Tiro as a friend. From Quintus' perspective, Tiro could not be a friend because he was not, and could never be, a Roman citizen (Williams, 2012).

Roman men did not confine their sexual desires to slaves and prostitutes. Some pursued freeborn male youths, despite social prohibitions. By 226 BCE, the sexual pursuit of freeborn male youths by men had become so common and problematic that a law (*Lex Scantinia*) was passed to protect them (Neill, 2009). The penalty was a fine. The law failed to stop the seduction of freeborn male youths and was later amended to strengthen its power (Cantarella, 1992). References to men pursuing freeborn male youths are common in love poems. Catullus (84–54 BCE) wrote: "Your honeyed eyes, Juventius, if someone let me go on kissing, I'd kiss three hundred thousand times, nor never think I'd had enough" (Neill, 2009, p. 195). Juventius came from an old noble family. When friends teased Catullus about desiring a free youth, he responded with insults that he will fuck his friends in the anus and mouth. Catullus erupted in fury when he learned that a colleague also loved Juventius. By the mid-first century BCE, most Roman writers, including Catullus, Horace, and Ovid (43 BCE–17/18 CE) routinely mentioned men in loving, sexual relationships with male youths or men (Neill, 2009). How long these relationships lasted or how they benefited the freeborn youths, besides affection and sexual pleasure, is unclear.

Male-male adoptions or unions were a common practice during the Roman Empire (Neill, 2009). Whether these unions represent devoted friendships or financial arrangements is open to debate. According to Boswell (1980), both Martial and Juvenal (c. 55–127 CE) mention somewhat disapprovingly attending public ceremonies uniting two Roman men, like a marriage. The ceremonies included the men's families, exchange of dowries, a banquet, and legal obligations. Martial noted that the two men being united were both adults and masculine: "The bearded Callistratus married the rugged Afer" (Boswell, 1980, p. 82). Because both men are masculine, Martial is puzzled by who is playing which sexual role in the relationship. Juvenal expressed reproof that male unions were too common: "I have a ceremony to attend tomorrow morning in the Quirinal valley … . What sort of ceremony? … Nothing special: A friend is marrying another man and a small group is attending" (Boswell, 1994, p. 81). Critics have complained that Boswell reads too much into these references, proposing instead that Juvenal and Martial are describing mutual adoptions by two men for its legal benefits, not loving (sexual) relationships (Shaw, 1994; Young, 1994). While male unions in ancient Rome were not gay marriages, neither were they simply business arrangements. Adoption or union ensured that the lower status individual would inherit his friend's assets and live comfortably. It strains rationality to believe that two unrelated people would adopt each other in a public ceremony for financial reasons and not be close friends. Further, it makes little sense that Juvenal and Martial would view Roman men adopting each other as "brothers" for inheritance benefits as a sign of moral decline. Although Juvenal and Martial are not specific about their concerns, they seem to object to the celebration of adult men uniting because they are violating Roman masculine norms and perhaps avoiding taking a wife and having children.

Popular literary sources during the empire depict devoted male friendships as prevalent and noble. In the *Satyricon*, perhaps the first European novel, Gaius Petronius Arbiter (c. 27–66 CE) depicts the excesses of the Roman wealthy class during the early empire (Neill, 2009). The story centers around Enclopius, a comic character, and his male partner, Giton, who are similar in age. Enclopius is attractive, and both men and women want to take him to bed. However, Enclopius is mainly interested in Giton, who lives with him and loves him. Enclopius and Giton are presented as a couple in a common law marriage for non-citizens (*contubernium*). Enclopius says that he and Giton have been together so long "that it had become a bond of blood" (Neill, 2009, p. 206). At one point in the novel, Enclopius and Giton endure a severe storm at sea. Fearing they may die, the pair tie themselves together to ensure they will be buried together. In *Ephesiaca*, a popular romance novel by Greek author Xenophon of Ephesus (second century–third century), the main characters, 14-year-old Anthia and 16-year-old Habrocomes, fall in love at the festival of Artemis (Neill, 2009). They then experience a series of improbable events before being reunited at the end. A subplot of the story involves Hippothoos, a pirate and friend of Habrocomes. Hippothoos is in love with Hyperanthes, a young man of similar age. A wealthy older man from Byzantium also loves Hyperanthes and convinces his parents to let him take the youth to Byzantium to "educate" him. Readers understand that Hyperanthes will be the man's concubine. Hippothoos eventually locates Hyperanthes, murders his captor, and rescues the youth. Sometime later Hyperanthes is killed and mourned by Hippothoos. An impoverished Hippothoos marries a rich elderly woman, with the aim of inheriting her fortune. When she dies, Hippothoos meets and settles down with another young man, Cleisthenes, and they live happily together as a couple. The novel ends with each couple, including Hippothoos and Cleisthenes, being reunited and going to bed "as they are inclined" (Boswell, 1994, p.73).

As noted earlier, several literary sources in this period refer to love between women. However, unlike devoted male friends, women who love women were often depicted disapprovingly. In Petronius' *Satyricon*, two wives, Fortunata and Scintilla, are at a banquet and drunk (Cantarella, 1992). They cling together, giggling and kissing each other. While Petronius does not condemn them, their behavior is not respectable. Fortunata is also a former prostitute. In Lucian's *Dialogues of the Courtesans*, Leaena has an affair with Megilla. While Lucian does not condemn the pair, he portrays Megilla, the lover, as masculine and aggressive. The popular novel, *Babyloniaka*, includes a subplot about a woman in love with another woman (Brooten, 1996). Roman beliefs about women loving women are not clear. Cantarella (1992) argued that Romans viewed women loving women as morally depraved and "against nature" because they violated women's passive sexual role. However, art historian and archeologist Lisa Auanger (2002) countered that the absence of significant condemnation in Roman texts of women who love, kiss, and touch other women allows the possibility of acceptance of loving relationships between women.

Friendship in Roman Culture

Friendship was a central value among Romans (Konstan, 1997; Williams, 2012). Friends are frequently mentioned in speeches, letters, plays, novels, and philosophical essays. The Senate even commissioned a public altar to Friendship in 28 CE (Williams, 2012). Like today, Romans used the word "friend" (*amicus*) to describe a variety of relationships, from casual acquaintances to close intimates and to enemies, although in a mocking or ironic way. True friends were highly valued in Roman culture, and false friends were a common concern. Politicians, military leaders, orators, and philosophers glorified close male friends, often contrasting the true friend with the friendly flatterer (Konstan, 1997; Williams, 2012). True friends had goodwill towards each other, while flatterers masqueraded as friends to take advantage. In the first century CE, Plutarch wrote a popular essay titled, "How to Distinguish a Flatterer from a Friend". In the late Middle Ages, as classical texts were rediscovered, Plutarch's essay on friendship and Cicero's *De amicitia* became popular again.

In *Moral Epistles*, Roman philosopher Seneca (c. 4 BCE–65 CE) presented true friendship as a close relationship between noble men of good character and equivalent social status (Konstan, 1997). The true friend was like a second self, or alter ego, with whom one could speak frankly (Williams, 2012). True friendship was voluntary, mutual, and pleasurable. Married spouses were not friends. Married spouses might grow to love each other, but true devoted friends loved and respected each other from the beginning (Cantarella, 1992; Hardman, 1993). While deeply affectionate, there is little evidence that close male friendships in the early Roman Republic were sexual (Neill, 2009). However, during the turbulent late Republic and monarchial Empire, notable devoted friendships between men of different social statuses appear to have included sexual affection (Konstan, 1997). By the early Empire, devoted Roman friendships resembled Athenian friendships—an adult man in an intimate relationship with a younger man or youth (Cantarella, 1992).

In the first century BCE during the late Republic, Roman statesman Cicero wrote an influential treatise, *De amicitia*, that reinterpreted classical Greek ideas about friendship (Williams, 2012). *Amicitia* refers generally to friendship. Unlike Greek which blurred the boundaries between sex, love, and friendship, Roman Latin distinguished between romantic love (*amor*), erotic love (*eros*), and friendship (*amicitia*). Cicero's *De amicitia* idealizes friendship as noble, spiritual, and non-sexual, even though his closest emotional relationships were with men and seemingly sexual. As a Stoic, Cicero believed that man should not be controlled by his desires, which does not mean ignoring sexual desire or prohibiting its expression. However, early Christian ascetics seized on the idea of managing one's desires and reinterpreted Cicero's comments as suppression of sexual desire (Williams, 2012).

In *De amicitia*, Cicero speaks to his dear friend, Titus Pomponius Atticus (110–32 BCE), in the voice of Laelius, who is pondering the nature and meaning of friendship after the death of his friend Scipio. Laelius asserts that true devoted friendship is based on love and affection: "[Friendship is] the goodwill that one feels toward someone, for the benefit of the person for whom one has affection, joined with an equal goodwill on his part" (Williams, 2012, p. 19). Laelius emphasizes the close alter ego state of devoted friendship: "What (is) sweeter than to have one with whom you are bold to speak as with yourself?" (Konstan, 1997, p. 150). That is, a devoted friend is someone who loves you like himself and with whom you can be candid. That level of confidence and comfort in a true friend is only possible between men of similar social standing. Yet Cicero's Laelius acknowledges the usefulness of friendships between men of different social classes (Williams, 2012). Classicist Richard Saller (1989) noted that Romans, being very status conscious, rank ordered their friends: "*amici* were subdivided into categories *superiores, pares* and *inferiores* (and then lower down the hierarchy, humble *clientes*). Each category called for an appropriate mode of behavior, of which the Romans were acutely aware" (p. 57). Close business alliances or congenial patronage involving individuals from different social classes could become friendships over time, although friendship between men of different classes required a fine balance. Laelius, again, states: "In a friendship it is crucial to be a peer to one's inferior" (Konstan, 1997, p. 135). It was equally important for the lower status individual not be envious of his friend's advantages.

First-century CE historian Valerius Maximus also wrote about *amicitia* in *Facta et dicta memorabilia* (Memorable Deeds and Sayings), offering Orestes and Pylades as examples of true friends (Williams, 2012). Orestes is the son of Agamemnon, who was murdered by his wife Clytemnestra. Orestes returns to Mycenae to avenge his father's death. He kills his mother and her lover, Aegisthus. In one version of the story, Pylades, Orestes' closest friend, convinces him to go through with the plan when his courage wavers. Valerius' reference to these mythic friends is significant because their relationship was viewed by ancient writers as erotic. Then Valerius compares his own close friendship with Sextus Pompeius (consul in 14 CE) to Alexander and Hephaestion, who were friends and lovers. While Valerius may not have had a sexual relationship with Sextus, he had no difficulty comparing the depth of his friendship with Sextus to legendary heroes who were sexually affectionate.

By the late Republic/early Empire, the nature and form of close male friendships had shifted among the nobles. It is unclear exactly how these changes influenced the broader culture, but the populace were witnesses. During this time, military commanders and Roman political leaders rose to power through their early subordinate/receptive sexual relationships and friendships with powerful older men (Neill, 2009). Julius Caesar and Mark

Antony are notable examples. At age 19, Caesar was stationed in Bithynia where he allegedly was the receptive partner of Nicomedes, the king. A Roman businessman who witnessed the relationship widely publicized it. For the rest of his life, Caesar was teased and mocked by this allegation, which he never denied. None of it appears to have fazed Caesar. Observers noted no reaction. Some critical Senators went so far as to refer to Caesar as the "Queen of Bithynia". After defeating the Celts in Gaul, Caesar's soldiers reportedly sang in triumph: "Caesar conquered the Gauls, Nicomedes conquered Caesar. Behold Caesar now triumphs, who subjugated Gaul; Nicomedes, who subjugated Caesar, has no victories now" (Neill, 2009, p. 200). Roman soldiers and the populace may have viewed Caesar's youthful activities as amusing, rather than moral failings, while giving more importance to his military victories. Perhaps the mockery about his sexual relationship with Nicomedes did not affect Caesar because he was also having affairs with Senators' wives. Roman orator Curio the Elder (?–53 BCE) referred derisively to Caesar as "every man's wife and every woman's husband" (Neill, 2009, p. 201). Caesar also famously loved Cleopatra of Egypt. After Caesar's death, Mark Antony began an affair with Cleopatra.

Antony also had devoted friendships with older, powerful men in his youth, allegedly engaging in receptive sex with them (Neill, 2009). According to Cicero, Antony, who came from a noble family, prostituted himself in his youth by exchanging sex for gifts. Cicero also claimed that Antony formed "a steady and fixed marriage" with Curio the Younger (Neill, 2009, p. 201). However, Cicero was no friend of Antony and may well have exaggerated. Antony viewed Cicero as a political enemy and at one point ordered his assassination. Even so, Jewish historian Titus Flavius Josephus (37–100 CE) noted Antony's close relationships with younger men when he came to power (Neill, 2009). While ruling the eastern province after Caesar's death, Antony asked Herod, the Judean king, to send his young handsome brother-in-law, Aristobulos, to the Roman court. According to Josephus, Herod declined to send Aristobulos because of Antony's reputation for seducing young men.

Some Roman emperors had male favorites who came from lower social classes and benefited greatly from the relationship. For example, in the second century, Emperor Hadrian (76–138 CE) famously maintained an affectionate, sexual relationship with Antinous, a handsome Bithynian Greek youth (Hardman, 1993). As a young, poor, non-Roman, Antinous greatly increased his status and access to resources as Hadrian's favorite. Although Hadrian was married, there is no record of Antinous having married. After Antinous drowned in the Nile at age 19, Hadrian deified him and founded the city of Antinopolis near where he died. Hadrian promoted the cult of beautiful Antinous throughout the empire. Thus, Antinous whose position was ethnically, socially, and sexually inferior to Hadrian (and to Roman citizens generally) was celebrated as a deity and worshipped across the empire at Hadrian's order. While it is unclear what the general population thought about Antinous, the Jews and early Christians strongly objected to the creation of deities and celebrating a man who was sexually receptive (Hardman, 1993; Neill, 2009).

Funerary Epitaphs and Burial Arrangements

Funerary epitaphs are a unique source of references to friendship in ancient Roman culture. People of all social classes publicly announced their close friendship with the deceased on funerary plaques and memorials (Williams, 2012). Funerary friendships epitaphs were more common in urban areas of ancient Rome than in rural sites. Friendship epitaphs sponsored by women were more common in the Iberian Peninsula than in other parts of the Roman Empire. Women identified women as intimate friends in funerary epitaphs. Slaves and freed persons also proclaimed their friendship with the deceased. Occasionally, a man and woman together commissioned an epitaph for a mutual friend. However, most funerary epitaphs commemorating friendships are from an individual for a same-sex friend. While these may not have been devoted friendships, they were significant enough for the surviving individual to pay for the memorial and engraving. Of note, when men or women referred to different-sex friends in funerary epitaphs, there is often a sexual connotation (Williams, 2012). There is no sexual connotation when men or women refer to a same-sex friend in an epitaph, which does not mean the friendship was non-sexual.

Men and women typically referred to the deceased as an "incomparable", "excellent", "dear", and "deserving friend" (Williams, 2012). Men often used the term *amicus* (friend) to refer to a close relationship with a non-relative male. Women used the term *amica*, implying very close personal friendships. Historian Craig Williams (2012) commented that Roman women could have used other terms, such as *familiaris* or *necessaria*, to denote a close relationship with a woman. However, women consistently chose the word for friend (*amica*). We cannot know whether the deceased thought of the other person as a friend, or what kind of friends they were. The public reference to friendship may have been an attempt to elevate one's status by declaring that the higher status deceased individual was a close friend (Williams, 2012). However, noblemen and women also sponsored funerary friendship epitaphs.

In addition to declaring one's friendship on a plaque, Roman friends sometimes arranged to be buried in shared space and not as a cost-saving measure (Williams, 2012). Unrelated same-sex pairs and sometimes groups of friends, some of whom were married couples, frequently arranged to be buried together. That is, some men and women felt such deep affection for a same-sex friend that they wished never to be apart and so arranged to spend eternity together in the same burial plot. The combined burial of unrelated same-sex adults again illustrates the value of friendship in Roman culture.

We do not know whether same-sex pairs buried together also had spouses. Since most people married, it may be that some friends preferred to spend eternity together, rather than with their spouses.

The Christianization of Rome and De-sexualization of Male Friendship in the Late Empire

By the second half of the second century, the Roman Empire was experiencing increasing challenges. Germanic tribes along the Danube and invaders from the Parthian (or Arsacid) Empire of ancient Iran in the east seriously threatened Roman borders, requiring sustained military efforts (Neill, 2009). Worse, military contact with the east introduced a plague that eventually killed five million people in the Empire. With resources stretched thin and defenses weakened or missing, invaders sacked and destroyed Roman cities and disrupted trade. Bandits roamed the countryside. Pirates controlled the seas and some ports. Earthquakes shook the ground. Under these apocalyptic conditions, Christianity began to take hold. Early Christian preachers declared that these catastrophes were God's punishment for Roman paganism and sexual excesses, such as adultery and sex with male youths (Neill, 2009). Several Christian sects were quite hostile to pleasure and sexual activity in general. Earlier in the first century, Saint Paul, who never married, preached that sex should be confined to marriage, mainly to manage temptations: "But if they cannot exercise self-control, let them marry, since it is better to be married than to be burnt up" (I Corinthians 7:9, NJB). For Paul, marriage was not a sacred institution blessed by God; it was a way to avoid hell. But once married, divorce was not an option. Paul laid the foundation for later Christianity's hostility toward sexual pleasure, especially non-procreative sex and same-sex sexual activities. Paul also reinterpreted the Stoic concept of Natural Law, referring to universal principles of order, to mean God's law. Two hundred years later, consistent with Paul's version of Natural Law and his negative view of sex and marriage, Clement of Alexandria proclaimed that "to have sex for any purpose other than to produce children is to violate nature" (Neill, 2009, p. 213).

After Emperor Marcus Aurelius' death in 180, there followed a series of short-lived emperors, political instability, and civil war (Neill, 2009). By 270, the Roman Empire had become a totalitarian state. Between 180 and 284, when Diocletian (244–311) ascended the throne and restored orderly government, 38 emperors briefly reigned, most of whom were assassinated. To establish a more orderly succession, Diocletian delegated a co-emperor and junior co-rulers. By this time, early Christians were fomenting civil unrest and increasingly vocal. Christians publicly denounced Diocletian's right to rule on religious grounds. Late in his reign, Diocletian began prosecuting Christians who refused to publicly sacrifice to the gods. There is no evidence of systematic persecution, despite later Christian claims (Nixey, 2017).

Historian and Anglican priest William Frend (1965) documented "hundreds, not thousands" of Christian martyrs during this period. Typically, Roman officials offered Christians multiple opportunities to sacrifice to the gods or flee before arrest.

Diocletian's orderly succession lasted about one year (Neill, 2009). In 306, Gaul and Britain declared Constantine Emperor of the East. In 312, Constantine converted to Christianity after seeing a vision. In 313, he granted religious freedom to Christians and linked the church to his government. Christianity's new prestige led to battles between rival sects over doctrine and ignited fanatical, terroristic campaigns to convert non-Christians (Konstan, 1997; Nixey 2017). Christian zealots organized and compelled mobs to smash "pagan" idols and temples, destroy "idolatrous" works of art, and burn classical literature that did not support Christianity. Thus, began an increasingly broad, intense, and long campaign by Christians to obliterate non-Christian classical art, architecture, and literature (Nixey, 2017). While some Roman citizens spoke out against the zealots and resisted the destruction of public temples, art, and books, threats of violence and actual violence by mobs, as well as the government's implicit backing meant that opposition could only delay defeat. In 324, Constantine defeated the emperors in the west and became the sole ruler of the Roman Empire. After Constantine's death, his sons, Constantine II (316–340), Constans (c. 323–350), and Constantius II (317–361), jointly ruled as co-emperors. In 342, Constans and Constantius issued a law prohibiting a man from marrying another man "as though he were a woman" (Cantarella, 1992, p. 175). The penalty was burning alive. There is no evidence that this law was enforced. It may have served as a threat against gender norm violations or as a political tool against enemies. Cantarella (1992) noted that male marriage was rare in the late empire and Christians may not have pushed for this law since they did not particularly value marriage.

After a series of short-lived Christian and non-Christian emperors, Theodosius I (347–395), the last emperor to rule both the east and west halves of the empire, gained the throne in 379. The next year, Theodosius declared Nicene Christianity the state religion and the only acceptable version of Christianity. The Roman Catholic Church was born. Theodosius also prohibited visiting temples and making sacrifices to the gods. In 395, the empire split in two. The western empire ended in 410 when the Visigoths captured Rome. In 438, Eastern Emperor Theodosian II (401–450) issued a compilation of laws known as the Theodosian Code. In the Code, a reference to male brothels from a 390 law by Theodosian I is missing, leaving a general prohibition against receptive male sex with men. One hundred years later in 533, Byzantine Emperor Justinian (c. 482–565) released a legal text (the *Institutiones*) summarizing the principles of law. This text referenced punishing men who take the active role in sex with men, citing a non-existent law as precedence: "he who exercises his shameful lust with a man is punished *gladio* on the basis of the *Lex Julia*" (Cantarella, 1992, p. 181). Any sexual activity between men was now against the law and punishable by death. This reference appeared in the Code of Justinian in 538, which served as a model for laws throughout Europe for centuries.

At the time, Roman laws against receptive male sex with men probably had little effect, but attitudes had begun to change. In the late fourth century, John Chrysostom (c. 349–c. 407) in a letter to members of the Antioch church (near modern Antakya, Turkey) complained about widespread male-male sexual activity among the laity and leadership. He stated unconvincingly that this was a new phenomenon: "A new and lawless lust has invaded our life … . (W)omankind is in danger of being superfluous when young men take their place in every activity" (Crompton, 2003, p. 141). While we do not know the prevalence of male-male sexual activities in the Antioch church, Chrysostom knew the practices of men in the late empire. He singled out male-male sexual activities as "new" and "monstrous" and deserving special attention. Chrysostom also blamed the destruction of Sodom on male-male sexual activities: "If any one disbelieves hell, let him consider Sodom, let him reflect on Gomorrah … . Would you wish also to know the cause for which these things were then done? It was one sin, a grievous one, yet but one. The men of that time had a passion for boys, and on that account they suffered this punishment" (Crompton, 2003, p. 141). Chrysostom echoes Hellenistic Jewish writer, Philo of Alexandria (c. 20 BCE–c. 50 CE), who first linked receptive male sex with men to God's destruction of Sodom. Philo's reconceptualization reflected Jewish hostility toward Greek customs, including the love of male youth. Early Christian leaders, believing that Christ (the New Covenant) supplanted Jewish Law (the Old Covenant), did not adopt the view that receptive male sex with men caused the destruction of Sodom until the third and fourth centuries (Neill, 2009). Later, in *The City of God*, Augustine (354–430) repeats Philo and Chrysostom's assertion about Sodom's destruction (Crompton, 2003). Augustine believed that sex was the original sin that damned humanity and male-male sexual activity was one of the worst sexual sins.

Ever vigilant to sin, early Christians viewed Roman male friendships with suspicion (Konstan, 1997). While philosophers and scholars vaunted friendship, most early Christian writers ignored classical texts on friendship, and many followers were uneducated. However, Clement of Alexandria is one Christian writer who commented on friendship. In the late second and early third centuries, Clement referred to a modified version of Aristotle's classification of friendship. He wrote that the best kind of friendship was based on virtue (*aretē*) and affection (*agapē*), which came from God. Increasingly, Christians abandoned reference to friendship and described solidarity with fellow Christians in kinship terms, as brothers and sisters through Christ. In the late fourth century, Paulinus of Nola wrote: "you are my brother by virtue of a greater parent than those who are united to me by mere flesh and blood. For where is that brotherhood in blood now? Where that former friendship [amicitia]?" (Konstan, 1997, p. 157). In his Confessions, Augustine contrasted his close friendship with a male youth who died to spiritual communion. His friend's death so devastated Augustine that he turned to God: "For I felt that my soul and his were one soul in two bodies, and therefore life was a horror to me, since I did not want to live as a half" (Neill, 2009, p. 224). Acknowledging the sexual part of his loving friendship, Augustine also condemned it: "Thus I contaminated the spring of friendship with the dirt of lust and darkened its brightness with the blackness of desire" (Neill, 2009, p. 224). Augustine now saw fellowship as a function of devotion to God: "He truly loves a friend, who loves God in his friend, either because He is in him, or so that He be in him" (Konstan, 1997, p. 172).

When church fathers wrote about friendship, they primarily focused on relations among monks, priests, and other followers who lived together in communities (Konstan, 1997). In the late fourth century, Saint Ambrose (c. 340–397), bishop of Milan, wrote in "On the Duties of Ministers": "[God] gave the form of friendship we follow, that we may perform the wishes of a friend, that we may open our secrets, whichever we have in our bosom, to a friend, and that we may not be ignorant of his hidden things" (Konstan, 1997, p. 150). Ambrose was not encouraging intimacy, which was dangerous. Rather, he encouraged self-disclosure to avoid secret sins and promote loyalty to the community.

By the fifth century, the Roman Empire was a Christian state. The view of devoted male friendships and male sexual activity with men had begun to change. Intimate friendships offered opportunities for sin which had to be guarded against. For early Christians, fellowship was found in sharing the love of God with believers. Christians viewed everyone as sinful by nature and tempted by pleasure, especially sexual pleasure. Sex should be strictly confined to marriage for the purpose of procreation. Even then, sex was problematic. For Christians, male-male sexual activity became a "monstrous" sin that violated God's law and drew His wrath on the community. These beliefs laid the foundation for the anti-pleasure, anti-sexual attitudes that have pervaded Christianized Western culture up to the present.

Here is where our historical survey of devoted same-sex friendships through Western culture ends. Extending this survey to the present would require additional chapters, given the voluminous amount of source material available on friendship after the Middle Ages. While this history is fascinating and provides rich material on women's friendships, my point has been made: Devoted male friendships were common across many historical cultures. Age- and status-different devoted male friendships, like those among military cultures, provided social opportunities for young men to rise in status and influence. Devoted friendships likely aided young men in acquiring resources to later marry and have children. In Classical Athens and the late

Roman Republic, devoted male friendships among age-similar social equals were evident. The social and reproductive advantages of male friendships between social equals are less obvious, although close friends make strong allies and loyal companions. In ancient Greece and Rome, we also find evidence of women in loving relationships with women, including numerous funerary epitaphs highlighting female friendships. Unfortunately, these sources reveal little about the nature and structure of female friendships.

Under strong Christian disapproval, devoted male friendships became less visible. Western culture remained largely sex-segregated. Same-sex friends remained the primary source of emotional support and meaning for men and women, although now they were non-sexual and less intimate. In the late eighteenth and nineteenth centuries, affectionate same-sex friendships resurfaced as lavishly romantic relationships (Vicinus, 2004). More recently, individualism and psychoanalytic perspectives on sexuality have further altered the expression of same-sex friendships in Western culture (Lewes, 1988; Weeks, 1985/1989).

Ancient and Imperial China and Devoted Friendships

So far, this historical survey has focused on ancient societies that contributed to Western culture. I would like now to quickly scan the history of two non-Western cultures, China and Japan, for themes of devoted male friendship. Evidence of devoted male friendships within these far eastern societies increases our level of confidence that such friendships are an adaptation for navigating sex-segregated environments to ultimately achieve social and reproductive outcomes. In addition, evidence for the persistence of devoted male friendships in these populous cultures for thousands of years—until colliding with hostile Western values about sexual sin—suggests that our contemporary versions of friendship and sexuality are culturally defined.

In the late Neolithic period, communities began to form along the Yellow River and Yangtze River. Around 8,000 years ago, agricultural communities began to appear in central China (History of China, 2020). The earliest written records of this culture appeared about 1250 BCE during the Shang Dynasty (c. 1600–1046 BCE). The geographic region acquired its name more than 1,000 years later from the Ch'in (Qin) Dynasty (221–207 BCE). During the Qin Dynasty, construction began on the Great Wall (Neill, 2009). The government also built a network of roads and unified existing laws. The territory of China greatly expanded westward during the Han Dynasty (202 BCE–220 CE). The post-Han dynasties experienced a series of weak emperors, manipulation by powerful families, corruption, and political instability. Stability returned with the Tang (618–907) and Song (960–1271) Dynasties, which also sparked tremendous innovation in literature and technology. Trade thrived through the Silk Road in the west and on the seas in the east. Invasion by Mongols in the early thirteenth century ended the Song Dynasty. Kublai Khan (1215–1294), grandson of Ghengis Khan, declared himself Emperor of China in 1271. The Yuan Dynasty (1271–1368) brought another period of great invention and creativity, such as the abacus (Neill, 2009). An advanced monetary system facilitated trade, and irrigation and sewage systems led to urban expansion. Cities offered sophisticated services, such as teahouses, wine shops, catering, and various arts and entertainment. The Ming Dynasty (1368–1644) further expanded Chinese territory into Korea on the east, Uzbekistan on the west, and Vietnam and Burma in the south. During the Ming Dynasty, Chinese businessmen and officials began interacting with Westerners, bringing them in regular contact with Christian values (Neill, 2009). By the late sixteenth century, Western missionaries had begun systematic efforts to proselytize in China (Crompton, 2003). In 1644, under a pretense of providing aide, the Manchu seized the throne and established the Qing Dynasty, the last imperial dynasty, which lasted until 1912. By the mid-nineteenth century, persistent condemnation of sexual sin by Western missionaries and businessmen had taken hold (Neill, 2009). By the early twentieth century, the Chinese population generally disapproved of same-sex sexual activities, and devoted male friendships drew suspicion.

For most of China's history, sex-segregation has been the rule. Governed by men, women have been largely confined to domestic spaces and physically separated from men when not serving them (Crompton, 2003). Confucian teachings, such as the *Book of Rites*, stressed the separation of men and women even within the home (Ebrey, 2020). Consistent with Confucian teachings, Han Dynasty laws codified the authority of family heads or senior males over other members of the family. Under Han law, men could divorce their wives on several grounds, but women had no specific right to divorce. Marriages could also end by mutual agreement. In traditional Chinese culture, marriage had a central role in linking clans or families together (Neill, 2009). Marriage was mandatory and by arrangement. Men who married (and produced children) were free to pursue love through male friendships and sexual relationships outside of marriage. Traditional Chinese culture viewed sex as natural and pleasurable, not sinful. However, women were expected to be faithful. Chinese women's roles were kinship based and included daughter, sister, wife, daughter-in-law, mother, mother-in-law, and grandmother.

Traditional Chinese societies were also class structured. For men, devoted friendships usually involved men from different social classes (Crompton, 2003). The lower-class individual received considerable social, health, and financial benefits from these relationships. The upper-class partner gained a loyal friend and companion who would not depose him. Love and affection, and sometimes sexual intimacy, held the friendship together. The structure of devoted female friendships is less certain because little information is available.

Zhou Dynasty

The primary sources on devoted same-sex friendships in Chinese history are histories of the imperial courts and literature (Neill, 2009). Western observers sometimes wrote about their experiences, usually because they were shocked. Literary texts provide insight into how nobles and occasionally commoners experienced their worlds. One of the most famous stories about Chinese devoted male friendships comes from a philosophical text, *Han Fei Zi* (Hinsch, 1990). In the late sixth century BCE, Duke Ling (c. 534–492 BCE), ruler of the feudal state of Wei, walks in an orchard with his friend and favorite, Mizi Xia, an official in the court. Mizi Xia picks a peach, takes a bite, and exclaims how delicious it is. He gives the peach to the duke, who praises him for disregarding his own appetite. Later generations poetically referred to the love between Mizi Xia and Duke Ling with the phrase "the Half-Eaten Peach". In an earlier story about a male favorite, a Zhou court official, Zhuang Xin, has long desired his lord, King Xiang Cheng (1055–1021 BCE), but has kept his feelings secret (Hinsch, 1990). One day, the shy official asks to hold the ruler's hand because he cannot simply take the king's hand. Upon hearing the request, Xiang Cheng's expression changes, but he says nothing. As explanation, the official tells the story of another ruler who was loved in secret by his boatman. One day while boating with the ruler the boatman sang about his unspoken love. The king was deeply moved and "responded" to the boatman (Hinsch, 1990, p. 23). When Zhuang Xin finishes the story, Xiang Cheng takes his hand and promotes him in the court. Being a male favorite, having a devoted friendship with a ruler, has obvious benefits, including rank in the court, power, better living conditions, better food, and access to resources to support one's family. These stories became legendary examples of how men should love men in power.

Devoted male friendships existed outside the Zhou courts as well. *The Classic Odes*, one of the earliest collections of Chinese poetry and popular songs and dating to before the seventh century BCE, presents friendships and experiences of ordinary people, such as farmers and soldiers (Hinsch, 1990). One *Odes* verse reads: "There is a beautiful man, clear, bright, and handsome. Unexpectedly we meet, fitting my desire" (p. 17). Another verse depicts admiration between two masculine soldiers: "How splendid he was! … . How strong he was! … . How magnificent he was! … . Side by side we chased two wolves. He bowed to me and said 'that was good'" (p. 17). Unfortunately, little information has survived about how these friendships were structured or functioned.

Han Dynasty

Male favorites were so common in Han courts that imperial biographers devoted entire chapters to them (Neill, 2009). The first ten Han emperors had several well-known male favorites documented by contemporary historians (Crompton, 2003). Male favorites frequently came from humble origins and rose to positions of influence, benefiting both themselves and their families. Most Han court male favorites had wives and children. In Sima Qian's biography of Emperor Wen (202–157 BCE), third of the Han monarchs, the author recounts how the emperor found his favorite. In a dream, Wen sees a boatman wearing a yellow cap and with a tear in the back of his robe below the sash (Hinsch, 1990). The boatman helps him ascend to Heaven. The opening in back of the robe suggests that the boatman is the receptive sexual partner. When the emperor awakes, he rushes to the lake in search of the boatman in his dreams. Wen finds Deng Tong, a peasant boatman, wearing a yellow cap and with an identical tear in his robe. The emperor takes Deng Tong back to the palace and makes him his concubine and favorite. Apparently, the transition from boatman to concubine is not difficult. While the biographer belittled Deng Tong's talents in the court, Qian related other stories that depict Deng Tong as the emperor's trusted companion and caretaker, eventually arousing Prince Liu Qi's jealousy (Neill, 2009). When Liu Qi (188–141 BCE) ascends the throne as Emperor Jing, he also has a male favorite: Zhou Ren, who came from humble beginnings. Emperor Jing bestowed wealth and titles on Zhou Ren and his children.

The most famous story of loving friends in this period is the "Cut Sleeve". As the story goes, Emperor Ai (27–2 BCE), tenth ruler of the Han Dynasty, had an intense friendship with a minor official in the court, Dong Xian (Hinsch, 1990). Their relationship was well-known. One afternoon Emperor Ai was napping with Dong Xian stretched across his sleeve. The emperor awoke but did not wish to disturb Dong Xian. Ai cut his sleeve and left, attending to official business. Courtiers noticed and began wearing robes with a cut sleeve in honor of Emperor Ai and Dong Xian's love for each other. Dong Xian was married and had children. His wife lived in the palace with him. Ai gave both Dong Xian and his father titles of marquis and grants of land (Neill, 2009). Emperor Ai was also married but reportedly not fond of women and he had no children. Ai tried unsuccessfully to make Dong Xian his successor.

Scholars have noted occasional references to devoted female friendships during the Zhou and Han periods (Neill, 2009). As in other cultures, male writers had little interest in what women did. However, Han politician and historian, Ying Shao (c. 140–206), commented on female couples in the imperial household: "When palace women attach themselves as husband and wife it is called *dui shi*. They are intensely jealous of each other" (Hinsch, 1990, p. 174). A specific term for devoted female friends suggests that they were prevalent enough to be named. Other Han texts occasionally refer to devoted friendships among female servants and slaves.

As noted earlier, the post-Han period experienced centuries of political instability. Yet during this time, powerful men continued to have male favorites, and legends about devoted male friendships grew (Neill, 2009). Devoted male friends became themes in literature. One popular fictional story initially attributed to the Zhou Dynasty but recently dated to the Three Kingdoms period (220–280) depicts a ruler in the state of Chu, Wang Zhongxian, who develops a devoted friendship with a young scholar, Pan Zhang (Hinsch, 1990). Hearing about Pan Zhang's remarkable work, Wang Zhongxian asks to meet him and receive copies of his writings. Pan Zhang is quite handsome. When the two met, they "fell in love at first sight and were as affectionate as husband and wife, sharing the same coverlet and pillow with unbounded intimacy" (Hinsch, 1990, p. 24). The pair die around the same time and are buried together on a hillside. A tree grows nearby with intertwining branches, as if embracing, and so people called it the "Shared Pillow Tree" in honor of the two friends and their devotion to each other. A celebrated pair of real-life friends include Pan Yue (247–300), a well-known poet, and Xiahou Zhan (243–291), a minor poet, who are referred to "sworn brothers" and "linked jade disks", a popular term for couples in a sexual relationship (Hinsch, 1990, p. 64). Reportedly, Pan Yue was exceptionally handsome and desired by men and women. His most well-known works are poems to his deceased wife. Third-century poets and devoted friends, Xi Kang (223–262) and Ruan Ji (210–263), and their sexual passion play into an amusing story about a Taoist scholar, Shan Tao (205–283), and his wife (Hinsch, 1990). Shan Tao considered Xi Kang and Ruan Ji his closest friends. While visiting, Shan Tao's wife spies on Xi Khang and Ruan Ji in their bedroom and observes them having sex. Upon returning to bed with her husband, she tells Shan Tao that his ability is not equal to theirs!

Tang and Song Dynasties

The Tang and Song Dynasties spawned a boom in prose literature as literacy improved (Hinsch, 1990). Reading became an entertainment. Popular literary themes were less romantic than in the past and frequently included everyday situations that ordinary people could relate to, often with bawdy or erotic overtones. References to male-male sexuality were common. In one story, the protagonist openly desires anal sex with his male friend: "When Wu Sansi saw his beloved's pure whiteness, he was immediately aroused. That night Wu summoned him so they could sleep together. Wu played in the 'rear courtyard' until his desire was completely satisfied" (Hinsch, 1990, p. 87). In a popular morality tale about the prodigal son of a wealthy family, the son's sexual attractiveness and sexual exploits with men (and exploitation) are featured: "Then one day a band of rogues came. Because of his exceptional good looks, he was repeatedly sodomized … . He indiscriminately associated with Buddhist and Taoist monks, robbers and thieves, and was a beloved to all of them. Day and night men excitedly played in his rear courtyard. One could hang a bushel of grain from his erect penis and it would still not go down!" (Hinsch, 1990, p. 88). Popular stories frequently depicted Buddhist and Taoist monks desiring sex with men, which readers accepted as given. Buddhist and Taoist vows required sexual abstinence from women, but not men. Besides monks and priests, students and government officials were also the subject of sexual jokes. While male-male attraction and sexual behavior were often vehicles for funny stories, male-male sexual activity itself was not the joke. In one story, a monk and disciple visit a patron. Upon arriving at the house, they see that the disciple's belt has come lose, spilling papers on the ground that had been tucked into his belt. The monk jokes, "It looks as though you have no bottom", to which the disciple replies, "If I hadn't you wouldn't be able to exist for a single day!" (Hinsch, 1990, p. 103). In another story, the humor centers on a new husband's sexual inexperience with women: On their wedding night, a man and a woman go to bed. The husband immediately grabs his wife's rear and attempts to have anal sex with her. The wife stops him and exclaims, "You're doing it the wrong way". The husband replies, "But I've been doing it that way since I was very young—what's wrong with that?" She retorts, "Well, I've been doing it since I was very young, too, and it wasn't that way" (Hinsch, 1990, p. 116). A third story jokes about men's unwillingness to give up their male partners after marriage. In the story, a man arranges a wife for his young male friend among his relatives so the friend can move freely within the family and not avoid anyone. One day, as the friend enters the man's bedroom, he is seen by the wife's mother who is visiting. She asks her daughter, "Which relative is he?" The wife replies, "He's my husband's husband" (Hinsch, 1990, p. 116).

Ming Dynasty

Ming emperors also had male favorites. According to historians, Ming emperor, Xizong (?–1627), set up two separate palaces because his male favorites and female concubines could not get along (Crompton, 2003). Novels, stories, and poems often featured male-male friendship and sexuality among students, husbands, merchants, and soldiers. In "The House of Gathered Refinements", a popular tragic Ming-era story by Li Yu (1611–1680), the subject is a ménage à trois between two married men and a male youth, spoiled by an envious, corrupt government official (Neill, 2009). Two well-educated young men, Jin and Liu, both married, open a shop together. The pair take in a beautiful lower-class young man, Quan, whom they both love and share. Quan sleeps at the shop and Jin and Liu take turns staying with him at night on the pretense of "guarding the shop", while the men enjoy the "flowers" of Quan's "rear courtyard". An evil official, Yan Shifan, also desires Quan, who rejects him. Yan orders Quan jailed, but he still refuses Yan's advances. Angered by Quan's refusals, Yan has him castrated. Eventually, eunuch Quan finds himself in the imperial household and has the opportunity to tell the emperor what has happened to him. Enraged, the emperor has Yan beheaded, and Quan uses his head as a urinal. While an unusual story, essentially lower-class Quan bonds with more powerful men to advance his position, although it costs him his reproductive ability. In another unusual novel, *Chronicle of Chivalric Love*, two masculine male friends discover their love for each other (Neill, 2009). This story reveals the expectation that devoted male friends differed in status and sexual roles. In the story, Zhang Ji is a courageous, military hero. He and his friend, Zhong Tunan, whose name is a pun on "seeking men", share a bed after a night of heavy drinking. After Zhang Ji falls asleep, Zhong Tunan somehow penetrates the solider without waking him. Zhang Ji dreams that he is no longer in control of his body. In the dream, he feels a sting, but it does not hurt. He does not know whether his body is a man's or a woman's. From this point on, the two are devoted friends, who stay connected as each lives his life. After many years, Zhang Ji and Zhong Tunan retire together with their families. There are several unexpected elements of this story, including the transformative nature of sex and the masculine hero taking the receptive sexual role. While Zhang Ji, the soldier-hero, would have considerable social status, he takes the receptive role in the friendship. In traditional Chinese Buddhist culture, sexual receptivity is not stigmatized and does not signify low social status. While Zhong Tunan's age, occupation, and social status are less clear, he is not presented as a hero, like Zhang Ji. The pair's friendship and sexual roles do not interfere with their marriages or abilities to produce many children.

Love and friendship between women is more frequently mentioned in Ming literature than in earlier eras. A famous example of female love in Chinese literature is Li Yu's play, *Pitying the Perfumed Companion* (or *The Fragrant Companion*) (Crompton, 2003). Reportedly, the play was based on actual events in Li Yu's household. In the play, a young married woman, Madam Fan, meets and falls in love with a beautiful girl, Cao Yuhua, at a Buddhist convent. Madam Fan is 17 years old, and Cao Yuhua is 15. Their love is so strong that they make vows of fidelity before the Buddha. In order to be together, Madam Fan convinces her husband to take the girl into their household as his concubine, so they both can share her. Other Ming writers also portrayed devoted female friendships among Buddhist and Taoist nuns (Neill, 2009). Convents may have been a convenient place for female friendships to develop, just as monasteries were for men. During this period, female unions or marriages were reported, particularly in Guangdong province east of Fujian.

Various sources also make references to devoted male friendship or brotherhood ceremonies in the southern province of Fujian (Crompton, 2003; Hinsch, 1990; Neill, 2009). Fujian male brotherhoods were so well-known that they were referred to as "the Southern Custom" (*nanfeng*) (Hinsch,

1990). Male brotherhoods may have been part of an older tradition. Writer Shen Defu (1578–1642) described these unions as involving an "adoptive older brother" (*quixiong*) and an "adoptive younger brother" (*qidi*) (Hinsch, 1990, p. 133). The age differences suggest unequal statuses. The pair participated in a formal ceremony with their relatives. The younger man then moved in with the older partner's family as a son-in-law. When the time came for the young man to take a wife, the partner arranged for a suitable wife and paid the bride price himself. Shen Defu said about the adoptive brothers: "They love each other and at the age of thirty are still sleeping in the same bed together like husband and wife" (Crompton, 2003, p. 226). The reference suggests sexual intimacy that continued after the younger man married. Certainly, the older partner was already married. Shen Defu noted that some adoptive brothers, who could not stay together, killed themselves rather than be apart.

Qing Dynasty and the End of Devoted Male Friendships

Initially, the new Manchu government stressed austerity and Neo-Confucian family values, although at least four of the Manchu emperors had male favorites (Crompton, 2003; Neill, 2009). The government passed laws prohibiting male rape and attempted to regulate prostitution with little success. Male prostitution was rampant and associated with the theater, with male actors functioning as prostitutes. Women were forbidden from performing in the theater, so young attractive male youths played female roles. The stage served as a display window for beautiful male youths who sold their sexual services. Into the early nineteenth century, Qing literature also featured devoted male friendships, usually between older and younger men who came from different social classes. These friendships were described as like marriages, although the friends also had wives. However, by the mid-nineteenth century, literary references to sexual intimacy between devoted male friends had sharply declined. Frequent contact with the West had introduced anti-sexual Christian values. Chinese culture began to echo negative Western attitudes about sexual activity between men (Neill, 2009).

In this very brief scan of devoted same-sex friendships in ancient and imperial China, I have drawn upon a fraction of texts to illustrate beliefs and practices spanning more than a thousand years of Chinese history. While the evidence presented is small in comparison to the span of time, the existence of devoted male friendships and male-male sexual intimacy throughout Chinese history is unmistakable. Overall, ancient and imperial Chinese literary sources portray devoted male friendships frequently and positively. We also see evidence of devoted female friendships particularly during the Ming Dynasty, although it is doubtful that female friendships only existed at this time.

Like most traditional cultures, Chinese societies were sex-segregated environments. In particular, men formed close friendships with other men, and some observers described these friendships as like marriages. Many devoted male friendships involved men of different ages and from different social classes. Devoted friendships were affectionate and sexual with little or no stigma placed on taking the receptive sexual role. Buddhism viewed sexual expression and pleasure as natural. The lower status friend in male friendships, particularly a male favorite, received significant social and financial benefits for himself and his wife and children. In short, for more than one thousand years, devoted male friendships, and possibly devoted female friendships, thrived in China until intruding anti-sexual Western values discouraged them. As contact with the West increased, references to devoted friendships in China almost vanished by the mid-nineteenth century.

Imperial and Feudal Japan and Devoted Male Friendships

Historian Louis Crompton (2003) claimed that Japanese history is barely noteworthy until the mid-sixth century when Buddhism arrives. While not exactly true, the introduction of Buddhism is a convenient starting point for this brief survey. First introduced from Korea, Japanese Buddhism was heavily influenced by Chinese Buddhism (Japan, 2020). Other important Chinese contributions followed, including art, calligraphy, literature, and philosophy. About 200 years after the introduction of Buddhism, a Japanese aristocrat, Kūkai (774–835), known later as Kōbō Daishi ("The Great Teacher"), studied Buddhism in China (Crompton, 2003; Neill, 2009). Returning in 816, Kūkai built a monastery and temple on Mount Koya in central Japan and founded one of the main branches of Buddhism (Shingon). Kūkai is also credited with bringing male-male love to Japan through Buddhism, although historical references to male love exist before this time. Kūkai was likely credited because male love and devoted friendships were prevalent among Buddhist monasteries. Japanese Buddhists could not marry and avoided sexual contact with women. However, sexual contact with male youths was not prohibited and was even celebrated, until the late nineteenth century.

Japanese Buddhism regarded the natural world as a reflection of the transcendent Divine (Neill, 2009). By contrast, medieval European Christianity at this time viewed the world as sinful and full of temptation. According to Shingon Buddhism, sexual activity is part of divine creation and, therefore, a holy act. Thus, appreciation of male beauty and love of male youths is an appreciation of the mystical beauty of the Buddha (Neill, 2009). A popular monastery text from 1598 entitled, *Kōbō Daishi's Book*, describes the "mysteries of devoted boys" (Schalow, 1992). One section describes hand signals for priests and acolytes to silently communicate their interest in each other. Another section describes how priests can recognize an acolyte's interest and slowly prepare him for anal sex. A third section describes seven tantric positions for anal sex with an acolyte. Acolytes who partnered with priests were called *chigo*. The priest partner was referred to as *nenja*. A *chigo* acolyte was particularly appreciated for his *nasake*: that is, empathy for the emotional and sexual needs of a *nenja* priest. From the tenth century on, many monasteries produced collections of prose and poetry that featured the love of male acolytes (Neill, 2009). From a story reportedly based on fact, the abbot of Ninna-ji, the headquarters for Shingon Buddhism, falls in love with a beautiful acolyte, Senju, who plays the flute, sings, and delights the abbot. Later another attractive youth, Mikawa, joins the monastery and catches the abbot's eye. Senju notices. Feeling dishonored, he avoids the abbot. At a dinner, the abbot sends for Senju, who reluctantly appears. The abbot asks him to sing, and Senju sings a sad song about being lost and abandoned. The abbot, overcome with emotion and desire, sweeps up Senju and takes him to bed. That night everyone in the monastery talks about what happened. The next day, they discover that Mikawa has left the monastery.

Many priests authored poems and texts expressing love and devotion for an acolyte. Quite possibly, acolytes experienced affection and love for their priest-lover, although their voices are missing. Acolytes may have benefited in various ways by an intimate relationship with an older, experienced priest or monk in the all-male community. The *chigo* acolyte had a senior defender/protector who could assist the novice in his studies and with social networking among influential members of the monastery. From about the early thirteenth century on, some priests or monks and acolytes made formal vows of fidelity and loyalty to each other similar to brotherhood vows (Leupp, 1995). In 1237, a 36-year-old monk, Samon Shūsei, at the Tōdaiji Temple in Nara, offered these written vows to his beloved acolyte, Ryūō-maru:

Item: I will remain secluded at Kasaki Temple until reaching age forty-one.
Item: Having already fucked ninety-five males, I will not behave wantonly with more than one hundred.
Item: I will not keep and cherish any boys except Ryūō-maru.
Item: I will not keep older boys in my own bedroom.
Item: Among the older and middle boys, I will not keep and cherish any as their *nenja*. (Leupp, 1995, p. 39)

Here we see a negotiation of boundaries and potential points of conflict between male friends as they formalize their friendship. While promising fidelity, Samon Shūsei allows himself five more sexual partners! Also, at the end of the text, the monk cleverly limits his vows to the present lifetime (Leupp, 1995). By the seventeenth century, special monk-acolyte devoted friendships were known as *kyodai musubi* ("brotherhood bonds") and marked by verbal and written oaths and a long-term commitment. The monk was the "older brother" (*anibun*) in the friendship, and the acolyte was the "younger brother" (*otōtobun*).

Shōgunate Military Rule

Beginning in the eleventh century and for 300 years, Japanese emperors "retired" from court and took vows as Buddhist priests (Neill, 2009). From the monastery, "cloistered emperors" continued to rule, while a figure-head emperor sat on the throne. This practice further aligned the government with religion, essentially creating mini-imperial courts in the monasteries. Subsequently, other aristocrats followed this pattern and lived in monasteries while continuing their involvement in the world. Noblemen also mimicked the imperial practice of acquiring male favorites. Rulers and the noble class had long sent their sons to monasteries to receive an education and gain spiritual instruction. Aristocratic men would have witnessed monk-acolyte friendships in their youth at the monastery and may well have participated in them.

The practice of cloistered emperors resulted in a weakened centralized government. Minor provincial officials and nobles established power bases in their provinces, including private armies (Neill, 2009). Constant conflict between provinces led to the formation of a corps of highly trained professional soldiers—the *samurai*. By the twelfth century, Japan had devolved to a feudal state. Military rulers (*shōgun*), nominally appointed by the emperor, ruled over regions managed by governors (*daimyo*), who relied on the samurai as a police force and army. Shōgunate military rule (*bakufu*) continued for 700 years, until imperial rule was restored in 1867. In his exceptionally researched text, *Male Colors: The Construction of Homosexuality in Tokugawa Japan*, Gary Leupp (1992) provides a detailed list of 26 shōguns and daimyos who had male favorites during this era of military rule. Minamoto Yoritomo (1147–1199), the first shōgun, had an intimate male favorite whom he made an officer in the imperial guard (Leupp, 1995). References to male favorites among the emperors, shōgun, and samurai mainly come from diaries from this period up to the Meiji Restoration (Crompton, 2003). In his diary, Fujiwara Yorinaga (1120–1156), a minister in the Regency, refers to two Heian emperors who had male favorites. Yorinaga also records his many sexual partners from servants to entertainers to nobles in his diary. One entry in 1148 reads: "Tonight I took Yosimasa to bed, and really went wild. It was especially satisfying" (Neill, 2009, p. 274). Several court officials' in their diaries mentioned that Emperor Shirakawa (1053–1129) had a beautiful young male concubine/favorite. Shirakawa's grandson, Emperor Toba (1103–1156), a devout Buddhist, also had a male favorite. Another court diarist noted that Emperor Go-Shirakaw (1127–1192) had a close male favorite, Fujiwara Nobuyori (1133–1159), who was appointed to several high positions in the court (Leupp, 1995). Favorites often received positions of authority, titles, and land. Being a favorite of a shōgun, daimyo, or samurai offered young men tremendous social advancement and honor, as well as benefits to his family. Consequently, families worked hard to draw the attention of samurai and shōgun to their beautiful teenage sons (Neill, 2990). The implications of such relationships were clear to everyone. Some parents even prepared their sons for life with a samurai by having them practice stretching their anus with dildoes.

Power struggles among the regional daimyo contributed to civil war until Tokugawa Ieyasu (1543–1616) established the Edo *bakufu*, also known as the Tokugawa shōgunate. The Tokugawa shōgunate marked a long period of peace and stability in Japan. Of 11 Tokugawa rulers between 1603 and 1837, eight had male favorites (Crompton, 2003). Of the remaining three rulers, one was only seven when he ruled, and one was an invalid. Ieyasu, the first Tokugawa shōgun, had 13 wives and concubines and 17 children, in addition to his male favorites. Ieyasu was often criticized for spending too much time with his male favorites. Tokugawa Ienari (1773–1841), the eleventh shōgun, ruled for 50 years (Crompton, 2003). Ienari had 55 children by 40 consorts but frequently bedded male actors from the Nō theater.

Around this time, Japan had its first direct contact with the West. In 1549, Jesuit Francis Xavier (1506–1552), blown off course while on a mission, landed in Japan. Xavier's account of this visit is the first Western observation of Japan. Before leaving, Xavier toured Buddhist monasteries and was appalled: "There are monks who love the sin abhorred by nature; ... . Nobody, neither man nor woman, young nor old, regards this sin as abnormal or abominable ... . The monks lodge many young sons of samurai within their monastery, and commit this crime with these boys whom they teach reading and writing ... . It has been the custom for a long time already" (Neill, 2009, p. 270). It is difficult to imagine that Xavier kept his views from his Japanese hosts. After Xavier's accidental visit, others followed deliberately. Italian Jesuit administrator, Alessandro Valignano (1539–1606), visited Japan several times between 1579 and 1603. In one early report, Valignano said of the daimyo rulers and samurai: "The gravest of their sins is the most depraved of carnal desires, so that we may not name it. The young men and their partners, not thinking it serious, do not hide it. They even honor each other for it and speak openly of it" (Neill, 2009, p. 270). Valignano blamed Japan's internal conflicts between daimyo on this "sin" and likely shared his opinion with everyone. Early Jesuit missionaries had some initial success in converting peasant and samurai aristocracy to Christianity. However, the missionaries were expelled 50 years later over their destruction of Buddhist temples and monasteries. By this time, Western traders and merchants had begun arriving in Japan, and they also disapproved of male-male sexuality (Crompton, 2003; Leupp, 1995).

Samurai and Attendants

At its peak, medieval Japan had over two million samurai. The samurai shared many similarities with the knights in Medieval Europe and Dorian warriors in ancient Greece (Neill, 2009). The samurai were highly trained masculine fighters who followed a strict code of chivalry and honor. Seventeenth-century writer, Ihara Saikaku (1642–1693) described samurai as "rough and brawny" men. They lived a life of simplicity in service to their lord and had a close affiliation with Buddhism. Many samurai had received an education in the Buddhist monasteries and likely observed or participated in intimate, sexual friendships with monks in their youth. The samurai typically had a male attendant in training to be a samurai himself. Becoming a samurai was a significant way to improve one's social situation. Young men could only become samurai by committing to a long period of training and servitude with an experienced samurai. The samurai and attendant spent most of their time together, living in an all-male environment. Although in later years samurai married women, for the first several hundred years of shōgunate rule only the love of men was thought worthy of a warrior. The samurai largely looked down on women, viewing them as "holes to be borrowed" for carrying children of samurai (Neill, 2009, p. 278).

In the all-male environment, a samurai's primary emotional relationship was with their attendant or *wakashu* ("young man") or other samurai. Samurai chose their *wakashu* attendants for their physical abilities and masculine good looks. Unlike monks, who preferred boys between the ages of 12 and 17, samurai preferred older male youths in their mid-to-late teens to early twenties because of the physical demands of the role (Neill, 2009). Service to a samurai, and later duties as a warrior, required physical strength, endurance, and fighting skills. An attendant was expected to be worthy of his master-teacher by being an excellent student. Saikaku noted that samurai "preferred big, muscular boys" and the warrior-attendant pair "bore cuts on their bodies as a sign of male love" (Neill, 2009, p. 279). Samurai and *wakashu* attendants often vowed loyalty and fidelity to each and sometimes manifested they vows with cuts on their arms or legs or by cutting off part of their fingers. The custom of samurai-*wakashu* devotion, mentoring, and training was known as *wakashudō* ("the Way of Youth"). Like Dorian warrior attendants, samurai *wakashu* were also receptive sexual partners with their samurai lords. Like Buddhist *chigo* acolytes, *wakashu* attendants were expected to demonstrate *nasake*: sensitivity to their masters' needs, including their sexual needs. Writers portrayed *wakashu* attendants' sexual submission to their samurai lords as pleasurable and emotionally satisfying for them. Although we do not if this was true, the culture viewed the samurai-*wakashu* friendships as satisfying and meaningful to both. Japanese culture venerated samurai-*wakashu* love and devotion. Consistent with this view, the pair's friendship generally continued after the *wakashu* became a samurai himself.

Samurai warriors followed a strict code of honor. A popular Saikaku story from 1688, illustrates this rigid code and the tragic consequences that can result (Crompton, 2003). In the "Tragic Love of Two Enemies" from the *Tales of the Samurai Spirit*, samurai Senpatji is ordered by his feudal lord to kill his best friend, also a samurai. He does so, with regret. Years later, Senpatji encounters a woman and her teenage son in a remote province. Unbeknownst to Senpatji, the woman is his friend's widow and the youth, Shynosuke, is his son. Senpatji befriends them and falls in love with Shynosuke. When the woman realizes who the samurai is, she demands that Synosuke kill him. He initially refuses but finally agrees and confronts Senpatji. The samurai replies, "I am happy to die at your hands. Come and kill me, and avenge your father" (Crompton, 2003, p. 421). The mother overhears this exchange. Admiring both men for their sense of honor, she stops them before they fight. She asks them to "Love each other again for this night" (p. 421). The next morning the mother finds them together in bed dead. While lying together, Shynosuke had run his sword through Senpatji's heart and through his own body. The mother then kills herself for causing the deaths of these honorable men.

As powerful, respected warriors, the samurai captured Japanese imaginations. The popularity of samurai and their influence on culture reached its zenith in the Tokugawa period (1603–1867), also known as the Edo period after the capital of Japan. During the Tokugawa period, tens of thousands of samurai were garrisoned in the capital at any one time under the pretext of protecting the figurehead emperor. The government wished to keep an eye on the warriors and prevent provincial factions from taking hold (Crompton, 2003; Leupp, 1995). The heavy concentration of samurai in the capital fueled their influence on the culture. The middle class began mimicking samurai customs and fashion. Citizens began learning versions of the warrior arts (*judo, kyodo,* and *kendo*) for sport and spiritual discipline. Samurai-*wakashu* attendant friendships became a favorite theme in popular literature, often referred to as *nanshoku*. Middle-class men began imitating the *nanshoku* friendships that they read about, witnessed in popular theater, or observed in public. Imitated *nanshoku* friendships may have been passionate, but they lacked the valor, honor, and commitment that distinguished samurai-*wakashu* attendant bonds.

Tokugawa Period

After 150 years of warfare, new military leadership under Tokugawa Ieyasu brought a long period of peace and stability (Neill, 2009). The Tokugawa period saw extensive rebuilding and the need for craftsmen, artisans, and laborers. Trade and economic prosperity increased. By the early seventeenth century, a growing class of merchants and craftsmen emerged in Japanese cities. In Confucian hierarchy, merchants and craftsmen ranked at the bottom of social classes (Crompton, 2003). However, with money to spend, they freely enjoyed popular entertainments, like theater and male prostitutes. By this time, Japanese cities, like Edo, had thriving theater districts. A large part of theater's popularity was because actors often doubled as prostitutes. Nō theater, a sophisticated stylized artform, developed in the fourteenth century and was hugely popular (Crompton, 2003). Nō plays frequently featured *nanshoku* themes. Short farcical spoofs, called *kyogen* plays, served as fillers between serious performances. In one *kyogen* play called *The Old Warriors*, a beautiful noble boy, a *chigo*, and his servant arrive in a provincial town (Neill, 2009). Hearing of his visit, local young men (*wakashu*) of the town organize a party. As the party begins, an older man arrives and demands to see the *chigo*. He is turned away but returns later with (older) men with weapons. The young men disarm the angry villagers by jumping in their arms and kissing them. The joke is that the older men discover they are lovers of young men (*wakashu*) rather than boys (*chigo*).

In the early seventeenth century, *kabuki* theater originated as dance companies of women, with no aspirations of being art (Neill, 2009). Kabuki was performed without masks, and its early appeal was the attractiveness of the female performers. However, early kabuki theater became so notorious as a front for prostitution that in 1629 the government banned women on stage. Young male actors began playing the parts of girls and women. Attractive young boys playing beautiful girls created a huge sensation, and kabuki theater became more popular than ever. 1n 1652, the government tried to ban *wakashu* kabuki by requiring that girl characters be played by men over the age of 15 (Crompton, 2003). This rule failed to diminish theater's popularity or its association with prostitution. Rather, popular young male actors/prostitutes became minor celebrities in the culture. A critical commentary about kabuki theater published in 1658 reads: "They have produced a theater called *wakashu kabuki* in which the dancers are young men. Many men were so enchanted by their charms that they ended up swearing their eternal love and becoming ill by seriously wounding their arms" (Neill, 2009, p. 290). As noted earlier, cutting one's arms refers to the custom of oath swearing among samurai *nanshoku*. In another story, a samurai from an outer province attending his first kabuki performance in Edo is so mesmerized by the beauty of the *wakashu* actor that he jumps on stage, cuts off his ear, and hands it to the actor as a sign of everlasting love. Critics frequently complained about the huge sums of money men spent at the theater being entertained by young men.

Popular Tokugawa author, Ihara Saikaku, often wrote stories about samurai set in contemporary seventeenth-century Japan (Neill, 2009). The *Great Mirror of Man Love* (*Nanshoku ōkagami*), published in 1687, featured 20 stories depicting samurai *nanshoku* with young men, and 20 tales about men with kabuki actor-prostitutes (Crompton, 2003). The samurai stories often involve men of similar ages who take brotherhood vows, with one man designated as the "older brother" and the other as the "younger brother". In the tale, "Two Old Cherry Trees Still in Bloom", two samurai, now 66 and 63, who had eloped together as teens, are still deeply in love (Schalow, 1992). From his 1685 collection, *Five Women Who Loved Love* (*Kōshoku gonin onna*), Saikaku describes the typical sexual progression of a young Japanese man: In his youth, he is the beloved of an older man who is in his 20s or 30s; when he comes of age, the man takes a youth of his own. Eventually, men marry and have children, although this does not necessarily mean the end of intimate relationships with men or male youths. In another Saikaku novel, *Life of an Amorous Man* (*Kōshoku ichidai otoko*), the protagonist, Yonosuke, at the age of 54, takes an accounting of his life. He muses that to date he has seduced 3,742 women and 725 men. In *A Boor's Tale* (*Denbu monogatari*), a popular story from this period by an anonymous author, friends argue about the superiority of (men) loving women versus loving male youths (*wakashu*), reminiscent of Plutarach's *The Dialogue on Love* (Leupp, 1995). Several friends meet at a river to escape the heat and begin a discussion about love: "Why don't we debate the issue? Is the Way of Women truly vulgar, and the Way of Youths really more refined?" (Leupp, 1995, p. 207). One man, called the Refined One, states that *wakashu* is better because it is preferred by samurai and priests. The woman-lover, the Boor, claims that love of women is better and profound. The Boor adds that women produce children and have made major contributions to society. However, as night falls, no one has won the debate, and the friends go home. The author apparently saw no reason to answer the question directly, although the names of the main characters may say it all.

The Meiji Restoration and the End of Samurai Nanshoku

By the early eighteenth century, the samurai *nanshoku* tradition was in decline (Neill, 2009). The long period of peace had lessened the necessity and importance of the warrior class and their customs. Popularity had reduced samurai honor, virtue, and "brotherhood" to a caricature. The theater, frequented by samurai and middle-class merchants, portrayed *nanshoku* as simply the love of beautiful young men and sexual gratification at a price. The association of *nanshoku* with masculinity and physical prowess was gone. The most desired male actor-prostitutes were slight, effeminate, and bawdy. By the early nineteenth century, samurai *nanshoku* had almost disappeared.

With the restoration of imperial power in 1867, there followed a period of rapid westernization as Japan sought to catch up to the industrial West and match their military capabilities. During this time, the Japanese became more self-conscious of how the West perceived them (Crompton, 2003). Westerners visited Japan frequently and did not disguise their reactions to what they saw. They were shocked by the public display of erotic art and the prevalence of phallic shrines. Western visitors could not fathom the lack of shame among the Japanese who engaged in mixed nude bathing, nor the acceptance of male love. The imperial government viewed visible male love as an embarrassment and liability and attempted to ban male-male sexual activity in 1873. The penalty was 90 days of imprisonment, although the law was ineffective. Under advisement by French legal experts, the government repealed the law ten years later (Crompton, 2003). However, by this time, male-male sexuality was socially disapproved. Since Japanese culture lacked the extreme religious condemnation of homosexuality that was so prevalent in the West, male love became impolite. Once widely popular, male love was now a shameful embarrassment. Japanese writers commented critically on male love among students and soldiers well into the twentieth century. Increasingly the culture ignored or refused to discuss male love.

In closing this section, Japan had a long tradition of devoted male friendships among religious orders, government officials, and the military. Monks had their *chigo* acolytes. Rulers had their male favorites, and samurai had their *wakashu* attendants. For the young, lower-status individual, devoted male friendships offered many social benefits. Bonding with an adult priest, government official, or samurai facilitated the youth's education, training, access to resources, and social advancement. While men in monasteries did not marry or have children, a youth's close relationship with respected priests or monks could facilitate better living conditions, social networking, and advancement in the religious community. Male favorites of an emperor, court official, or shōgunate ruler significantly improved their lives and gained significant social status, power, and wealth. Many male favorites were married and had children. Samurai warriors were cultural heroes and achieving samurai status provided honor and social advantages that also benefited one's wife and children. Although early samurai did not marry, later samurai did. While devoted male friendships may not have always been sexual, Japanese culture did not stigmatize male-male sexuality or the receptive sexual role until negative Western sexual attitudes took hold. Numerous references to friends exchanging vows suggest that devoted friendships or brotherhood bonds were common and respected in Japanese culture. For 700 years, samurai *nanshoku* relationships were respected and widely popular. During the Tokugawa period, the urban middle-class imitated samurai *nanshoku* friendships, although the prevalence of *nanshoku*-like relationships among ordinary citizens is unknown. Popular culture's reconceptualization of *nanshoku* relationships as pleasurable entertainments, the decline of the warrior class, and increasing contact with the West contributed to a general disapproval of male-male sexuality in late nineteenth-century Japan.

Concluding Remarks about Devoted Friendships

I have argued that devoted same-sex friendships are an adaptation for life in sex-segregated environments. In this chapter, I provided a brief historical survey of devoted same-sex friendships from early civilizations in Mesopotamia through advanced civilizations in Greece, Italy, China, and Japan, up to the near present. Table 4.1 summarizes this data. Across these cultures and throughout history, segregation of men and women has been common, and devoted male friendships have been pervasive. Devoted male friendships have had various names, such as blood brothers, adoptive brothers, sworn brothers, *erastēs* and *erōmenos*, true friends, male favorites, *nenja* priest and *chigo* acolyte, and samurai *nanshoku*. Devoted male friendships have also been referenced euphemistically as "The Cut Sleeve" or "The Half-Eaten Peach". At other times, devoted male friendships have been referenced by the names of legendary friends, such as Gilgamesh and Enkidu, Achilles and Patroclus, Orestes and Pylades, David and Jonathan, and Alexander and Hephaestion.

Devoted male friendships have taken at least three common forms. Most frequently, devoted friendships have involved an adult, higher status male mentor with a lower status male youth novice. This form of devoted male friendship has been common among warrior-military cultures, such as the ancient Sumerians, Indo-European invaders and their descendants (the Celts, Scythians, and Germanic tribes), Romans, and feudal Japan. The adult mentor-friend functioned as teacher, protector, superior officer, sponsor, and companion for the youth. The adult mentor-friend helped the youth navigate the male hierarchical military environment and society. The youth gained knowledge, combat and survival skills, allies, status, social skills, better living conditions, and resources to support a family. Without a mentor-friend, male youth in warrior-military cultures would have found it difficult to improve their lives or survive for long. The mentor-novice pair sometimes exchanged vows in public ceremonies to signify their special relationship and commitment to each other. Although the training period ended when the male youth reached adulthood or married, evidence suggests that the devoted friendship often continued. Devoted friendships among men close in age appear to have involved differences in social status. Achilles and Patroclus and Alexander and Hephaestion are good examples.

The ruler-favorite is a second common form of devoted male friendships. Since most cultures were sex-segregated, the imperial courts were largely male societies, although rulers and government officials had ready access to women. Typically, the favorite was a handsome young lower status male who gained considerable power and wealth because of his unique relationship with the ruler/official. Evidence suggests that male favorites were often married, and the favorite's position benefited his wife, children, and sometimes his extended family. The third common form of devoted male friendships is found among religious orders, like Japanese Buddhist priests/monks and their acolytes. Priest/monk-acolyte friendships were age- and status-structured similar to warrior-attendant friendships in military cultures. Acolytes gained a teacher, protector, mentor, sponsor, and companion.

Table 4.1 Devoted Same-Sex Friendships from Early Civilizations in Mesopotamia through
Advanced Civilizations in Greece, Italy, China, and Japan

Civilizations	Reference	Time period
Early farming communities	Goddess worship and fertility sex (suggestive)	Beginning appx. 9000 BCE
Indo-European warrior people		Invasion from appx. 4000–1000 BCE
Germanic tribes, Celtic people, and Scythians	Male initiation/mentoring; blood brotherhoods; male sexual relationships	Beginning appx. 1700 BCE
Hittites	Hittite Law I #36	Appx. 1650–1100 BCE
Ancient Mesopotamia		
Sumeria, Akkadia, Babylonia, and Assyria	Gilgamesh and Enkidu in the poem *Gilgamesh*	Compiled appx. 2100 BCE; Gilgamesh reigned between 2800–2500 BCE
Middle East		
Early Israelites	Ruth and Naomi in the Book of Ruth*	Compiled fifth century BCE; events date to the thirteenth century BCE
	David and Jonathan in 1 and 2 Samuel	Compiled late seventh century BCE; events date to the eleventh and tenth centuries BCE
Ancient Greece		
Archaic Greece	Achilles and Patroclus in *The Odyssey*	Compiled eighth century BCE; events date to the thirteenth and twelfth centuries BCE
North Aegean Islands	Sappho's love poems; sisterhoods in the *thiasoi*; novels depicting female couples*	Late seventh century BCE through 215 CE
Dorians	Male initiation/mentoring; brotherhoods	Beginning appx. 1200 BCE
Athens (Classical period)	Adult-youth courting; lifelong devoted male friendships among peers	Beginning appx. fifth century BCE
Hellenistic Greece	Alexander and Hephaestion; spread of Greek customs, including adult-youth relationships and warrior-attendant devoted friendships	Beginning 336 BCE

(Continued)

Table 4.1 Continued

Civilizations	Reference	Time period
Roman Republic and Empire	Burial of pairs of unrelated same-sex adults*	Appx. first century BCE through Roman Empire
	Funerary same-sex friendship epitaphs: especially, female friends*	Appx. first century BCE through Roman Empire
	Male unions: e.g., Manlius Torquatus and friend; Callistratus and Afer	Appx. first century BCE through Roman Empire
	Julius Caesar and Nicomedes, King of Bithynia	First century BCE
	Cicero's *De amicitia* to Atticus: e.g., Laelius and Scipio	Appx. first century CE
	Hippothoos and Hyperanthes, then Cleisthenes in *Ephesiaca*	First century CE
	Valerius Maximus' *Facta et dicta memorabilia*: e.g., Orestes and Pylades; Valerius and Sextus Pompeius	First century CE
	Enclopius and Giton in *Satryicon*	First century CE
	Emperor Hadrian and Antinous	Second century CE
Ancient and Imperial China		
Zhou Dynasty	King Xiang Cheng and Zhuang Xin	Appx. tenth century BCE
	Duke Ling and Mizi Xia (Half-Eaten Peach)	Late sixth century BCE
Han Dynasty	Emperor Wen and Deng Tong	Second century BCE
	Emperor Jing and Zhou Ren	Second century BCE
	Emperor Ai and Dong Xian (The Cut Sleeve)	First century BCE
	Devoted female friendships in court called *dui shi**	First century BCE
Post-Han period	Poets Pan Yue and Xiahou Zhan (Linked Jade Disks)	Third century
	Poets Xi Kang and Ruan Ji	Third century
	Ruler Wang Zhongxian and Pan Zhang (The Shared Pillow Tree)	Third century
Tang and Song Dynasties	Devoted male friends and male-male sexuality in novels and popular stories	Seventh through thirteenth centuries
Ming Dynasty	Emperor Xizong and male favorites	Seventeenth century
	Jin, Liu, and Quan in "The House of Gathered Refinements"	Seventeenth century
	Zhang Ji and Zhong Tunan in *Chronicle of Chivalric Love*	Seventeenth century
	Madam Fan and Cao Yuhua in *The Fragrant Companion**	Seventeenth century
	Female devoted friendships/sisterhoods among Buddhist and Taoist nuns;* female unions in Guangdong province east of Fujian*	Seventeenth century on
	Male devoted friendships/brotherhoods in Fujian (The Southern Custom)	At least late sixteenth century on

(Continued)

Table 4.1 Continued

Civilizations	Reference	Time period
Qing Dynasty	Manchu emperors had male favorites	Seventeenth and eighteenth centuries
	Literature depicts adult and young men in devoted male friendships	Seventeenth to mid-nineteenth century
Imperial and feudal Japan	Kūkai (Kōbō Daishi) founds Shingon Buddhism	Appx. 816
	Terms identified for priest (*nenja*) and acolyte (*chigo*) in loving sexual relationships	Ninth century on
	Emperor Shirakawa had male favorites	Late eleventh to early twelfth century
	Emperor Toba had male favorites	Early twelfth century
	Emperor Go-Shirakaw and Fujiwara Nobuyori	Late twelfth century
	Samurai established; custom of samurai-*wakashu* attendant devoted friendships begins	Twelfth century on
	Minamoto Yoritomo, first shōgun, had male favorite; 26 shōguns and daimyos had male favorites during shōgunate military rule	1185–1867; twelfth century on
	Monk and acolyte devoted friends make vows to each other	Early thirteenth century on
	Devoted monk-acolyte friendship called "brotherhood bond" (*kyodai musubi*)	Seventeenth century
	Eleven shōguns had male favorites; Edo middle-class imitate samurai *nanshoku* friendships; Nō and *wakashu* kabuki theater feature *nanshoku* themes; *A Boor's Tale* debates love of *wakashu* and women	1603–1867 (Tokugawa period)

*Specific references to female friendships

Without an adult mentor-friend to sponsor him and make introductions, young Buddhist acolytes likely had difficulty achieving advancement in the religious community.

Although devoted male friendships are prevalent across historical cultures, evidence for devoted female friendships is sparse. Historically, men have been uninterested in women's activities and left them out of the record. Even so, a few examples can be found, such as the special friendship between Ruth and Naomi and sisterhoods among girls in the *thiasoi* of North Aegean Islands. In Rome, funerary epitaphs celebrate female friends and combined burials of unrelated adult women suggest that Roman women had very close friendships. References to female couples (*dui shi*) in the Han Dynasty court, female marriages in the Guangdong province, and female couples in novels and plays support the existence of devoted female friendships in ancient Chinese culture. We know little about how devoted female friendships were structured, although there are obvious advantages for women who have close female allies and companions within sex-segregated environments.

Critics may argue that variability in how friendships have been defined makes comparison across cultures impossible. I disagree. Differences across cultures warrant caution in making comparisons, but comparisons are quite useful. We also readily accept other concepts that vary widely across cultures, like "adulthood", "marriage", and "family", and understand that these concepts have common features and value. Devoted friendships are similar. There is logic and consistency in the concept of devoted male friendships that permit cautious comparisons across cultures.

Others may complain that I have deliberately blurred the distinction between friends and lovers. I have. However, many historical cultures have not differentiated between friends and lovers, although Western culture does. Again, the persistence of passionate, intimate, long-term devoted male friendships across cultures is the critical feature, not whether friends had sex. Our modern preoccupation with sexuality as a defining characteristic of people and relationships makes it difficult for us to move past sex and imagine other ways of being. Devoted male friendships in past cultures have often involved sexual intimacy, but sex did not define those relationships. Historical cultures described in this chapter have viewed sexual expression within devoted male friendships in a variety of ways: As a function of power, a sign of submission, affirmation of social roles, a spiritual connection or communion with a life force, and even simply as pleasure. For these cultures, love and commitment within established social roles defined devoted friendships, not sex.

Some critics may believe that, like today, a few men are attracted to men and these are the people depicted in the historical record in devoted male friendships. In other words, I have only demonstrated the existence of a small proportion of men-who-love-men across cultures. Nothing more. However, historical men in devoted friendships were not early versions of gay men, and the prevalence of devoted male friendships across historical cultures exceeds the small proportion of same-sex attracted men found in contemporary Western culture. Among warrior-military cultures, for example, devoted male friendships were widespread. Further, the profiles of devoted male friends in historical cultures run counter to the characteristics of gay men in contemporary Western culture. In warrior-military cultures and many imperial courts, men in devoted friendships are described as masculine, while contemporary gay men are usually presented as gender nonconforming or effeminate (Bailey, Vasey, Diamond, Breedlove, Vilain, & Epprecht, 2016). Never masculine! Further, men in historical devoted friendships nearly always had wives and children, unlike gay men today. Were men in historical devoted friendships simply restricted in sexual outlets? Were they behaviorally bisexual, consistent with their culture, but not actually sexually attracted to male youths or men? In sex-segregated cultures, male contact with women was often restricted but outside of religious orders men were not completely cut off from female sexual partners. In many cultures, men were not prohibited from having additional female sexual partners even after marriage. Abundant evidence demonstrates that men in devoted friendships felt a deep, passionate love for their companions, above that experienced with women.

This model of attraction, love, and same-sex friendships found in historical cultures contrasts sharply with how people experience themselves and form relationships in contemporary Western culture. In the next chapter, I will examine contemporary ideas about sexual attractions, personal identities, and social reality.

Take Home Points

- Humans have lived in sex-segregated cultures, until very recently.
- Across historical cultures, adult men frequently formed mentoring relationships with male youths or young men that became devoted friendships. Typically, devoted male friends differed in age, social status, and role.
- Having an adult mentor-friend offered direct advantages for survival and indirect reproductive benefits to young males within sex-segregated societies.
- Limited evidence suggests that in many cultures women also formed devoted friendships with girls or young women.
- Sex-negative attitudes in Western culture have significantly contributed to the disappearance of devoted male friendships.

References

Alessi, P. T. (2003). *Golden verses: Poetry of the Augustan age*. Indianapolis, IN: Hackett Publishing.

Auanger, L. (2002). Glimpses through a window: An approach to Roman female homoeroticism through art historical and literary evidence. In N. S. Rabinowitz & L. Auanger (Eds.), *Among women: From the homosocial to the homoerotic in the ancient world* (pp. 211–255). Austin, TX: University of Texas Press.

Babylonia (2020). *Wikipedia*. https://en.wikipedia.org/wiki/Babylonia.

Bailey, J. M., Vasey, P. L., Diamond, L. M., Breedlove, S. M., Vilain, E., & Epprecht, M. (2016). Sexual orientation, controversy, and science. *Psychological Science in the Public Interest, 17*(2), 45–101.

Boswell, J. (1980). *Christianity, social tolerance, and homosexuality: Gay people in Western Europe from the beginning of the Christian era to the fourteenth century*. Chicago, IL: University of Chicago Press.

Boswell, J. (1994). *Same-sex unions in premodern Europe*. New York: Villard Books.

Bramanti, B., Thomas, M. G., Haak, W., Unterländer, M., Jores, P., Tambets, K., ... Burger, J. (2009). Genetic discontinuity between local hunter-gatherers and Europe's first farmers. *Science*, *326*(5949), 137–140.

Brooten, B. J. (1996). *Love between women: Early Christian responses to female homoeroticism*. Chicago, IL: University of Chicago Press.

Cantarella, E. (1992). *Bisexuality in the ancient world*. New Haven, CT: Yale University Press.

Cochran, G., & Harpending, H. (2009). *The 10,000 year explosion: How civilization accelerated human evolution*. New York: Basic Books.

Crompton, L. (2003). *Homosexuality & civilization*. Cambridge: Belknap Press.

Curry, A. (2013). Archaeology: The milk revolution. *Nature*, *500*(7460), 20–22.

Dover, K. J. (1989). *Greek homosexuality*. Cambridge, MA: Harvard University Press.

Ebrey, P. (2020). Women in traditional China. Asia Society Center for Global Education. https://asiasociety.org/education/women-traditional-china

Frend, W. H. C. (1965). *Martyrdom and persecution in the early church: A study of conflict from the Maccabees to Donatus*. Oxford: Blackwell.

Garnier, R., Sagart, L., & Sagot, B. (2017). Milk and the Indo-Europeans. In M. Robeets & A. Savalyev (Eds.), *Language dispersal beyond farming* (pp. 291–311). Amsterdam, The Netherlands: John Benjamins Publishing.

Goetze, A. (1950/1974). The Hittite laws. In J. B. Pritchard (Ed.), *Ancient near Eastern texts relating to the Old Testament* (pp. 188–196). Princeton, NJ: Princeton University Press.

Greenberg, D. F. (1988). *The construction of homosexuality*. Chicago, IL: University of Chicago Press.

Hardmann, P. D. (1993). *Homoaffectionalism: Male bonding from Gilgamesh to the present*. San Francisco, CA: GLB Publishers.

Herm, G. (1975). *The celts: The people who came out of darkness*. New York: St. Martin's Press.

Hinsch, B. (1990). *Passions of the cut sleeve: The male homosexual tradition in China*. Berkeley, CA: University of California Press.

History of China (2020). *Wikipedia*. https://en.wikipedia.org/wiki/History_of_China

Hofmanová, Z., Kreutzer, S., Hellenthal, G., Sell, C., Diekmann, Y., Díez-del-Molino, D., ... Burger, J. (2016). Early farmers from across Europe directly descended from Neolithic Aegeans. *Proceedings from the National Academy of Sciences*, *113*(25), 6886–6891.

Homer. (1938). *The Iliad* (W. H. D. Rouse, transl.). New York: New American Library.

Horner, T. M. (1978a). *Jonathan loved David: Homosexuality in Biblical times*. Philadelphia, PA: Westminster.

Horner, T. M. (1978b). *Eros in Greece: A sexual inquiry*. New York: Aegean Books.

Indo-European migrations (2020). *Wikipedia*. https://en.wikipedia.org/wiki/Indo-European_migrations

Japan. (2020). *Wikipedia*. https://en.wikipedia.org/wiki/Japan

Konstan, D. (1997). *Friendship in the classical world*. Cambridge, United Kingdom: Cambridge University Press.

Kuin, I. N. I. (2017). Being a barbarian: Lucian and otherness in the second sophistic. *Groniek*, *49*(211), 131–143.

Leupp, G. P. (1995). *Male colors: The construction of homosexuality in Tokugawa Japan*. Berkeley, CA: University of California Press.

Lewes, K. (1988). *The psychoanalytic theory of male homosexuality*. New York: Meridian.

Mitchell, S. (2004). *Gilgamesh: A new English version*. New York: Free Press.

Neill, J. (2009). *The origins and role of same-sex relations in human societies*. Jefferson, NC: McFarland & Company.

Nemet-Nejat, K. R. (1999). Women in ancient Mesopotamia. In B. Vivante (Ed.), *Women's roles in ancient civilizations: A reference guide*. Westport, CT: Greenwood.

Nissinen, M. (1998). *Homoeroticism in the Biblical world: A historical perspective* (K. Stjerna, transl.). Minneapolis, MN: Fortress.

Nixey, C. (2017). *The darkening age: The Christian destruction of the classical world*. London: Pan Macmillan.

Norton, R. (1993). The historical roots of homophobia. In W. Leyland (Ed.), *Gay roots: An anthology of gay history, sex, politics, and culture* (pp. 69–92). San Francisco, CA: Gay Sunshine.

Olalde, I., Schroeder, H., Sandoval-Velasco, M., Vinner, L., Lobón, I., Ramirez, O., … Lalueza-Fox, C. (2015). A common genetic origin for early farmers from Mediterranean cardial and Central European LBK cultures. *Molecular Biology and Evolution*, 32(12), 3132–3242.

Saller, R. P. (1989). Patronage and friendship in early imperial Rome: Drawing the distinction. In A. Wallace-Hadrill (Ed.), *Patronage in ancient society* (pp. 49–62). London: Routledge.

Sandars, N. K. (1972). *The epic of Gilgamesh*. London: Penguin Books.

Schalow, P. G. (1992). Kūkai and the tradition of male love in Japanese Buddhism. In J. I. Cabezón (Ed.), *Buddhism, sexuality, and gender* (pp. 215–230). Albany, NY: State University of New York Press.

Sergent, B. (1986). *Homosexuality in Greek myth* (A. Goldhammer, transl.). Boston, MA: Beacon.

Shaw, B. (1994). A groom of one's own? *The New Republic*. https://newrepublic.com/article/79049/groom-ones-own

Sumer (2020). *Wikipedia*. https://en.wikipedia.org/wiki/Sumer

Taylor, T. (1996). *The prehistory of sex: Four million years of human sexual culture*. New York: Bantam Press Books.

Uyeda, J. C., Hansen, T. F., Arnold, S. J., & Pienaar, J. (2011). The million-year wait for macroevolutionary bursts. *Proceedings of the National Academy of Sciences*, 108(38), 15908–15913.

Vanggaard, T. (1972). *Phallós: A symbol and its history in the male world*. New York: International Universities Press.

Vicinus, M. (2004). *Intimate friends: Women who loved women, 1778–1928*. Chicago, IL: University of Chicago Press.

Ward, A. (2008). Mothering and the sacrifice of self: Women and friendship in Aristotle's Nicomachean ethics. *Thirdspace*, 7(2), 32–57.

Weeks, J. (1985/1989). *Sexuality and its discontents*. London: Routledge.

Westboro Baptist Church. (2020). *Godhatesfags.com*. https://www.godhatesfags. com/

Williams, C. A. (2012). *Reading Roman friendship*. New York: Cambridge University Press.

Young, R. D. (1994). Gay marriage: Reimagining church history. *First Things*, 47, 43–48. http://www.leaderu.com/ftissues/ft9411/articles/darling.html

Chapter 5

Labeling Love and People
Sexual Attractions and Identities

Most of us have felt sexually attracted to someone at some point in our lives. Probably many times. Those who interact frequently with a range of people may experience sexual attraction fairly regularly. It happens something like this: We notice a handsome man or a beautiful woman on the street or while standing in line for coffee. Our eyes meet for a moment, and we both smile. Or we meet someone new at a party and feel quite pleased by their interest and close contact. We feel excited and special. Or we recognize an awkward erotic feeling for a friend or a colleague at work during an exchange and blush. We feel nervous. Self-conscious. Heart pounding. We lose our train of thought and stumble over words. We want to be physically close to the other person—and not talking. Everything around us seems to disappear. Sexual or romantic fantasies may captivate our thoughts for days (and nights). If we are brave enough to propose meeting later for coffee, or a drink, or dinner, we may discover that the other person says yes. We may find that they like our company. If we manage not to do something stupid while having coffee or dinner, we may find that the individual is even willing to have sex with us! If the sexual encounter turns awkward and disappointing which can happen when expectations are high, the attraction may end then and there. But if all goes well and the experience is enjoyable, the attraction may grow. Some people only recognize their attraction after good sex. If we have shared interests, complementary personalities, and more time together, the excitement and pleasure may develop into love.

While love is indeed grand, it is not rational or logical. Without doing anything deliberate, we may again notice a handsome man or beautiful woman and feel an erotic tug. For many of us, sexual attraction feels automatic and not conscious. It seems to just happen. Why that person? Why now? We may not know exactly who or what triggers sexual attraction in us, but we may have a pretty good idea of who or what we are *not* attracted to. For instance, many people might say they are definitely not attracted to someone of the same sex. Not now. Not in the past. Never. Some people might acknowledge that they deeply love a same-sex best friend, enjoy time together, and profoundly miss their friend when apart but deny any possibility of sexual attraction or sexual intimacy with their friend. French philosopher Michel Montaigne (1580/1993), for example, acknowledged his close friendship and profound love for his friend, Étienne de la Boétie: "If I am pressed to say why I love him, I feel that my only reply could be: 'Because it was he, because it was I'" (p. 97). Montaigne is an insightful, articulate fellow, but his best explanation is simply that he and Étienne love each other because of who they are.

People today appear to experience sexual attraction, love, and friendship quite differently from our ancestors, even recent ancestors from a few hundred years ago. Although we perceive our sexual attractions as automatic and unconscious, in truth, sexual attractions are filtered through our experience of ourselves and social circumstances. How we experience ourselves is a function of numerous individual and social factors, including gender, age, race/ethnicity, nationality, skin color, temperament, body image, health, self-esteem, mood, developmental history, social status, social history, family dynamics, relationship status, proximity to others, size and structure of the community, and the prevailing cultural norms to name a few. As automatic as it seems, sexual attraction is not simply a reaction to a stimulus; it is a social experience. An individual's experience of sexual attraction is a function of their predispositions for attraction, their personal history, and the culture in which they live.

Throughout this text, I have described how sexual attraction and love have been central to male-female mating pair-bonds and devoted same-sex friendships at least since the time of early human hunter-gatherers. Different-sex sexual attraction and love solved the problem of sustaining sexual activity between reproductive partners frequently enough to promote pair-bonding, conceive a child, and ensure parental investment in offspring within the context of a hunter-gatherer culture and its social conventions. Self-selection of a reproductive mate had advantages but so did arranged marriages. Further, devoted friendships solved the problem of navigating complex same-sex social environments to survive, thrive, and acquire resources to obtain a quality reproductive mate and support a family within a hunter-gatherer culture and its social conventions. Devoted male friendships have been observed across cultures and throughout history, which strongly supports the hypothesis that devoted same-sex friendships are adaptive traits. The passionate attachment and sexual intimacies of historical devoted male friendships are quite different from contemporary male friendships and how most men think about and experience their sexuality. Gay men are an exception. Both gay men and lesbian women are more likely than heterosexual men and women to have sex with friends, although not necessarily with their best friends (Nardi & Sherrod, 1994).

In Chapter Four, I identified anti-sexual Judeo-Christian attitudes within Western culture and our cultural emphasis on the individual as major factors accounting for how sexuality and devoted male friendships are expressed today. While not specific to sexuality, a recent study published in *Science* illustrates the powerful cultural influence of the Western Roman Catholic Church on how we think about ourselves and experience social reality. Across 440 regions within 36 countries, researchers examined the duration of exposure to the Catholic Church's policies, the intensity of kinship-based institutions, and 24 psychological outcomes related to individualism, cooperation, and conformity (Schulz, Bahrami-Rad, Beauchamp, & Heinrich, 2019). Over the past 1,500 years, Europeans with longer exposure to the Catholic Church's policies and pronouncements on marriage and family grew more individualistic, less obedient to elders, more focused on the nuclear family and less focused on kin, more prosocial toward strangers, and more sensitive to relational contexts of fairness compared to people in regions with less exposure to the Catholic Church. Unquestionably, the Roman Catholic Church has suppressed native beliefs and traditional practices and dominated the psychology of European people under its influence (Neill, 2009). Over the past 1,500 years, the Catholic Church has significantly altered European attitudes toward marriage, family, friendship, and same-sex sexuality. Recent non-religious ideological pressures such as individualism, capitalism, and the invention of sexual kinds of people in the late nineteenth century (e.g., the homosexual/gay/lesbian) have also significantly affected how people experience and interpret their lives (Neill, 2009). In this chapter, I explore the effect of recent ideological pressures on sexuality and identity.

Contemporary Westerners living in secular democracies may find it difficult to believe that Christianity ever had such power over people's thoughts and way of life. Today, we live in a largely technological society detached from close-knit kin groups with civil governments of elected officials that assure citizens of inalienable human rights. But, we are not so far from the past. Most moral arguments today around sexual and gender minority rights, gender transitioning, gay marriage, contraception, abortion, euthanasia, and even immigration and gun rights echo familiar Christian platitudes and predictions of societal disaster (e.g., God's punishment) if we do not follow God's natural laws. Popular Christian televangelists blame gay people for high divorce rates, terrorist attacks, and natural disasters (Pat Robertson Controversies, 2019). People living in the Christianized late Roman Empire, or in medieval Europe during the Inquisition, or among the Puritans in colonial America experienced intense pressure to conform to approved religious standards or be exiled or killed. Like early Christians in Rome, Islamic Republics and Islamic extremists today are busy pursuing the same oppressive theocratic goals of a conformist religious state.

In this chapter, I explore the conceptualization of sexual attraction in contemporary Western culture. I contrast the modern experience of exclusive attraction and sexual identities with historical patterns of bisexuality and argue that people's experience of exclusive (hetero)sexual attraction is a culturally imposed constraint.

Inventing Sexual Kinds of People

In our current culture, sexual attraction reflects specific sexual orientation identities (Stein, 1999). That is, people are grouped or defined and self-defined by their sexual attractions. Typical sexual orientation identity labels are *heterosexual* or *straight* (different-sex attracted), *gay* or *lesbian* (same-sex attracted), *bisexual* (attraction to both sexes), and various other terms (e.g., pansexual, biromantic) representing non-heterosexual attractions. Identity labels reflect social norms and are not adopted to accurately represent an individual's sexual attraction or their sexual behavior. People choose a sexual orientation identity for many reasons. They may select an identity out of pride, defiance, or to gain social benefits associated with conforming to community expectations and avoid social stigma.

Sexual orientation refers broadly to one's sexual attraction to same-sex or different-sex partners, or both, or to one's identity. Sexual orientation is a multi-dimensional concept that encompasses identity, sexual attraction, behavior, fantasy, and romantic attraction (Kauth, 2000). These dimensions are not entirely congruent and provide different but overlapping information about the individual. Sometimes researchers use identity labels (e.g., heterosexual, gay) as proxies for exclusive sexual attraction and behavior, which is not entirely accurate. Conscientious investigators acknowledge this limitation. Researchers sometimes categorize people by sexual behaviors (e.g., men-who-have-sex-with-men or MSM) to avoid the mismatch between identities and behavior, although the categories do not reflect how people view themselves. Adding to the confusion, researchers assess sexual attraction, behavior, and identity in various ways depending on their aims, employing different methods and formats, dissimilar response options, and even idiosyncratic assessment periods. Unsurprisingly, self-report methods yield somewhat different results compared to physiological assessments like sexual arousal or pupil dilation. Reporting formats (e.g., paper-and-pencil survey and computer-assisted interview) assure different degrees of anonymity, which affects how candidly people respond to sexual questions. Non-standard response options also change what people report. Inconsistencies and imprecision in sexual orientation measurements make it difficult to compare data across studies, although fuzzy measures have not stopped sexual orientation research. In a recent paper, Bailey, Vasey, Diamond, Breedlove, Vilain, and Epprecht (2016) provided a comprehensive review of methodological issues in assessing sexual orientation and the state of research findings on same-sex attraction.

The idea that there are two natural kinds of people—those who are exclusively attracted to men or to women—dates to the late nineteenth century (Stein, 1999). Philosopher Michel Foucault (1990) famously claimed in the introduction to his *History of Sexuality*: "Homosexuality appeared as one of the forms of sexuality when it was transposed from the practice of sodomy onto a kind of interior androgyny, a hermaphrodism (*sic*) of the soul. The sodomite had been a temporary aberration; the homosexual was now a species" (p. 43). Implicit but surprisingly not mentioned in Foucault's statement is the simultaneous birth of the "heterosexual". The homosexual/gay/lesbian and the heterosexual are inextricably linked. In *The Invention of Heterosexuality*, Jonathan Ned Katz (1995) explores this twin birth and how the exclusive heterosexual came to be defined as normal and natural.

Expanding on Foucault, gender and critical theorist David Halperin (1990) observed winkingly that "Sexuality is thus the inmost part of an individual human nature. It is the feature of a person that takes the longest to get to know well, and knowing it renders transparent and intelligible to the knower the person to whom it belongs. Sexuality holds the key to unlocking the deepest mysteries of the human personality" (p. 26). Halperin attributed the birth of "homo-sexuality" as a concept to Charles Gilbert Chaddock's English translation of Richard von Krafft-Ebing's enormously influential medical text, *Psychopathia Sexualis*. According to Halperin (1990), "Before 1892 there was no homosexuality, only sexual inversion" (p. 15). Of note, Chaddock also used the term "hetero-sexuality" in the same text, but he was not the first to use these terms. German-Hungarian activist, Karoly Maria Kertbeny, had already used "homosexual" and "heterosexual" in an 1868 letter to Karl Ulrichs, a German activist who had published texts defending men who love men. Ulrichs (1994) had invented a typology of sexual attraction (and a separate terminology) based on gender inversion. In Ulrichs' model, *true* men loved women, making female attraction a male trait, and *true* women loved men, making male attraction a female trait. Men who loved men were like-women and possessed a female soul. Women who loved women had a male soul. Ulrichs viewed these characteristics as inherent traits and not behavioral preferences.

The popularity of *Psychopathia Sexualis* helped to spread the idea that people either possessed inherent same-sex or different-sex attractions (Halperin, 1990; Katz, 1995). Sigmund Freud must have been aware of Krafft-Ebing's work, but he did not view kinds of sexual attraction as exclusive or fixed. Like Ulrichs, Freud (1905/1953) incorporated gender inversion into his conception of sexuality and made sexuality central to his theory of development. He hypothesized that exclusive same-sex attraction represented a fixation in an early stage of psychosexual development. Even so, Freud did not view same-sex attraction as a mental illness and even hypothesized that same-sex eroticism was essential to friendship (Lewes, 1988). Nevertheless, Freud (1915/1987) referred to male-female sexuality as "normal", meaning typical, and the ultimate outcome of psychosexual development.

Later psychoanalysts, like Sandor Rado and Edmund Bergler, disagreed with Freud on homosexuality. Rado and Bergler saw male-female sexual attraction as biological and *essential* to psychological health (Lewes, 1988).

Further, both viewed same-sex attraction as a mental disorder. Published in 1952, the first edition of the American Psychiatric Association's *Diagnostic and Statistical Manual of Mental Disorders* (DSM) reflected post-Freudian psychoanalytic thinking. Homosexuality appeared in DSM I as a Sociopathic Personality Disturbance. Psychoanalysts were also highly skeptical of the concept of bisexuality (Lewes, 1988). Bergler (1962) proclaimed emphatically in one text: "BISEXUALITY—a state that has no existence beyond the word itself—is an out-and-out fraud, involuntarily maintained by some naïve homosexuals, and voluntarily perpetrated by some who are not so naïve" (p. 80). In contrast, biologist Alfred Kinsey (1948; 1953) had published data from a large sample demonstrating that many men and women engaged in bisexual behavior. Remarkably, 46% of adult men and 28% of women reported having both male and female sexual partners. Kinsey argued that there were not just two kinds of sexual people: "The world is not to be divided into sheep and goats. Not all things are black nor all things white. It is a fundamental of taxonomy that nature rarely deals with discrete categories. Only the human mind invents categories and tries to force facts into separated pigeon-holes" (1948, p. 639).

In the late 1940s and early 1950s, Kinsey (1948; 1953) shocked the world with evidence that people engaged in a surprising variety of sexual behaviors. Kinsey and colleagues had conducted lengthy face-to-face interviews with more than 12,000 men and nearly 6,000 women. He aimed to approximate the general population with a large enough convenience sample. Unfortunately, the sample included a disproportionate number of male prisoners, prostitutes, and the sexually adventurous. Kinsey and colleagues categorized participants' sexuality on a 7-point scale based on the sex of partners with whom they had experienced an orgasm. They categorized just 50% of men and 70% of women as exclusively heterosexual based on their reported sexual behavior. (See Table 5.1). A small percentage of men and women reported only same-sex partners (4% and 2%, respectively). However, 10% of men were exclusively same-sex partnered for at least three years between the ages of 16 and 55. Two-to-six percent of unmarried women and less than 1% of married women were exclusively same-sex partnered between the ages of 25 and 35.

Kinsey's argument against discrete sexual kinds of people fell on deaf ears. Despite several valiant efforts by sociologists confirming the concept of bisexuality (e.g., Greenberg, 1988; Rust, 2000; Weinberg, Williams, & Pryor, 1994), leading sex researchers have continued to express doubt that bisexuality is a sexual orientation, at least for men (Bailey et al., 2016). Not long ago, researchers published a study implying that men who identify as bisexual are not being honest about their sexual attractions (Rieger, Chivers, & Bailey, 2005; see Carey, 2005). The authors concluded that bisexual-identified men exhibited a genital arousal pattern much like gay men, even

Table 5.1 National Studies of Sexual Orientation Identity and Same-Sex Contact

Authors; study country	N	Sex	Heterosexual/ straight	Gay or lesbian	Bisexual	Same-sex contact
Kinsey et al. (1948); United States	12,214	Men	50.0%*	4.0%*	46.0%*	37.0% ever
Kinsey et al. (1953); United States	5,940	Women	70.0%*	2.0%*	28.0%*	13.0% ever
Mercer et al. (2013); United Kingdom (England, Scotland, Wales)	15,162	Men	97.1%	1.5%	1.0%	8.0% ever
		Women	97.3%	1.0%	1.4%	11.5% ever
Ward et al. (2014); United States	34,557	Men	97.8%	1.8%	0.4%	----
		Women	97.7%	1.5%	0.9%	----
Richters et al. (2014); Australia	20,094	Men	96.7%	1.9%	1.3%	6.6% ever
		Women	96.3%	1.2%	2.2%	13.8% ever
Copen et al. (2016); United States	9,175	Men	95.1%	1.9%	2.0%	6.2% ever
		Women	92.3%	1.3%	5.5%	17.4% ever
Fu et al. (2019); United States	2,021	Men	93.0%	4.4%	1.8%	7.0% past year
		Women	92.8%	2.7%	2.9%	6.0% past year

*Categorized by sexual behavior, not identity

though many participants responded sexually to both sexes. Study authors argued that bisexual men in the study were more *strongly* aroused to men than women, drawing heavy criticism from gay and bisexual activists and other researchers. Later, investigators conducted a follow-up study, and this time they recruited bisexual men who had a history of long-term sexual relationships with both sexes, as well as self-reported bisexual arousal (Rosenthal, Sylva, Safron, & Bailey, 2011). Contrary to the earlier study, bisexual men demonstrated a strong arousal pattern to *both* sexes, unlike gay and heterosexual men. Nevertheless, Bailey (2009; 2016) and others continued to claim until recently that male sexual orientation is sex-specific and categorical, ignoring bisexual men.

Prevalence of Sexual Kinds of People

Recent studies in Western countries using rigorous national probability sampling methodologies and computer-assisted data collection find remarkably similar results regarding the prevalence of modern sexual kinds of people. Probability sampling methodologies attempt to reflect the national population, and computer-assisted survey formats are more private and, therefore, may elicit more honest responses than completing a paper survey or responding in person to an interviewer. Three national surveys from the United Kingdom (UK; England, Scotland, and Wales; the 2010–2012

National Surveys of Sexual Attitudes and Lifestyles) of participants, aged 16–44 (Mercer, Tanton, Prah, et al., 2013), and one large national survey of Americans (the 2013 National Health Interview Survey), aged 18–64, found that collectively 97–98% of men and women identified as heterosexual (Ward, Dahlhamer, Galinsky, & Joestl, 2014). (See Table 5.1). Across studies, only 1–2% of participants identified as gay or lesbian. Slightly more men than women identified as same-sex-attracted. Less than 1.5% of participants identified as bisexual, with women choosing this label slightly more often than men. However, the UK studies also asked about same-sex sexual contact and found that 8% of men and nearly 12% of women reported ever having a same-sex sexual partner (Mercer, Tanton, Prah, et al., 2013).

A large national study of Australian adults (the Second Australian Study of Health and Relationships), employing computer-assisted telephone interviews, revealed that 96% of men and women, aged 16–69, identified as heterosexual (Richters, Altman, Badcock, Smith, de Visser, Grulich, Rissel, & Simpson, 2014). Only 1–2% of respondents identified as gay or lesbian, but 7% of men and 14% of women had engaged in some same-sex sexual activity. More women than men identified as bisexual. This study also compared sexual identities to self-reported sexual attractions. Most heterosexual-identified men (96%) reported exclusive attraction to women, and 90% of bisexual men reported attraction to both sexes. However, only 56% of gay men had an exclusive attraction to men; 42% reported some attraction to both sexes. Among heterosexual-identified women, 88% indicated an exclusive attraction to men, and 93% of bisexual women reported attraction to both sexes. Interestingly, nearly 60% of lesbian-identified women also reported attraction to both sexes. At least in this Australian sample, people with non-heterosexual identities were more fluid in their attractions.

A smaller national representative sample of Americans (the 2011–2013 National Survey of Family Growth), aged 18–44, found a slightly lower proportion of self-identified heterosexuals and a larger group of bisexuals (National Health Interview Survey; Copen, Chandra, & Febo-Vazquez, 2016). Over 6% of men and more than 17% of women had ever engaged in same-sex sexual activity. Variability in responses in this study compared to previous studies may be due to differences in the purpose of the research and in how questions were asked. The National Health Interview Survey primarily examined health behaviors, while the National Survey of Family Growth included many questions about sexuality.

Finally, a recent national representative sample of Americans (the 2015 Sexual Exploration in America Study), aged 18–91, focused on sexual experiences and found moderate variability in responses compared to other studies (Fu, Herbenick, Dodge, Owens, Sanders, Reece, & Fortenberry, 2019). Most men and women (93%) identified as heterosexual. Over 4% of men and nearly 3% of women identified as gay or lesbian, and 2–3% identified as bisexual. About 6–7% of respondents reported having engaged in same-sex sexual activity in the past year. In examining concordance between identity and attraction, 96% of heterosexual-identified men reported exclusive attraction to women, while 93% of heterosexual-identified women reported only attraction to men. In sum, recent national representative studies across three countries have shown that between 90 and 98% of men and women identify as heterosexual while between 1 and 4% identify as gay or lesbian. Women are more likely than men to identify as bisexual. Across studies, sexual orientation identity and attraction appear to correspond fairly well.

Sexual Attractions and Social Stigma:

These recent national studies largely depict sexual orientation as binary and exclusive: that is, heterosexual vs. *non-heterosexual* (not simply gay or lesbian), with the majority of people identifying as heterosexual. As noted earlier, Bailey and colleagues (2009; 2016) concluded until recently that male sexual orientation is categorical and heavily skewed toward female attraction, suggesting that for men sexual arousal *is* sexual orientation. At the same time, they have questioned whether women have a sexual orientation at all. If they do, it is unclear to what it is oriented. Studies of women's genital arousal patterns have found a relatively flat pattern (Chivers, 2005; Chivers, Seto, & Blanchard, 2007). In other words, heterosexual-identified women have exhibited similar arousal patterns to preferred and non-preferred sexual partners, even sometimes reporting higher subjective arousal to non-preferred partners! Lesbian-identified women, however, have exhibited an arousal pattern similar to men: that is, stronger arousal to a preferred (same-sex) partner. Why heterosexual-identified women would have a non-specific (bisexual or pansexual) sexual arousal pattern is unclear. Given this pattern, are heterosexual-identified women really heterosexual?

Psychologist Lisa Diamond (2008) has described women's non-specific sexual orientation as *sexually fluid*, meaning a capacity for situation-dependent flexibility in sexual responsiveness. Such flexibility may occur often, a few times, or once. In a prospective study of non-heterosexual women, Diamond (2008) found that two-thirds of women changed their sexual orientation identity at least once, and half of them changed their identity more than once over a decade. Women tended to align their identity with their current monogamous relationship, whether with a man or a woman. This is not something men do. From an evolutionist perspective, it makes some sense that women's sexual arousal is more non-specific or contextual than men's arousal because women have a greater reproductive investment. There is more at stake for women in every sexual encounter. For women, the social circumstances of an encounter may be more relevant for triggering arousal than a specific partner.

Despite experiencing sexual orientation differently, contemporary men and women tend to identify themselves as exclusively heterosexual. Is it possible that the studies described above are wrong? I contend that the data presented above reflect the socially privileged convention of heterosexuality and the stigma associated with non-heterosexuality. The data do not represent sexual attraction free of culture. Because same-sex sexual contact is stigmatized in contemporary cultures, it is quite possible that at best only people who strongly (or exclusively) feel same-sex attraction will report it because that experience is incontrovertible. Those who weakly or moderately feel same-sex attraction may deny the phenomena (at least to themselves) or choose not to report it, even when the consequences are minimal. If this hypothesis is true, as the culture becomes more tolerant, we should see increasing rates of bisexuality but not necessarily higher rates of exclusive same-sex behavior. In a fascinating study, researchers found exactly that. Using data from the nationally representative General Social Survey of American adults, investigators compared sexual behavior and attitudes between 1972 and 2014, a period of increasing social acceptance of gay and lesbian people (Twenge, Sherman, & Wells, 2016). Remarkably, the number of people who reported at least one same-sex partner since age 18 *doubled* between the early 1990s and the early 2010s. For men, the rate increased from nearly 5% to 8%, while for women the rate rose from 4% to almost 9%. By 2014, almost 10% of American adults reported at least one same-sex experience in adulthood. Bisexual behavior accounted for the increased rates, climbing from 3% to nearly 8%, and women accounted for the largest jump in bisexual activity. Yet the proportion of people who reported exclusive same-sex activities remained static for those 40 years.

To understand how social stigma may have prevented people from engaging in or reporting bisexual behavior, we need to examine social attitudes about same-sex sexuality between 1972 and 2014. In the early 1970s, only 11% of adults believed that same-sex sexual activity was "not wrong at all", but by 2014 almost half of the adults surveyed agreed with this statement (Twenge, Sherman, & Wells, 2016). Recall that in 1972 homosexuality was still a psychiatric disorder, and same-sex sexual acts (e.g., sodomy) were illegal in the United States. Gay men and lesbians could be arrested for merely associating in bars. Arrests were often made public by a notice in the local newspaper, which could result in being fired and becoming a pariah in the community. However, by 2014, the U.S. Supreme Court had ruled that state sodomy laws are unconstitutional. What is more, same-sex marriage was legal in 20 states! Just one year later in 2015, the U.S. Supreme Court struck down state bans on gay marriage, legalizing same-sex marriage in all 50 states. Same-sex couples rushed to get married, and same-sex marriage announcements began appearing in local newspapers. During this 40-year period, gay, lesbian, bisexual, and transgender (LGBT) people became increasingly visible. In the 1970s, gay people portrayed on television were two-dimensional, tragic characters. In 1997, Ellen DeGeneres "came out" on the cover of *Time*, while her character "came out" on national television. DeGeneres lost her advertisers and her prime-time television show. However, by 2014, DeGeneres' new popular day time television program had been running for more than ten years and is still on the air as this book goes to press. By 2014, gay, lesbian, and bisexual actors and characters were highly visible on television in such programs as *Orange is the New Black* (Netflix), *Modern Family* (ABC), *Transparent* (Amazon Prime), *Looking* (HBO), *American Horror Story* (FX), *The Flash* (CW), and *How to Get Away with Murder* (ABC) to name a few.

Despite huge cultural shifts during this 40-year period, these changes did not benefit everyone, and not all attitudes were positive. In 1979, Jerry Falwell founded the Moral Majority in response to the growing gay and lesbian rights movement in America. The Moral Majority influenced national politics for ten years. The emergence of HIV/AIDs in the early 1980s fueled additional backlash against gay rights for more than a decade. Violence against gay men and lesbians remained high between 1972 and 2014. Today, sexual orientation-motivated violence is the third most prevalent hate crime in America after attacks targeting racial and ethnic minorities and non-Christians (Federal Bureau of Investigation, 2019).

So, are we to believe that between 1972 and 2014 the United States somehow created more people with attraction to both sexes? That seems unlikely. However, the culture dramatically changed during those 40 years. Possibly, in a more tolerant culture, individuals could engage in same-sex sexual activities with less social condemnation. Stigma associated with same-sex attraction and behavior lessened but did not disappear, and the culture did not actively promote same-sex attraction and behavior for everyone as we have seen in historical cultures. We should ask: If a reduction in social stigma could lead to increased bisexual activity in the population, what effect might a large cultural change have? If culture can greatly influence which sex people find attractive, then what are researchers measuring when they ask people about their sexual attractions?

In the past 150 years, two mutually exclusive kinds of sexual people emerged in Western culture whose identities are presumed inherent and essential to their sense of self: the heterosexual and the homosexual/gay/lesbian. Most people today report conforming to one of those two identities. While sexual scientists now view women, but not men, as sexually fluid (e.g., Bailey et al., 2016), most people today identify as heterosexual. Identifying oneself as heterosexual is a very different way of being than in past cultures, over thousands of years. Yet contemporary culture and sexual science appear to accept that these identities and behavioral patterns reflect our true selves—who we are and have always been. Consistent with this view, sexuality researchers conduct countless studies to identify possible biological explanations for exclusive same-sex attraction. However, the causes of exclusive other-sex attraction are not investigated. The assumption is that exclusive other-sex attraction needs no explanation because it is the norm.

How do we reconcile such dramatic differences in how people experience themselves and express sexual attractions between past and present? Was the past a fiction? Was the historical record simply biased toward the experiences of a few elite bisexual individuals who had access to wealth and education? Certainly, the historical record is biased towards those who were educated and those in power. We know little about the lives of ordinary people in history who were uneducated and attracted little attention. Should we believe contemporary research findings about exclusive sexual attraction and arousal among men because these phenomena are better measured now? If our current measures can accurately identify heterosexual and non-heterosexuals, does this information represent an essential truth about people? Perhaps our knowledge from biologic studies of gay men and lesbian women apply outside of contemporary Western culture—to past cultures where straight, gay, and lesbian identities did not exist. If we accept the validity of contemporary heterosexual and gay/lesbian identities and self-reported attractions as essential truths, then we should reject the long history of male bisexuality across cultures as overblown or inaccurate. On the other hand, if we accept the well-documented history of male bisexuality across cultures, then we are presented with the possibility that contemporary social discourse and cultural stigma have constrained sexual expression. In the next section, I attempt to reconcile these conflicts and lay the foundation for an alternative way of conceptualizing contemporary sexual attractions and our experience of them.

Constructing Sexual Kinds of People and Social Reality

By the early twentieth century, the concepts of the exclusive heterosexual and the homosexual/gay/lesbian had begun to take hold in Western cultures, promoted mainly by physicians, psychiatrists, and medical writers (Foucault, 1990; Katz, 1995). In this conceptualization, the heterosexual and the homosexual/gay/lesbian were believed to have their own distinct personality and behavioral traits. Through the early-to-middle century, psychologists and psychiatrists described the homosexual/gay/lesbian as cross-sexed, extending Ulrichs' idea that same-sex attracted people represented a third sex (Kauth, 2000; Ulrichs, 1994). Besides attraction to men, gay men were believed to possess other feminine characteristics, like softer physical features, emotionality, theatricality, passivity, and an interest in fashion and decorating (Bérubé, 1990). Gay men were also thought to exhibit anti-masculine traits, such as underdeveloped and weak muscles, little body hair, narrow shoulders and broad hips, large buttocks, low athleticism, poor coordination, and a dislike of sports. During World War II, American psychiatrists watched for feminine/anti-masculine features in men during their enlistment physicals in a misguided and unsuccessful attempt to weed out gay men from the military (Bérubé, 1990). Officials worried that the inclusion of gay men would weaken the military's fighting ability, which might cause the United States to lose the war. Similarly, psychologists and psychiatrists attributed masculine characteristics to lesbian women, such as broad shoulders, big frame, rough physicality, rugged facial features, good coordination, aggressiveness, and love of sports. Lesbians were also attributed anti-feminine traits, including a lack of desire for children and disinterest in domesticity and marriage.

By mid-century, psychiatrists officially declared the homosexual/gay/ lesbian mentally ill (American Psychiatric Association, 1952). In addition to mental illness, other psychiatrists labeled the homosexual/gay/lesbian a sexual predator and a threat to society. According to Bergler (1962), since homosexual/gay/lesbian people cannot reproduce—ignoring that gay and lesbian people have heterosexual parents and that many same-sex attracted people have married different-sex spouses and had children!—the only way gay and lesbian people could continue to exist is if they recruited new members. Bergler (1962) asserted that the homosexual/gay/lesbian population multiplied by seducing unsuspecting children into participating in gay sex. The experience of gay sex was somehow so powerful and rewarding that it transformed the child into a same-sex attracted person. Homosexual/gay/ lesbian people were now a public health hazard. One notorious mid-century educational film (*Boys Beware,* 2020) shown in schools warned children and adolescents to beware of the lone, sinister, gender nonconforming man; he was out to seduce straight boys and turn them gay. Although very few gay men and lesbian women (like heterosexuals) have any sexual interest in children, the stereotype of the creepy homosexual/gay/lesbian child-molester stuck and has not gone away. The "threat" of the homosexual /gay/lesbian sexual predator resurfaces regularly. Anita Bryant's "Save Our Children" campaign used this trope successfully to fight gay rights ordinances in the late 1970s. The cliché of the gay pedophile is revived each time men publicly accuse Roman Catholic priests of abusing them as boys. Religious leaders have denounced gay men and lesbians as immoral and haters of family and God (Herman, 1997). Until relatively recently, same-sex sexual behavior between consenting adults was a crime, and socializing in public places was enough to get gay men or lesbians arrested and have their names printed in the local newspaper. Being publicly identified as gay or lesbian could cost you your job. While some attitudes have changed, few states today have laws that protect gay men and lesbians from being fired from their jobs because of their sexual orientation, denied housing, or refused services, like health care. Why would anyone choose to align themselves with such a repugnant social identity?

In contrast, the heterosexual was the opposite of the homosexual/gay/lesbian. The heterosexual was normal, natural, and healthy. Medical and mental health professionals in the mid-twentieth century presented the heterosexual man as typically masculine: strong, muscular, hairy, broad-shouldered, physically coordinated, aggressive but protective, motived to provide for his family, logical, fond of team sports and cars and, of course, attracted to women (Katz, 1995). Any feminine traits, like empathy or cooking, were appropriately balanced by the heterosexual man's overtly masculine characteristics. Similarly, medical and mental health professionals portrayed the heterosexual woman as feminine: soft, curvy, sexy, kind, gentle, emotional but empathetic, social yet domestic, and yearning for a husband and children to fulfill her life (Katz, 1995). Of course, these cartoonish stereotypes misrepresented many different-sex attracted people, but it hardly mattered. The mythic heterosexual was the model for society—what everyone should be or aspire to be. Research on individual differences in gender expression has further reinforced the idea that heterosexual men love masculine activities and heterosexual women enjoy feminine activities (Bailey et al., 2016), downplaying the fact that many heterosexual men and women do not fit the stereotypes. Researchers have argued that what is important is that as a group, gay men and lesbians differ on average from heterosexual men and women—the norm. Further, religious leaders have presented heterosexual men and women as living embodiments of God's plan for creation (Herman, 1997). Heterosexuals have gone forth and multiplied. Heterosexuals create children and a loving family, although, of course, gay men and lesbian women also form families. Given this cultural idealization of heterosexuality, why would anyone not identify as heterosexual? The socially approved response could not be clearer. The point here is not whether there are mutually exclusive sexual kinds of people but that one sexual kind is highly stigmatized and another is revered.

An unfortunate consequence of the creation of exclusive heterosexuals and exclusive homosexuals/gays/lesbians has been the overt sexualization of same-sex friendships (Nardi, 1992; Spencer, 2019). Two hundred years ago, Western men and women penned romantic letters to their close same-sex friends, expressing their strong love and devotion, without their relationships being sexualized (Foster, 2007; Vicinus, 2004). Friends wrote about longing to be together, promising to greet the other with sweet kisses when they rejoined. Whether friends actually kissed when they met is beside the point. The reference to kissing was not read as sexual desire, even if the desire was real. In that era, men and women often shared a bed with same-sex friends (and sometimes strangers), without anyone thinking that something sexual was happening (Duberman, 1989). Although we do not really know what friends (or strangers) did together in bed behind closed doors, sharing a bed was not viewed with suspicion. However, today same-sex friends who express love and affection for each other, who long to be together, and who sleep in the same bed would immediately generate strong beliefs that they are gay, and probably already having sex. The sexualization of same-sex friendships most threatens heterosexual men who have the most to lose (in status) by being perceived as gay. The fear of being seen as gay (and the fear that one might be gay) likely inhibits male friendship and intimacy (Nardi, 1992; Spencer, 2019). New friendships are difficult enough without the worry that a gesture of affection might make the friend and others view you with disgust. The problem is compounded if the potential friend is openly gay, lesbian, or bisexual. Some heterosexual men and women may feel pressure to avoid developing a close friendship with a gay/lesbian or bisexual person because other people might think there is a sexual attraction or a sexual relationship.

Forms of Social Constructionism

The exclusive heterosexual and exclusive homosexual/gay/lesbian are socially constructed sexual kinds of people. They are "real" in that these are the stock identity options for people to label themselves and for interpreting one's erotic and sexual experiences. When Foucault described the creation of a sexual kind of person (the homosexual), he became the spokesman for a collection of century-old ideas that I will refer to as *social constructionism*. These general ideas have other names in different disciplines, like Anthropology, which does not matter to this argument. Overall, social constructionism holds that social reality is a function of social discourse; that is, language and social discussion within a culture define and set limits on how people experience the world and themselves (Berger & Luckmann, 1966; Foucault, 1990). From this perspective, language and social discourse construct social reality through words, concepts, beliefs, religious practices, laws, and social customs. Through numerous social interactions within ever-present culture, people mold themselves to fit available social roles and identities that exist only in that way in that culture. To extend this idea further, cultures have their own unique rules and roles and, consequently, produce different ways of being and different social realities.

This is not a rehash of 40-year-old arguments in academia about constructionism versus biology. I will present a new perspective on old ideas that have not disappeared but have spread. The premise of constructionism is alive and well in efforts by liberal social activists, hard-right political conservatives, and loud voices in the echo chambers of social media to control the narrative and bully others into accepting their beliefs. While different opinions have value, personal beliefs are not science and cannot erase the products of our evolutionary history any more than they can stop a virus from spreading.

A strong version of social constructionism asserts that cultures are independent from each other and unique (Gagnon, 1990). Within this framework, similarities across cultures are merely superficial resemblances, so comparing social phenomena across cultures makes no sense. We should expect to see wildly varied cultures with little in common. Strong social constructionism also holds that everything, including biology and science, is influenced and shaped by social discourse (words/language). Objective social reality does not exist, because social phenomenon does not escape subjective interpretation. From a strong constructionist perspective, biological factors, motivational drives, and predispositions have little or no influence on human behavior and identity, nor on the social reality that we create for ourselves. Biological factors are like background noise. Social reality is the symphony. What matters from a strong constructionist perspective is that social discourse surrounds us and sets the conditions for interpreting our experience. Thus, strong constructionist positions hold that the invention of the word "homosexual" in the late nineteenth century was necessary for people to recognize and explain their same-sex attraction as a unique identity (Foucault, 1990). In other words, before the homosexual/gay/lesbian was invented, same-sex attracted people did not exist because no concept or social framework existed for this experience. While sexual attraction and behavior existed earlier, in the past, different attractions were viewed as preferences, like preferring strawberry over chocolate ice cream. Likewise, from this perspective, before the word "heterosexual" was invented, different-sex attracted people did not exist because there was no such concept. For strong constructionists, social discourse is reality.

However, the long-held premise behind strong social constructionism (the Sapir-Whorf hypothesis)—that words limit our reality, and concepts cannot exist without words for them—has been refuted repeatedly (McWhorter, 2014). For example, early claims that Hopi Indians did not track time because they did not have words to denote *before*, *after*, or some *future* time, consistent with the Sapir-Whorf hypothesis, were simply untrue. These claims were products of overzealous anthropologists who drew quick conclusions. Hopi Indians indeed had verb tense markers to denote time. Beyond the Hopi Indians, cultures have been shown to have an awareness of concepts without terms for them, refuting the other leg of strong constructionism. While English does not have an equivalent for the German word *schadenfreude*, meaning delight in the another's misfortune, English speakers still find it funny to see someone walk into a wall or slip and fall down. Further, contrary to strong constructionist predictions, cultures are not wildly variable or unlimited in variation. Cultures show remarkable similarities. As noted earlier, human cultures share several universal features (Brown, 1991).

Regarding sexual kinds of people, Foucault correctly observed that the homosexual/gay/lesbian was a unique sexual type that first appeared in the late nineteenth century, but he was not a careful historian. Sexual kinds of people had been identified earlier (Neill, 2009). Before creation of the word "homosexual", men who preferred anal sex with men were called *sodomites*. Sodomy often referred to male-male anal sex but could include oral sex, masturbation, and even bestiality. Contrary to Foucault, sodomy was not simply a behavioral characteristic. Sodomites were sexual kinds of people who differed from other (normal) people. Beginning with the attribution of Sodom's destruction centuries ago, sodomites have been characterized as lecherous, immoral, immoderate, aggressive, antisocial, and largely same-sex attracted (Crompton, 2003; Neill, 2009). Sodomites were not the only kind of same-sex attracted person recognized in history. In *The Myth of the Modern Homosexual*, Rictor Norton (1997) documented that for at least 200 years before the term "homosexual" was invented, there existed in European cities subcultures of primarily same-sex attracted people who adopted various social labels for themselves, such as *molly, madge cull, bugger, Ganymede, Gany-boy, queen, queer, punk, sodomite*, and *tribade*. This is interesting because mollies and others labeled *themselves* rather than culture forcing them to conform to pre-determined roles. Social recognition that some people preferred certain sexual practices goes back even further. In ancient Rome, adult men who preferred the receptive sexual role with men were called *pathic*, from the Greek word for passive (*pathikos*) (Neill, 2009). *Pathic* men were characterized as weak, unmanly, and feminine, which sound like personality traits. As we have seen, in other cultures, same-sex love had no specific term but was referenced euphemistically as "The Cut Sleeve" and the "The Half-Eaten Peach". In short, cultures have recognized same-sex attracted people long before the term "homosexual" was invented. A specific term for, say, same-sex attracted people, has not been necessary for a culture to recognize the phenomenon.

While a strong version of social constructionism is overly restrictive and refutable, a modest version has merit and support. Despite many similarities, cultures indeed differ in important ways, including around issues of sexuality. What is more, these differences are difficult to detect for people outside of those cultures who miss the nuance of native language, concepts, and customs. Observers must be cautious when comparing cultures, especially those in the past. Observers must also be attuned to their own inherent cultural biases. Cultures are similar in that they reward conformity and punish nonconformity. As observers of our own culture, unless one is a minority in some fashion, it may be difficult to appreciate the enormous social pressure experienced by all members of a culture to conform to approved ways of being. Social pressure is particularly evident when people are chastised or punished for violating social norms, so many members of a culture conform to expectations and avoid stigma. For the most part, people conform to the social and sexual roles available or assigned to them. If someone could go back in time and conduct a survey in ancient Sparta and Rome asking men to identify their sexuality, time-traveling researchers would probably find that men label themselves as *masculine men*. They would not describe themselves as attracted to men and women and not because the term "bisexual" did not exist at the time. For ancient Spartan and Roman men, their masculine role was their sexuality. Masculine sexuality included sex with male youth and women, either sequentially or concurrently, at different periods in their lives. Deviation from the masculine role in Roman culture would have invited social disapproval.

What we see in the larger context of history is that cultures establish general frameworks for how people experience their lives and view themselves. In cultures that have promoted bisexuality, many if not most men (and perhaps many women too) appear to have engaged in sex with males and females. Those who did not follow social norms were likely called out. Some perhaps were even punished. With the Christianization of Western culture more than 1,500 years ago and other cultures more recently, approved sexuality became increasingly restricted to activities between (consenting) different-sex adults. Same-sex experiences and age-disparate sexual experiences were disapproved and punished. Consistent with current cultural norms, when researchers today ask people in Western cultures to label their sexuality, most men and women identify themselves as heterosexual and report only attraction to different-sex people, because heterosexual is what they should be. It is the normal, natural, socially approved way of being. Non-heterosexuality is wrong and stigmatized, even though there is greater acceptance of non-heterosexuality today. A small proportion of men and women find that they cannot fit the rigidly defined heterosexual role and adopt a non-heterosexual identity.

Looking across the larger context of history, contemporary people appear to have suppressed or lost their capacity for sexual attraction and behavior with males and females. Western culture has denied this possible sexual experience and shamed it when it occurs. Thus, contemporary men and women are not lying when they identify as exclusively heterosexual. This is their social reality—just as the social reality for ancient Spartan and Roman men was to have sexual relationships with male youth, girls, and women. When sexual science researchers are unaware of or forget the long historical record of bisexuality, they risk believing that exclusive sexual identities, attraction, and behavior among people today are independent of culture. Researchers are in part assessing participants' *correspondence* with Western cultural norms about sexuality. It is unsurprising that most people see themselves as consistent with today's expectations that they should be—must be—heterosexual.

Challenging the Conclusions of Sexual Arousal Studies

Sexual scientists have long viewed physiological studies of sexual arousal as the "gold standard" for assessing sexual attraction (Bailey et al., 2016). The assumption is that physiological arousal (i.e., an erection, vaginal congestion), unlike self-report which is vulnerable to social bias, cannot be faked or is extremely difficult to fake. A physiological response is considered almost automatic and reflexive, involving minimal cognitive processing; an individual observes a preferred sexual stimulus and becomes aroused. The thinking is that any cultural influence on physiological sexual arousal should be small. A comparable set of sexual stimuli should produce similar results with a similar sample of participants from any culture. Thus, physiological studies of sexual arousal have been viewed as *objective* and valid compared to self-report. As noted earlier, most physiological studies of sexual arousal have found that men produce a categorical sex-specific response—attraction to either men or women—while women show a non-specific or fluid response (Bailey et al., 2016). These findings are consistent with the slim history of bisexuality among women across cultures but inconsistent with the lengthy historical record of bisexuality among men.

If sexual attraction and love are in part the glue that holds male-female pair-bonds together and the connection for same-sex-devoted friendships within sex-segregated societies, as I have argued, we can expect that women would experience some level of sexual arousal to both men and women. Contemporary studies have demonstrated that women's sexual arousal pattern is even less specific than that! In a fascinating arousal study, Meredith Chivers and colleagues (2007) showed 20 lesbian women, 27 heterosexual women, 17 gay men, and 27 heterosexual men several brief video scenes while continuously recording their genital arousal and subjective sexual arousal. Study participants viewed men and women engaging in same-sex sexual activity, solo masturbation, and nude exercise. They also saw videos of male-female human sexual activity and bonobo chimpanzees engaged in sexual activity. As expected, participants were more aroused by sexual scenes than non-sexual scenes. Surprisingly, women evidenced greater sexual arousal overall to female stimuli than to male stimuli. Lesbian-identified women did not drive this finding, although lesbian women's responses were more categorical, like men's responses, and demonstrated a preference for female stimuli. Heterosexual-identified women also found women sexually arousing. Like similar studies, heterosexual women were not sex-specific in their genital or subjective arousal responses. That is, heterosexual women generally found *sexual activity* arousing, whether the scenes involved two men, two women, or a man and woman together, or bonobos engaged in sex. For heterosexual women, the sex of actors in the videos, or the species, mattered less than what they were doing, and the more explicit the sexual activity presented, the stronger the arousal response. Heterosexual women even showed a small arousal response to viewing women (but not men) exercising in the nude. Chivers and colleagues (2007) suggested that observing a woman's vulva is not a typical experience for most women and so it may have implied a sexual context. When viewing the male exercise video, women may have perceived men's non-erect, flaccid penis as non-sexual.

Chivers and colleagues (2005; 2007) have argued that for women, the context of sexual activity matters more than the sex of partner. This response is quite different from men who reliably demonstrate sexual arousal to their preferred sex of partner, supporting the idea that sexual orientation is different for women and men (Bailey et al., 2016). But why would women have a sexual orientation cued to sexual context rather than sex of partner? Chivers and colleagues (2007) proposed that rapid vaginal lubrication may offer women some protection from injury during penetration, regardless of whether the partner is preferred. That explanation makes some sense, given that ancestral women likely had less control than men over whether and when they had sex. This explanation also makes sense from the perspective that men and women have different levels of investment in reproduction, and so should respond differently to sexual situations. Women have considerable investment in reproduction. For women, sexual attraction and arousal may precede or occur simultaneously with sexual activity. Flexible sexual arousal may offer women the opportunity to benefit from various intimate (human) relationships to their social and reproductive advantage. A flexible sexual arousal pattern is consistent with my hypothesis that ancestral women living within sex-segregated environments employed sexual attraction and love to support devoted female friendships, indirectly benefiting their reproductive success. Further, if women generally have a flexible sexual arousal pattern, then contemporary women are not exclusively heterosexual as they frequently report. Thus, the data reported in Table 5.1, at least for women, are depicting correspondence with social convention or expectations, not actual attractions nor the capacity for attraction.

The online pornography website, Pornhub, offers confirming evidence that women find women sexually attractive, although women who view online porn are a select group. Pornhub is one of the biggest online porn sites in the world and publishes an annual summary of online activity. For 2019, Pornhub reported 42 billion visits in the year and more than 115 million daily visits—a 25% increase in daily visits over 2018 (The 2019 Year in Review, 2019)! By far, the greatest traffic originated from the United States. Countries with the next most frequent visits were Japan, the United Kingdom, Canada, France, Germany, Italy, Philippines, Australia, and Mexico. Overall, "lesbian" was the third most searched term on Pornhub (after "Japanese" and "hentai", referring to perverse animated sexual videos) and the *most frequently viewed* category of pornography among women for the year. Further, women viewed "lesbian" pornography 147% more often than men. These 2019 figures are similar to 2018. For men, "lesbian" was only the eighth most viewed category; "Japanese" was number one.

Chivers and colleagues (2007) also found that men demonstrated a reliable arousal pattern that was specific to sex of partner. Self-identified heterosexual and gay men generally showed stronger arousal (penile erection) to their preferred sex of partner and to the intensity of sexual activity depicted. The correlation between genital and subjective arousal was quite high for heterosexual and gay men (.82 and .85, respectively) but moderate for heterosexual and lesbian women (.56 and .58, respectively). In the study, heterosexual men were quite aroused by female-female sexual activity and solo female masturbation but, unlike women, men were not aroused by scenes of exercise or bonobos engaged in sex. Of note, Chivers and colleagues (2007) found that heterosexual men demonstrated *significant* penile erection to male-male sexual activity, although not to solo male masturbation. This intriguing finding is easily missed in the authors' lengthy discussion about women's arousal pattern. As explanation, Chivers and colleagues (2007) reported that at least one study has found that heterosexual men can suppress their penile response to socially disapproved (same-sex) sexual stimuli (Adams, Motsinger, McAnulty, & Moore, 1992), although another study did not detect activation in brain areas associated with suppression of sexual arousal (Safron, Barch, Bailey, Gitelman, Parrish, & Reber, 2007). Chivers et al.'s comment implies that heterosexual men may have been trying to suppress their arousal, which is odd. Were they not really heterosexual? Why were heterosexual men turned on by seeing two men having sex, but not aroused by watching male masturbation? Were heterosexual men able to suppress their arousal when viewing male solo masturbation but not when viewing two men engaged in sex? Were men only partially successful in suppressing their arousal? Would we expect to see active (brain) suppression of socially disapproved sexual arousal to men among heterosexual men who have been conditioned since birth *not* to perceive males as sexual objects? Men's social conditioning to deny or suppress same-sex arousal may be so well learned that it is automatic and unconscious, but not perfect. Still, heterosexual-identified men who show attraction to men risk stigmatization and loss of status, even if only in the eyes of the researcher who sees the data. By contrast, heterosexual-identified women are not stigmatized for attraction to females and, in fact, are encouraged by men to do so. Heterosexual men view women's sexual interest in women as erotic.

In their conclusion, Chivers and colleagues (2007) state that "men do demonstrate moderate increases in genital responding to films of their non-preferred gender target engaged in sexual intercourse; therefore, the difference in women's and men's sexual arousal patterns is one of *degree* rather than *kind*" (p. 1118, emphasis added). Of note, this conclusion is absent from later reviews of the sexual arousal literature, which take the strong position that male arousal is categorical and sex-specific (Bailey et al., 2016). As noted previously, research demonstrating a bisexual arousal pattern among bisexual men (Rosenthal, Sylva, Safron, & Bailey, 2011) was also dismissed in later reviews (Bailey et al., 2016), because some men use the term "bisexual" for reasons other than to accurately describe their sexual attractions.

The view that male sexual arousal is categorical and sex-specific is further challenged by evidence that physiological arousal patterns differ between men with an *exclusive* heterosexual orientation versus a *mostly* heterosexual orientation (Savin-Williams, Rieger, & Rosenthal, 2013). Using pupil dilation to assess sexual arousal, researchers found that mostly heterosexual men display more pupil dilation to males than exclusively heterosexual men. Greater pupil dilation was associated with greater sexual arousal. Yet mostly heterosexual men did not exhibit less pupil dilation to females than exclusively heterosexual men. Another study using an eye-tracking paradigm found that 24 mostly heterosexual men demonstrated significantly greater visual attention to genital areas when viewing images of naked men and male couples engaged in sex compared to 49 exclusively heterosexual men (Morandini, Veldre, Holcombe, Hsu, Lykins, Bailey, & Dar-Nimrod, 2019). In addition, mostly heterosexual men reported less disgust to erotic male images. The authors concluded that visual attention by mostly heterosexual men to erotic male stimuli was driven by sexual attraction. Again, exclusive and mostly heterosexual men did not differ in visual attention to erotic female stimuli. Consistent with these findings is evidence that young men are increasingly willing to acknowledge some same-sex attraction and label themselves as something other than exclusively heterosexual (Savin-Williams, 2017). As cultural tolerance for gay men has increased in recent years, young men appear more willing to acknowledge and demonstrate some attraction to men. Together, this evidence suggests that men have a broader spectrum of sexual attraction and arousal than has been presented. Thus, I assert that the data reported for men in Table 5.1 also reflect conformity to social convention and expectations, rather than actual sexual attractions or capacity for attraction.

If somehow researchers could go back in time and assess penile tumescence and subjective arousal among ancient Spartan and Roman men while they viewed various sexual stimuli, I am not convinced that Spartan and Roman men would demonstrate a categorical sex-specific pattern. Such a response would be inconsistent with the considerable historical evidence of bisexual attraction and behavior among men. Nor would these men exhibit a flexible arousal pattern like contemporary women in the Chivers study. I suspect ancient Spartan and Roman men would display an arousal pattern that reflects more of a continuum of attraction to males and females. Because traits naturally vary, I would expect that in our thought experiment a small proportion of Spartan and Roman men may be more strongly or even exclusively aroused by male stimuli. Although Spartan and Roman cultures mandated marriage and children, men who were exclusively attracted to males should be less reproductively successful than men who were attracted to males and females. In addition, ancient Spartan and Roman men who were exclusively attracted to women should experience some reproductive costs, because having few close male friends may make it difficult to navigate an all-male social environment and acquire resources to support a family.

In the larger context of history, cultures set conditions for how people think about themselves and how they experience sexual arousal. In cultures that promote bisexuality, many if not most men (and perhaps many women too) have appeared to have been attracted to and engaged in sex with males and females. Those who did not follow these social norms were viewed as odd and even punished. However, for more than 1,500 years, Christianized Western culture has promoted social conventions that have punished male-male sexual experiences (not so much female-female sexuality) and strongly rewarded exclusive male-female sexuality. Particularly in the past 150 years, since the invention of the exclusive heterosexual, men have been socially conditioned to respond sexually to girls and women and not to think of male youth and men as sexual partners. For at least the past 150 years, same-sex attraction has been seen as incompatible with being a masculine man. This construction of male sexuality is so pervasive that men need not consciously avoid or deny attraction to men because it is simply not conceivable. Yet not imagining the possibility does not make the experience impossible, as we have seen in some sexual arousal studies of men. Contemporary women have not been required to deny their attraction to women, and men even encourage women's sexual interest in women. While research data regarding contemporary sexual attractions are not false, interpretations of these data have been overly broad and lack historical context. When researchers are unaware of or forget that sexual arousal is performed within a culture that shapes personal perception, they risk believing that their data demonstrate an underlying truth that is free of social influence. If sexual identity and arousal data collected in research settings are indeed limited to a specific time and place in a culture, then researchers must be more conservative in their conclusions.

As this book goes to press, a group of researchers (Jabbour et al., 2020) published new analyses of sexual arousal data on almost 600 bisexual-identified men across eight studies (representing the US, United Kingdom, and Canada) and found robust evidence for a *continuum* of arousal, rather than categorical arousal. Researchers examined whether bisexual men's responses to their less arousing sex surpassed that of other men and whether the difference between bisexual men's responses to their less and more arousing sex was less than that of other men. In other words, bisexual men should show more arousal to their less-arousing sex compared to heterosexual- and gay-identified men and smaller differences between their arousal to men and women compared to heterosexual and gay men. Indeed, researchers found the inverted U-shaped curve on the Kinsey scale predicted for bisexual men. The paper's authors speculated that earlier studies may have missed these findings because of small sample sizes and low statistical power as well as recruitment of transitional bisexual men through gay-oriented publications and events. I suspect that the cultural expectation that bisexual men do not exist—a belief shared by some researchers—also made it difficult to find bisexual men and "see" them as bisexual. Indeed, evidence of men's arousal to males and females is not new.

Sexual Attraction and Love Support Mating Pair-Bonds and Same-Sex Friendships

Adaptation does not take place in a vacuum. Relatively stable physical and social environments over long periods of time set conditions for early human reproductive success in the distant past. Heritable traits associated with reproductive success in stable environments get carried forward to future generations. While the environment must be generally stable over time, various elements may have affected an individual early human's survival and ability to raise their children to reproductive age, including the presence of predators, parasites and disease, availability of food and water, weather conditions, shelter, injury, and others. For humans, the social environment is critically important for survival. While the social environment must also be generally stable over time, the individual early human had to navigate the community to develop social support, alliances, friendships, and kinship networks to access resources and acquire a quality mate in order to raise their children to reproductive age. Various factors may affect the individual's ability to survive and reproduce in the social environment, including their gender, social status, social skills and abilities, size of the community, religion, language, culture, technology, and the presence of hostile groups. Most early human cultures, until relatively recently, have been sex-segregated. An important aspect of complex social environments is the community's construction of social reality. Words, language, and social conventions established how early humans organized their groups, structured their relationships, and experienced themselves and events around them. These collective social environments also set conditions for reproductive success. In my view, an evolutionary theory best accounts for the many pressures on early human survival and reproduction and provides the most parsimonious explanation for the lengthy historical record of mating pair-bonds and devoted male friendships. A major implication of this idea is that most men (and probably most women) have the capacity for sexual attraction to and love of males and females. In the next section, I explore the implications and limitations of this idea.

A Capacity for Attraction to Males and Females

Historical and modern humans appear to be predisposed to form long-term reproductive mating relationships and close same-sex friendships. Over many generations, evolution has favored ancestral humans who exploited sexual attraction and love to (1) support male-female mating pair-bonds in order to raise large-brained, verbal, social children to reproductive age and (2) promote devoted same-sex friendships to navigate same-sex social environments, facilitate alliances, and acquire resources to obtain a quality mate and raise children to reproductive age. Our early ancestors' reproductive success carried forward heritable traits for long-term mating pair-bonds and devoted friendships. Once formed, various social factors emerged to support the continuation of both kinds of passionate, intimate attachments, even after attraction and love faded. Social expectations functioned to maintain mating pair-bonds and devoted friendships, including obligations to each other, benefits from the relationships, the needs of children (within mating pair-bonds), avoidance of loneliness, fear of reprisal if one ended the relationship, and lack of personal resources or status to pursue other options. In sum, if sexual attraction and love were integral to both mating pair-bonds and devoted same-sex friendships, then most humans have the capacity for attraction to males and females.

The hypothesis that men and women have the capacity for attraction to males and females is consistent with the considerable historical record, at least for men, and not a new idea. Freud (1905; 1915) incorporated bisexual attraction in his theories of psychosexual development and proposed that erotic attraction is central to all close friendships. Later Kinsey (1948; 1953) demonstrated that many men and women in America have bisexual experiences. He cautioned that people do not neatly fit into mutually exclusive sexual categories. More recently, Weinberg, Williams, and Pryor (1994) and Rust (2000) described the prevalence of men and women who experience attraction to both males and females, without arriving at a causal theory. Twenty years ago, I described a rough version of this idea that most men and women have the capacity for attraction to males and females (Kauth, 2000). I argued that the social benefits of close, erotic same-sex relationships within sex-segregated environments provided indirect reproductive advantages. About the same time, ecologist Rob Kirkpatrick (2000) and evolutionary psychologist Frank Muscarella (2000; 2005) separately presented an alliance theory of male-male sexual attraction and behavior in all-male environments. While focused mainly on explaining male-male attraction and alliances, Muscarella also speculated about female-female sexual attraction and alliances.

A capacity for attraction to males and females does not suggest that people must consciously experience such attractions. Social conventions and stigma function to regulate people's thoughts, feelings, and behavior and how they experience themselves. Sexual expression within a friendship is subject to social convention, circumstances, and individual factors. Across diverse cultures, many devoted male friendships appear to have included sexual affection.

Normal Variation Explains Exclusive Attraction

As a complex trait, sexual orientation is expected to vary. For some men and women, the sex of partner may be relevant only to the kind of relationship pursued, such as a reproductive relationship. Others, while attracted to males and females, may prefer one sex, if a choice is possible. As an old persistent trait, sexual orientation likely has a genetic basis and multiple influences to best exploit environmental conditions. Sexual orientation predispositions may result from different versions of a gene (a heterozygous trait) or multiple genes (a polygenic trait) (LeVay, 2011). Heterozygous traits involve dominant and recessive versions (alleles) of a gene. The most well-known example of a heterozygous trait is the shape of green peas—smooth (dominant) or wrinkled (recessive). Heterozygous human characteristics include blood type and curly or straight hair. Heterozygous traits have a limited range of variation. Given its complexity and variability, human sexual orientation likely involves multiple genes. Polygenic human traits are common and include eye color, skin color, hair color, body shape, height, and weight. Neuroscientist Simon LeVay (2011), who identified differences in brain structures between gay and heterosexual men, has argued that sexual orientation is a complex, polygenic trait, although he accepts that sexual attraction in men is categorical. In a recent review of the literature, Swift-Gallant and Breedlove (2019) argued that sexual orientation has multiple etiologies (genes, hormones, and immunological responses), although they focused primarily on androgen overexposure or insensitivity on same-sex attraction. Swift-Gallant and Breedlove viewed sexual orientation among men as polar rather than categorical.

If sexual orientation is polygenic, then this effect likely establishes a capacity for attraction that can be modified—promoted or restricted—by hormonal or immunological factors and even social factors. If so, then normal variation among relevant genes should produce a small percentage of men and women who experience only attraction to one sex. The reproductive cost of exclusive same-sex attraction (even given mandatory marriage and expectations to produce children across historical cultures) would keep the prevalence of exclusive same-sex attraction low, but not zero. Normal polygenic variation would also be expected to produce a small percentage of people who experience low sexual attraction or none at all. These folks may comprise a big portion of those who identify as asexual. Normal polygenic variation in sexual orientation would be expected to produce a modest proportion of men and women who experience only attraction to different-sex partners. People with an exclusive different-sex attraction might experience few direct reproductive costs but considerable indirect costs, including reduced social support and more limited access to resources within sex-segregated environments as a result of difficulty forming close same-sex friendships. If sexual orientation is polygenic, combinations of genes turned on or off should frequently result in the capacity for attraction to males and females. If having both different-sex and same-sex attractions provide reproductive benefits as I have argued, a sizable proportion of people in the population should have this capacity.

The idea that exclusive attraction is a byproduct of variation in sexual orientation is consistent with the biological evidence for female and male homosexuality. Evidence in support of a biological cause for same-sex attraction, mostly male-male attraction, comes from a variety of research that has examined shared genes (twin and family studies, genetic studies), androgen exposure and response (prenatal exposure studies, physical and gender characteristics studies), fraternal birth order (studies on number of older siblings and hypothesized maternal immune response), maternal fecundity (sexy, fertile mom studies), and kin selection (altruism studies). The current evidence does not point to a single causal factor. While the prenatal androgen exposure theory has the most support (Bailey et al., 2016), prenatal androgen exposure alone is not enough to produce same-sex attraction among women (Grimbos et al, 2010), and the timing or duration of prenatal androgen alone is insufficient to explain same-sex attraction among men (Martin & Nguyen, 2004; Skorska, Geniole, Vrysen, McCormick, & Bogaert, 2015). Numerous studies have shown that adult same-sex attraction in men and women is associated with childhood and adult gender nonconformity (Bailey & Zucker, 1995; Lippa, 2008). Bailey and colleagues (2016) have argued that gender nonconformity is not solely a product of social learning and culture. Gender nonconformity may have an underlying innate disposition. Androgen over/under exposure has been proposed as possible causes of gender nonconformity among gay men and lesbian women. However, linking gender nonconformity to adult same-sex attraction fails to account for gender conforming masculine gay men and feminine lesbian women, as well as gender nonconforming effeminate straight men and butch straight women.

In a recent study, psychologist Ashlyn Swift-Gallant and colleagues (2019) classified heterosexual and non-heterosexual men based on biomarkers associated with male-male sexual attraction. Researchers recruited 827 men via Facebook and at a Pride Festival. Participants were categorized as heterosexual or non-heterosexual based on reported sexual identity, attraction, and behavior. Biomarkers included non-righthandedness, familiality (gay or bisexual male relatives), and fraternal birth order (older male siblings). Men with older brothers have an increased chance of having same-sex sexual interests, which is hypothesized to result from the mother's cumulative immune response to a male fetus (Blanchard, 2018). Using a latent profile analysis approach, Swift-Gallant and colleagues (2019) found that men clustered into four groups: 1) Those who had no biomarkers (by far the largest subgroup); 2) those who had older male siblings; 3) those who were non-right-handed; and 4) those with gay and bisexual male family members. Of significant note, many heterosexual and non-heterosexual men evidenced *no* biomarkers and were in group 1, the most gender conforming subgroup. The most female-typical group was the fraternal birth order subgroup, which also scored highest on the Big 5 personality trait of Agreeableness.

Non-heterosexual men in the non-right-handedness group showed fewer masculine traits but no greater feminine traits than heterosexual men. In short, there appear to be different pathways or etiologies for the development of same-sex attraction in men, which implies different subgroups of same-sex attracted men. Also, a large proportion of non-heterosexual men show *none* of the typical attributes linked to male homosexuality: gender nonconforming traits, non-right-handedness, and being the youngest male. The usual etiological suspects explained very little. Obviously, scientists have not found the cause of male-male sexual attraction.

In their recent review of the literature on neuroendocrine influences on same-sex attraction, Swift-Gallant and Breedlove (2019) explained the mixed study findings as due to subgroups of lesbian women and gay men. For instance, prenatal androgen exposure is associated with gender nonconforming ("butch") lesbian women but not gender conforming ("femme") lesbian women. Thus, androgen exposure may modify women's sexual attraction capacity, but it probably does not cause same-sex attraction. Swift-Gallant and Breedlove also found support for androgen insensitivity among feminine or gender nonconforming, non-righthanded gay men with older brothers and who prefer receptive anal sex but not for masculine, righthanded gay men with no or few older brothers and who prefer penetrative anal sex. Again, hormone response and possible immunological effects (e.g., fraternal birth order) may modify men's sexual attraction capacity, but they are unlikely causes of same-sex attraction. Swift-Gallant and Breedlove (2019) concluded that same-sex attraction has multiple etiologies. Taking this a step further, if one rejects the assumption that same-sex attraction is something "gone wrong" and is perhaps just normal variation, then quite possibly different-sex attraction also has multiple etiologies.

The model of sexual orientation attraction presented here asserts that most people have the capacity for attraction to males and females. Sexual orientation is likely a polygenic trait. Normal variation in these genes results in a few people who are exclusively attracted to one sex. People who are exclusively same-sex attracted (or exclusively other-sex attracted) are born that way for the most part. Cultures may frustrate, suppress, or facilitate an individual's exclusive attraction, but cultures do not create sexual attraction beyond one's innate capacity.

A Mate and/or Devoted Friend

Long-term reproductive mating pair-bonds and devoted same-sex friendships have persisted across historical same-sex segregated cultures in varied but recognizable forms. I have argued that these adaptive traits drive humans to find a reproductive mate and to form close friendships. These drives function to form passionate, intimate attachments with people. Historically, these relationships have been specific to sex within same-sex environments. That is, a "reproductive mate" has been a different-sex person and a "friend" has been a same-sex person, but aside from the reproductive function that the mate performs, these roles need not be sex-specific or exclusive. A reproductive mate can be a best friend and vice versa. Creating a family is not limited to different-sex couples. Blurred roles were obvious in some of the historical examples of devoted male friendships in Chapter Four. Contemporary gay men and lesbian women who form a union with their partner or marry may be satisfying their drive to find a mate and form a family, whether or not they reproduce. Sex surrogates, artificial insemination, and adoption make it possible for a variety of families to have children. Further, our present culture allows broader definitions of pair-bonds and family than ever before. A pair-bond does not require making babies, and a family is who we hold dear, whether they are related or not.

Over the past 40 years or so, Western cultural values have shifted toward thinking of a spouse as one's best friend (Feiler, 2017). While a spouse-friend seems like an economical, efficient relationship, there are costs. The expectation may be that the spouse-friend takes the place of a best friend, rather than existing in addition to a best friend. While it is possible for a spouse to be a best friend, this dual role places a huge burden on spouses to function simultaneously in different, sometimes incompatible, roles. Close relationships can be difficult at best. When one needs a sounding board about issues with their spouse, who do you turn to when your best friend is also your spouse? A spouse may be a good friend but cannot be a friend in the way that a separate best friend can be. For practical reasons, these roles are best kept separate. Further, combining the spouse and friend roles may limit one's social network and limit the opportunity for multiple meaningful personal relationships. From my view, contemporary gay and lesbian couples have managed to avoid this problem by keeping the spouse and best friend roles separate and maintaining close friendships outside of the pair-bond.

Of course, men and women can be friends. In previous cultures, sex-segregation and the low social status of women made it difficult, if not impossible, for men and women to be friends. Our present culture allows men and women to mix socially and form close friendships in ways that were not possible in earlier times. Different-sex friendships can be long-standing, affectionate, and deeply intimate, although feelings of sexual attraction and sexual expression can confuse close male-female friendships and complicate respective marriages. Our present culture views friendships as non-sexual but sees adult male-female (non-kin) relationships as inherently sexual.

Men and women have a lot to offer each other. Generations of enforced sex segregation limited those opportunities for exchange and friendship. Yet despite greater socializing among men and women today, men like hanging out with their buddies, and women like spending time with close female friends. Given our evolutionary history, a preference for same-sex socializing makes perfect sense and is not a problem that needs solving. However, learning to have fulfilling mixed sex friendships is worth working on.

Sex Research in Cultural Context

Research on the nature and origin of sexual orientation has mainly focused on explaining homosexuality as a deviation from normative heterosexuality (Stein, 1999). Researchers have focused on how same-sex attracted people are dissimilar to different-sex attracted people. With masculine male and feminine female heterosexuals as the model, gay men and lesbian women are frequently portrayed as a mix of gendered traits and often cross-gendered. While current texts on human sexuality now describe same-sex attraction as a natural variation, not long ago, gay men and lesbian women were portrayed as a "special population". Not long ago, sociology courses covered homosexuality as deviant behavior, and bisexuality barely received mention. Changes in social attitudes have contributed to a small increase in research on bisexual men and women. However, I am not aware of sexual scientists who are actively investigating the origin of bisexuality or male-female sexual attraction. I sincerely hope this book inspires sexual scientists and scholars to question the current research program on sexual orientation. Sexual scientists exist in the same culture that conceptualizes exclusive (normative) heterosexuals and exclusive (deviant) homosexuals/gays/lesbians. Sexual science researchers cannot help being influenced by the culture in which they live.

Contemporary sex research exists within a particular time and place in history. The limitations of data from a particular time and place cannot be appreciated without a larger understanding of the history of sexuality. How much history should comprise the history of sexuality? The amount of context may depend on the research question. Certainly, the history of sexuality is not simply the published scientific literature within the past 15 years. The history of sexuality is older than the past 150 years. The history of sexuality is older than Western culture and overlaps multiple disciplines of study. However, at times, the current social experience of self and sexuality is exactly what researchers need to examine to understand, for example, health disparities among people with LGBT and related identities and how to address the health and social needs of a particular group of people.

With a greater historical context absent, conclusions regarding a narrow slice of human sexuality in this time and place may be easily mistaken for an underlying truth. While few researchers would argue that the most objective of sexual arousal data apply comparably across cultures or to people in the past or future, some investigators treat their "objective" research data as if this is true. Contemporary Western sexuality is a paragraph on a page in the book of human history. I urge contemporary sexual science researchers to be cautious and more aware of the cultural limitations of their findings.

Knowledge about sexualities and friendships through history and across cultures can help researchers appreciate how present culture affects the way people think about and express their sexuality. Researchers who see their findings within a larger cultural and historical context appreciate that current social reality regarding human sexuality will change.

Summary

In this chapter, I examined contemporary conceptions of sexual orientation as central to one's self identity and the idea that people are exclusively heterosexual or gay/lesbian. This modern concept of distinct sexual kinds of people is inconsistent with the lengthy historical record of male bisexuality. The idea that sexual attraction and love function to support both reproductive mating pair-bonds and devoted same-sex friendships leads to the conclusion that most people today have the capacity for attraction to both males and females, consistent with the historical record. As a complex polygenic trait, normal variation in sexual orientation should result in a moderate proportion of people who experience attraction to males and females and a small proportion who experience attraction only to one sex. Contemporary sex researchers, particularly those engaged in biological and physiological research, often fail to frame their findings within a cultural and historical context, implying that their work is independent of culture and represents an underlying truth. When viewed within the broader context of historical male bisexuality, recent research findings on sexual identity and arousal suggest that culture strongly influences how people experience their sexuality. The broader historical-cultural context also reminds us that how we see ourselves and live our lives today will change.

Concluding Remarks

I close this book with concluding remarks about the evolution of human mating pair-bonds, devoted friendships, and sexual attraction. First, the evolutionary model of human mating pair-bonds and devoted same-sex friendships presented here is broader, richer, and more parsimonious than evolutionary theories focused on mating alone. From my perspective, evolutionary theorists often give little significance to the same-sex social context in which our early ancestors spent most of their time. There are some exceptions—Lionel Tiger, Frank Muscarella, Rob Kirkpatrick, me, and a few others. The evolutionary model of human mating pair-bonds and devoted same-sex friendships presented here is richer and more parsimonious than proximal theories about the origin of same-sex sexual attraction and exclusive sexual kinds of people (e.g., theories regarding androgen exposure or sensitivity). Critics may believe that my description of devoted male friend-ships is just a version of male-male alliances, but devoted male friendships are qualitatively different from cooperative alliances. In not distinguishing between kinds of male alliances, theorists perpetuate the idea that all alli-ances function in the same way and serve the same purpose. They do not. Further, cross-cultural research focused on the *function* of sexual attractions to facilitate survival and reproductive success is potentially more productive than examining individual differences between sexual kinds of people who are relatively recent in origin. Frankly, the individual differences approach is limited in value and reinforces the idea that small differences between socially constructed groups are important. Those differences are relevant when identifying health disparities among stigmatized social groups. Those differences are less relevant when examining the function of sexual attrac-tions. Following the trail of function will reveal how attraction and sexuality influence everyday life, such as casual acquaintanceships, close friendships, work relationships, personal identity, community engagement, and the acquisition of status and resources.

Second, given the sex-segregated social environments in which early humans lived, devoted same-sex friendships may have been just as impor-tant and essential as finding a reproductive mate. Successfully navigating the same-sex social environment was necessary for survival and for acquiring access to resources *before* one could be reproductively successful. In most or all cultures, devoted male friendships allowed fortunate men (at least) to acquire enough status and resources to gain a mate and raise children to reproductive age. Although the evidence is far more limited, I suspect that devoted female friendships contributed to women's level of social support, childcare assistance and, ultimately, reproductive success. Thus, the desire for a close same-sex friend—a companion, a second self—runs very deep among humans and is as strong as the desire for a reproductive mate.

Third, my emphasis on history and cultural context throughout this text should not be read as a devaluation of biology. My evolutionist perspective on reproductive mating pair-bonds and same-sex friendships is grounded in the idea that humans are biological organisms with large social brains, which have allowed humans to create complex social relationships and reali-ties for themselves. Culture sits on top of but does not supplant biology or physical ecology. Only if an individual reproduces do their heritable traits get transmitted to their children and their children's children. In my model, evolution has produced people today who have a strong desire to form mat-ing pair-bonds and devoted same-sex friendships because these relationships promoted survival and reproductive success among our early ancestors. From ancient times to the present, cultural values and social discourse have shaped how people think about themselves, their spouse, and their friends.

The sexualization of people dates back to at least the early Christian zealots who took control of Rome and, with it, emerging Western culture. Our present culture invented exclusive sexual kinds of people about 150 years ago, and since then, men and women have largely thought of themselves as gay/lesbian or heterosexual. While there are cracks in this rigid typology, it is still dominant. I have argued that both our evolutionary and cultural histories are important for understanding contemporary human sexuality. Without that larger context, we may naively believe that how people view themselves and live their lives today is the way it has always been and must be.

Finally, some readers may be disappointed that I have not proposed dismantling current social conventions and creating radically different sexualities and loving relationships. Changing social conventions was not my goal. I have no manifesto for how society should be. As I have noted previously, evolution is a historical solution to ancient problems regarding reproductive success. Evolution is a product or outcome, not a prescription. Evolutionary theory can help us understand how our ancestors lived their lives and how we have been shaped by that history, but it cannot tell us how we should live our lives. If there is an underlying message here, it is that we carry our past in our bodies, and how we live in the present environment depends on how we have constructed our social reality through culture and technology. Therein lies the future. Not only are we less sex-segregated than in past cultures, we are learning (I believe) that history has disadvantaged us in how we relate to each other. Not only has medical and reproductive technology disrupted who is reproductively successful, technology now makes possible gene editing to remove or modify deleterious traits that killed our ancestors at an early age or prevented them from reproducing. Our technology makes it possible to redirect human evolution by redefining reproductive success. Francis Bacon said that knowledge is power. If we are actively engaged in the social discourse of our culture, we can alter how we think about ourselves, our relationships, and the social rules we live by. We participate in the construction of our social reality.

Take Home Points

- Most men and women today identify as exclusively heterosexual, but the historical record suggests that most men (at least) have a capacity for attraction to males and females.
- People conform to cultural conventions about social reality. In part, research on sexual orientation measures people's correspondence with social conventions.
- Current sex research can benefit from greater cultural and historical context and a focus on the function of sexual attraction.
- Understanding human evolutionary and cultural histories has the potential to alter social discourse and change our present reality.

References

The 2019 year [In review] (2019, December 11). *Pornhub insights.* https://www.por nhub.com/insights/2019-year-in-review

Adams, H. E., Motsinger, P., McAnulty, R. D., & Moore, A. L. (1992). Voluntary control of penile tumescence among homosexual and heterosexual subjects. *Archives of Sexual Behavior, 21*(1), 17–31.

American Psychiatric Association. (1952). *Diagnostic and statistical manual of mental disorders.* Washington, DC: Author.

Bailey, J. M. (2009). What is sexual orientation and do women have one? In D. A. Hope (Ed.), *Nebraska Symposium on Motivation: Vol. 54. Contemporary perspectives on lesbian, gay, and bisexual identities* (pp. 43–63). New York: Springer.

Bailey, J. M., Vasey, P. L., Diamond, L. M., Breedlove, S. M., Vilain, E., & Epprecht, M. (2016). Sexual orientation, controversy, and science. *Psychological Science in the Public Interest, 17*(2), 45–101.

Bailey, J. M., & Zucker, K. J. (1995). Childhood sex-typed behavior and sexual orientation: A conceptual analysis and quantitative review. *Developmental Psychology, 31*(1), 43–55.

Berger, P. L., & Luckmann, T. (1966). *The social construction of reality: A treatise in the sociology of knowledge.* Garden City, NY: Doubleday & Company.

Bergler, E. (1962). *Homosexuality: Disease or way of life?* New York: Collier.

Bérubé, A. (1990). *Coming out under fire: History of gay men and women in World War Two.* New York: Plume.

Blanchard, R. (2018). Fraternal birth order, family size, and male homosexuality: Meta-analysis of studies spanning 25 years. *Archives of Sexual Behavior, 47*(1), 1–15.

Boys Beware. (2020, February 16). *Wikipedia.* https://en.wikipedia.org/wiki/Boys_ Beware

Brown, D. E. (1991). *Human universals.* Boston, MA: McGraw-Hill.

Carey, B. (2005, July 5). Straight, gay or lying? Bisexuality revisited. *The New York Times.* http://www.nytimes.com/2005/07/05/health/05sex.html

Chivers, M. L. (2005). A brief review and discussion of sex differences in the specificity of sexual arousal. *Sexual and Relationship Therapy, 20*(4), 377–390.

Chivers, M. L., Seto, M. C., & Blanchard, R. (2007). Gender and sexual orientation differences in sexual response to sexual activities versus gender of actors in sexual films. *Journal of Personality and Social Psychology, 93*(6), 1108–1121.

Copen, C. E., Chandra, A., & Febo-Vazquez, I. (2016). Sexual behavior, sexual attraction, and sexual orientation among adults aged 18–44 in the United States: Data from the 2011–2013 National Survey of Family Growth. *National Health Statistics Report, 88,* 1–14. Hyattsville, MD: National Center for Health Statistics.

Crompton, L. (2003). *Homosexuality & civilization.* Cambridge: The Belknap Press.

Diamond, L. M. (2008). Female bisexuality from adolescence to adulthood: Results from a 10-year longitudinal study. *Developmental Psychology, 44*(1), 5–14.

Duberman, M. B. (1989). Writhing bedfellows" in antebellum South Carolina: Historical interpretation and the politics of evidence. In M. B. Duberman, M. Vicinus & G. Chauncey, Jr. (Eds.), *Hidden from history: Reclaiming the gay and lesbian past.* New York: New American Library.

Federal Bureau of Investigation. (2019, November 12). 2018 hate crime statistics. https://ucr.fbi.gov/hate-crime/2018/resource-pages/hate-crime-summary

Feiler, B. (2017, October 12). Should your spouse be your best friend? *The New York Times.* https://www.nytimes.com/2017/10/12/style/should-your-spouse-be-your-best-friend.html

Foster, T. A. (2007). *Long before Stonewall: Histories of same-sex sexuality in early America.* New York: New York University Press.

Foucault, M. (1978/1990). *The history of sexuality. Volume I: An introduction* (R. Hurley, transl.). New York: Vintage Books.

Freud, S. (1905/1953). Three essays on the theory of sexuality. In J. Strachey (Ed.), *The standard edition of the complete psychological works of Sigmund Freud (Vol. 7)* (pp. 123–246). London: Hogarth.

Freud, S. (1915/1987). *A phylogenetic phantasy. Overview of the transference neuroses* (A. Hoffer & P. Hoffer, transl.). Cambridge, MA: Harvard University Press.

Fu, T. C., Herbenick, D., Dodge, B., Owens, C., Sanders, S. A., Reece, M., & Fortenberry, J. D. (2019). Relationships among sexual identity, sexual attraction, and sexual behavior: Results from a nationally representative probability sample of adults in the United States. *Archives of Sexual Behavior, 48*(5), 1483–1493.

Gagnon, J. H. (1990). Gender preference in erotic relations: The Kinsey scale and sexual scripts. In D. P. McWhirter, S. A. Sanders & J. M. Reinisch (Eds.), *Homosexuality/heterosexuality: Concepts of sexual orientation* (pp. 177–207). New York: Oxford University Press.

Greenberg, D. F. (1988). *The construction of homosexuality.* Chicago, IL: University of Chicago Press.

Grimbos, T., Dawood, K., Burriss, R. P., Zucker, K. J., & Puts, D. A. (2010). Sexual orientation and the second to fourth finger length ratio: A meta-analysis in men and women. *Behavioral Neuroscience, 124*(2), 278–287.

Halperin, D. M. (1990). *One hundred years of homosexuality and other essays on Greek love.* New York: Routledge.

Herman, D. (1997). *The antigay agenda: Orthodox vision and the Christian right.* Chicago, IL: University of Chicago Press.

Jabbour, J., Holmes, L., Sylva, D., Hsu, K. J., Semon, T. L., Rosenthal, A. M., Safron, A., Slettevold, E., Watts-Overall, T. M., Savin-Williams, R. C., Sylla, J., Rieger, G., & Bailey, J. M. (2020). Robust evidence for bisexual orientation among men. *Proceedings of the National Academy of Sciences, 117*(31), 18369–18377.

Katz, J. N. (1995). *The invention of heterosexuality.* New York: Dutton.

Kauth, M. R. (2000). *True nature: A theory of sexual attraction.* New York: Kluwer.

Kinsey, A. C., Pomeroy, W. B., & Martin, C. E. (1948). *Sexual behavior in the human male.* Philadelphia, PA: W. B. Saunders.

Kinsey, A. C., Pomeroy, W. B., Martin, C. E., & Gebhard, P. H. (1953). *Sexual behavior in the human female.* Philadelphia, PA: W. B. Saunders.

Kirkpatrick, R. C. (2000). The evolution of human homosexual behavior. *Current Anthropology, 41*(3), 385–414.

LeVay, S. (2011). *Gay, straight, and the reason why: The science of sexual orientation.* New York: Oxford University Press.

Lewes, K. (1988). *The psychoanalytic theory of male homosexuality.* New York: Meridian.

Lippa, R. A. (2008). Sex differences and sexual orientation differences in personality: Findings from the BBC internet survey. *Archives of Sexual Behavior, 37*(1), 173–187.

Martin, J. T., & Nguyen, D. H. (2004). Anthropometric analysis of homosexuals and heterosexuals: Implications for early hormone exposure. *Hormones and Behavior, 45*(1), 31–39.

McWhorter, J. H. (2014). *The language hoax: Why the world looks the same in any language.* New York: Oxford University Press.

Mercer, C. H., Tanton, C., Prah, P., Erens, B., Sonnenberg, P., Clifton, S., ... Johnson, A. M. (2013). Changes in sexual attitudes and lifestyles in Britain through the life course and over time: Findings from the National Surveys of Sexual Attitudes and Lifestyles (Natsal). *Lancet, 382*(9907), 1781–1794.

Montaigne, M. (1580/1993). *The essays* (J. M. Cohen, transl.). London: Penguin Books.

Morandini, J. S., Veldre, A., Holcombe, A. O., Hsu, K., Lykins, A., Bailey, J. M., & Dar-Nimrod, I. (2019). Visual attention to sexual stimuli in mostly heterosexuals. *Archives of Sexual Behavior, 48*(5), 1371–1385.

Muscarella, F. (2000). The evolution of homoerotic behavior in humans. *Journal of Homosexuality, 40*(1), 51–77.

Muscarella, F., Cevallos, A. M., Siler-Knogl, A., & Peterson, L. (2005). The alliance theory of homosexual behavior and the perception of social status and reproductive opportunities. *Neuroendocrinology Letters, 26*(6), 771–774.

Nardi, P. M. (1992). Sex, friendship, and gender roles among gay men. In P. M. Nardi (Ed.), *Men's friendships* (pp. 173–185). Newbury Park, CA: SAGE.

Nardi, P. M., & Sherrod, D. (1994). Friendship in the lives of gay men and lesbians. *Journal of Social and Personal Relationships, 11*(2), 185–199.

Neill, J. (2009). *The origins and role of same-sex relations in human societies.* Jefferson, NC: McFarland & Company.

Norton, R. (1997). *The myth of the modern homosexual: Queer history and the search for cultural unity.* London: Cassell.

Pat Robertson Controversies. (2019, October 1). *Wikipedia.* https://en.wikipedia.org/wiki/Pat_Robertson_controversies

Richters, J., Altman, D., Badcock, P. B., Smith, A. M. A., de Visser, R. O., Grulich, A. E., ... Simpson, J. M. (2014). Sexual identity, sexual attraction, and sexual experience: The second Australian Study of Health and Relationships. *Sexual Health, 11*(5), 451–460.

Rieger, G., Chivers, M. L., & Bailey, J. M. (2005). Sexual arousal patterns of bisexual men. *Psychological Science, 16*(8), 579–584.

Rosenthal, A. M., Sylva, D., Safron, A., & Bailey, J. M. (2011). Sexual arousal patterns of bisexual men revisited. *Biological Psychology, 88*(1), 112–115.

Rust, P. C. R. (Ed.) (2000). *Bisexuality in the United States: A social science reader.* New York: Columbia University Press.

Safron, A., Barch, B., Bailey, J. M., Gitelman, D. R., Parrish, T. B., & Reber, P. J. (2007). Neural correlates of sexual arousal in homosexual and heterosexual men. *Behavioral Neuroscience, 121*(2), 237–248.

Savin-Williams, R. C. (2017). *Mostly straight: Sexuality fluidity among men.* Cambridge: Harvard University Press.

Savin-Williams, R. C., Rieger, G., & Rosenthal, A. M. (2013). Physiological evidence for a mostly heterosexual orientation among men. *Archives of Sexual Behavior*, 42(5), 697–699.

Schulz, J. F., Bahrami-Rad, D., Beauchamp, J. P., & Henrich, J. (2019, November 8). The church, intensive kinship, and global psychological variation. *Science*, 366(6466), eaau5141.

Skorska, M. N., Geniole, S. N., Vrysen, B. M., McCormick, C. M., & Bogaert, A. F. (2015). Facial structure predicts sexual orientation in both men and women. *Archives of Sexual Behavior*, 44(5), 1377–1394.

Spencer, S. (2019, November-December). The great cover-up. *The Gay and Lesbian Review/Worldwide*, 26(6), 15–18.

Stein, E. (1999). *The mismeasure of desire: The science, theory, and ethics of sexual orientation*. New York: Oxford University Press.

Swift-Gallant, A., & Breedlove, S. M. (2019). Neuroendocrine influences on human sexuality. *Oxford research encyclopedic. Neuroscience.* https://oxfordre.com/neuroscience/view/10.1093/acrefore/9780190264086.001.0001/acrefore-9780190264086-e-250

Swift-Gallant, A., Coome, L. A., Aitken, M., Monks, D. A., & VanderLaan, D. P. (2019). Evidence for distinct biodevelopmental influences on male sexual orientation. *Proceedings of the National Academy of Sciences*, 116(26), 12787–12792.

Twenge, J. M., Sherman, R. A., & Wells, B. E. (2016). Changes in American adults' reported same-sex sexual experiences and attitudes, 1973–2014. *Archives of Sexual Behavior*, 45(7), 1713–1730.

Ulrichs, K. H. (1994). *The riddle of man-manly love: The pioneering work on male homosexuality, volumes 1 & 2*. (M. A. Lombardi-Nash). Buffalo, NY: Prometheus Books.

Vicinus, M. (2004). *Intimate friends: Women who loved women, 1778–1928*. Chicago, IL: University of Chicago Press.

Ward, B. W., Dahlhamer, J. M., Galinsky, A. M., & Joestl, S. S. (2014). Sexual orientation and health among U.S. adults: National Health Interview Survey, 2013. *National Health Statistics Reports*, 77(77), 1–10.

Weinberg, M. S., Williams, C. J., & Pryor, D. W. (1994). *Dual attraction: Understanding bisexuality*. New York: Oxford University Press.

Index

Note: Page numbers in italics refer to tables

For Product Safety Concerns and Information please contact our EU
representative GPSR@taylorandfrancis.com
Taylor & Francis Verlag GmbH, Kaufingerstraße 24, 80331 München, Germany

www.ingramcontent.com/pod-product-compliance
Lightning Source LLC
Chambersburg PA
CBHW070410270326
41926CB00014B/2770

* 9 7 8 0 3 6 7 4 2 7 2 6 9 *